Can Poetry Matter?

Can Poetry Matter?

Essays on Poetry and American Culture

by Dana Gioia

GRAYWOLF PRESS • SAINT PAUL

Grateful acknowledgment is made to the editors of the periodicals in which these essays, many of which have been revised for book publication, were first published: the *Atlantic*, the *Nation*, the *Hudson Review*, the *Kenyon Review*, *Poetry*, the *Ontario Review*, *Verse*, the *Southern Review*, the *Antioch Review*, *Nebo*, *On Common Ground*, *AWP Newsletter*, and the *New York Times Book Review*.

Publication of this volume is made possible in part by a grant provided by the Minnesota State Arts Board, through an appropriation by the Minnesota State Legislature, a grant from the Wells Fargo Foundation Minnesota, and a grant from the National Endowment for the Arts. Significant support has also been provided by the Bush Foundation; Marshall Field's Project Imagine with support from the Target Foundation; the McKnight Foundation; and other generous contributions from foundations, corporations, and individuals. To these organizations and individuals we offer our heartfelt thanks.

Published by Graywolf Press
2402 University Avenue, Suite 203
Saint Paul, Minnesota 55114
All rights reserved.

www.graywolfpress.org

Published in the United States of America

ISBN 1-55597-370-1

2 4 6 8 9 7 5 3 1

Library of Congress Control Number: 2002102971

Cover design: Jeanne Lee

Acknowledgments

⟶

One may write poems for God alone, but critical prose is composed for editors. I have been fortunate to work with editors who not only encouraged my independence but also tolerated my missed deadlines, obsessive revision, and naive disregard for assigned word lengths. My deepest debt of gratitude goes to Frederick Morgan and Paula Deitz of the *Hudson Review,* who published nearly a third of these pieces, and to Elizabeth Pochoda, formerly of the *Nation,* who always made me feel that my work mattered as much to her as to its author. But special thanks are also due to Donald Bruckner of the *New York Times Book Review;* David Daniel, formerly of *AWP Newsletter;* Ted Gioia, formerly of *Sequoia;* Henry Hart, Robert Crawford, Ashley Brown, and Robert McPhillips of *Verse;* Paul Lake of *Nebo;* Joyce Carol Oates and Raymond Smith of the *Ontario Review;* Joseph Parisi of *Poetry;* Mark Sanders of *On Common Ground;* David St. John, formerly of the *Antioch Review;* Frederick Turner, formerly of the *Kenyon Review;* and to William Whitworth, who commissioned the title essay of this volume for the *Atlantic,* and Corby Kummer, who guided it through publication. Finally, I would like to thank Ellen Foos and Anne Czarniecki of Graywolf Press whose patience and professionalism helped bring this book into being.

Contents

For Mary

who deserves sonnets in folio
this meager prose

Introduction to Tenth-Anniversary Edition

⸺

NO ONE EXPECTED the huge response that "Can Poetry Matter?" generated, especially not its author. Although no one believes me, I did not set out to create a controversy. I was simply trying to address—as directly and candidly as possible—the increasing isolation of American poetry in our culture. On occasion I had the sense that I might be expressing an arguable proposition, but ironically those passages have been the ones to escape scrutiny. What stirred debate and even denunciation in some circles were assumptions that seemed to me utterly beyond argument— especially the notions that poetry had once been popular in the United States, that a larger and more diverse audience might be good for the art, and that contemporary poetry might occupy a meaningful place outside the university. I thought those propositions self-evident. Not everyone agreed.

When the original essay appeared in the April 1991 issue of the *Atlantic Monthly,* the editors warned me to expect angry letters from interested parties. When the hate mail arrived typed on the letterheads of university writing programs, no one was surprised. What astonished the *Atlantic* editors, however, was the sheer size and intensity of the response. "Can Poetry Matter?" eventually generated more mail than any article the *Atlantic* had published in decades.

The letters arrived in three familiar varieties—favorable, unfavorable, and incomprehensible. What was unusual was that they were overwhelmingly positive. Hundreds of people wrote—often at great length—to express their agreement, frequently adding that the article had not gone far enough in criticizing certain trends in contemporary poetry. The responses came from a great cross section of readers—teachers, soldiers, lawyers, librarians, nuns, diplomats, housewives, business executives, ranchers, and reporters—mostly people who were not then normally heard in the poetry world. As their testimonies demonstrated, they cared passionately for the art but felt isolated and disenfranchised from the official academic culture of poetry. An outsider myself, who worked in an office during the day and wrote at night, I felt a deep kinship with their situation. I probably learned more from those readers than they learned from me. Their comments provided clear and candid insight on the place poetry still occupied in the lives of many Americans.

For me the real response to "Can Poetry Matter?" will always reside in those individual letters, which have never entirely stopped coming. But meanwhile a larger and noisier public reaction began. Newspapers and magazines ran articles on the essay. Reporters phoned for interviews. Radio and television producers scheduled shows. The essay was reprinted, recorded, excerpted, and translated. Academic conferences offered panels to debate the essay's assertions. Nobody wrote a song, but there was a poetry slam parody in Boston.

When the book appeared in 1992, the controversy had not yet died down, at least in literary circles, and a small battalion of critics decided to fire a few shots in this new skirmish of the Culture Wars. By then I felt quite detached from the spectacle, which I realized often had little to do with the book itself. There was even a certain pleasure in having so many distinguished antagonists. Unpopularity is an acquired taste, but it can be a practical addition to an author's diet. "I would rather be attacked than unnoticed," said Samuel Johnson quite sensibly. "For the worst thing you can do to an author is to be silent as to his works."

Silence was not the fate of *Can Poetry Matter?* The book received an extraordinary number of both loudly negative and boisterously positive reviews—some of them longer than the title essay itself. Two other essays in the book had previously attracted widespread notice—"Notes on the New Formalism" and "Business and Poetry." Their republication was greeted with special horror by certain critics who lamented the recent revival of formal verse and questioned the possibility that serious poets might not only survive but somehow thrive outside the academy. As the next decade would demonstrate, those two trends, however at odds with conventional literary opinion, would become indisputable facts of literary history.

When a writer publishes something that becomes famous, the only sensible reaction is gratitude. I still marvel at my sheer good luck in gaining the attention of the intellectual community. The notoriety gave me the opportunity to quit my job and become a full-time writer. But I was also grateful when my fifteen minutes of fame came to an end. By then I understood the wisdom in the reclusive Philip Larkin's remark, "I don't want to go around pretending to be me." Not only is it hard work, but one constantly wishes for a better role.

Literary influence is a sloppy phenomenon. When a piece of writing gains enough notoriety to create controversy, the responses it generates often have little to do with the original text. The work has somehow struck a nerve, usually by examining an issue others have obscured or ignored. When all the repressed energy is suddenly released, it takes its own shape. For most respondents, the text itself is merely a point of departure. The author needs to step aside and let the public debate pursue its own dialectic. The culture is now at work, and the author has become only one of the spectators.

Can Poetry Matter? opened up the public conversation about American poetry to a large number of readers and writers who had previously felt excluded. For many, the book's impact was as much emotional as intellectual. It gave them the strength of their own convictions—which were often utterly unlike the author's. Literary culture is essentially a conversation. When a substantial number of new people enter the exchange—especially from segments of society not previously represented—they raise new questions that change the course of events. By critiquing the role of academic institutions in fostering poetry and insisting that contemporary poetry had a constituency outside the university, *Can Poetry Matter?* invited a number of new participants from all walks of life and of every literary opinion to join the conversation. Once they started talking, there has been no shutting them up. Their arrival has made the poetry scene less orderly and well-mannered—occasionally even anarchic—but it has also made it more democratic, diverse, and vital.

This line of reasoning, however, has an uncomfortable but inevitable implication. If the book's importance was to help enlarge and enliven the public conversation about American poetry, then the vehement rejection it generated in some circles was as important and helpful as the approval it found elsewhere. Meaningful differences of opinion made the discussion more energetic and substantial. Ultimately, for the culture at large, the specific issues being debated mattered less than the unexpected fact that poetry had suddenly proved worth arguing about.

In the decade since *Can Poetry Matter?* was first published, the state of

American poetry has changed radically—often in ways suggested by the title essay. Although the university writing programs critiqued in the book remain largely the same, they have lost their monopoly on contemporary poetry because the literary culture around them has experienced a vast renewal by reconnecting poetry with a broader audience. There are now countless poetry festivals, book fairs, reading series, discussion groups, and conferences based in the community rather than the academy. Although the state of poetry criticism and reviewing remains deplorable, it has been augmented by increased coverage in the general press. Many newspapers have begun printing poems and poetry columns. There are also numerous on-line columns and reviews. A network of local and syndicated poetry radio shows have also appeared as well as poetry segments on national shows like *The Writer's Almanac*. There is now a Poetry Book Club, and it is not unusual to find a poetry volume or anthology on the best-seller list. Audio books of poetry, which until recently were considered specialized items, are now commonly found in large chain bookstores.

Nonacademic institutions now also play a larger role in the poetry world. The bookstore and public library have reemerged as centers for literary activity, especially readings and lectures. Meanwhile, older poetry organizations have developed ambitious new programs to serve a broader public. The Poetry Society of America's "Poetry in Motion" has placed poems on buses, trains, and subways in major cities from New York to Los Angeles. The Academy of American Poets' National Poetry Month campaign has successfully promoted events in schools, libraries, bookstores, and the media. The U. S. Poet Laureateship has gradually changed from an honorific office into an active position for promoting the art among the American population, and many states and cities have instituted or renovated laureates of their own.

Poetry has become an increasingly public and performative art. Readings incorporating music and even dance have become common; usually taking place in theaters, concert halls, or parks. (One former U. S. Poet Laureate is currently touring with a string quartet.) Meanwhile the Internet has fostered an immense amount of activity—from mainstream sites like *Poetry Daily* to more specialized on-line journals, literary home pages, and chat rooms. Collectively, these innumerable sites have created a new, decentralized, electronic bohemia.

Not all of these trends are entirely new, but their rapid growth and public acceptance over the past ten years have been astonishing. The sort of urban literary activity that previously existed only in exceptional places like Manhattan or Berkeley is now found in hundreds of cities across the country. It is impossible to say what role *Can Poetry Matter?* played in this populist renascence. Whether the book served as one of the catalysts or was merely an early manifestation of a Zeitgeist already in the making is less important than the cultural events that followed.

The main effect of this new activity has been to revitalize, democratize, and decentralize the presentation and discussion of American poetry. A skeptical critic might justifiably claim that never has so much bad poetry been presented to so many people, but that observation misses the bigger and more important fact. At the beginning of the twenty-first century, a broad and diverse coalition of Americans has created a public space for poetry. This huge populist revival happened almost entirely outside the university. For the first time in half a century the academic poetry world is balanced by an equally large amount of activity in the general culture. The quality of these new enterprises is very uneven, but that is also true of most academic activity, and one can reasonably hope that competition between the two spheres will eventually make both stronger. The new populist revival is now transforming literary culture with such speed and reach that one wonders what the future will bring. It is a time of enthusiasm and experiment. No one today would dare claim that poetry is dead. The ancient unkillable phoenix has risen from the ashes and magnificently taken flight.

Dana Gioia

Preface

I HAVE READ poetry as long as I have been able to read. Before that, my mother, a woman of no advanced education, read or recited it to me from memory. Consequently, I have never considered poetry an intrinsically difficult art whose mysteries can be appreciated only by a trained intellectual elite. Poetry is an art—like painting or jazz, opera or drama—whose pleasures are generally open to any intelligent person with the inclination to savor them. Critics, justly obsessed with the difficulty of interpreting poetical texts, often forget the sheer immediacy of the medium's appeal. Study may deepen and training refine one's taste for poetry, but the appetite itself is not an especially sophisticated thing. Poets as dissimilar as Walt Whitman and Philip Larkin remind us how poetry answers a primitive, even primal urge. There are difficult masterpieces, of course, just as there are works of startling simplicity. Sometimes difficult poems fascinate a reader the most. As T. S. Eliot observed, readers can often be most devoted to poems they do not entirely understand. While it is a critic's task to analyze a literary work, the reader needs only to experience it. A critic must not only understand but respect that difference—even while chiding an audience to experience a work more fully.

I must also warn the reader that I do not believe that all serious criticism must address a professional literary coterie. Although some matters of scholarship and theory pertain mostly to specialists, other subjects naturally concern a broader constituency of readers. Just as political discourse often profits by leaving the caucus room, so does some criticism gain by looking beyond the seminar table. Different audiences compel a critic to ask different questions. There is a type of criticism that benefits from speaking in a public idiom to a mixed audience of both professional *literati* and general readers—groups that do not entirely share common assumptions. Such criticism has traditionally been at the center of literary culture. As poetry criticism abandoned a public voice, the literary public began, not surprisingly, to abandon poetry. To write responsible public criticism has become increasingly difficult in our age of intellectual specialization. But if literature is to continue as an important force in American culture, then to reinvent a public idiom capable of serious criticism is a necessary enterprise.

All of the essays collected in this volume were written while I worked in business. Whatever the other burdens my employment put on my literary aspirations, the job allowed me to write about whatever interested me most—however odd or unfashionable. It also freed me from the necessity of adopting an academic style. I wrote these essays with the conviction that poetry appeals to a broader audience than is usually acknowledged. I tried to find a style that satisfied the demands of my fellow writers and critics but was also accessible to the common reader. By the common reader, however, I did not imagine an uninformed or unreflective individual. Nor did I assume the incurious mass audience of the popular media. I kept before me the idea of the general reader on whom both Samuel Johnson and Virginia Woolf felt the vitality of literature depended—the intelligent, engaged nonspecialist. Whether such individuals ever read most of the essays was immaterial. What mattered was keeping my responsibilities to them in mind as I explored each issue.

Criticism is hardly less autobiographical than poetry or fiction. These essays reveal more about me than I care to admit. Perhaps most obvious, they betray their author's identity as a poet. Surely they also disclose the perspective of a critic working outside the academy. Rereading these pieces, I was struck by how important various accidents of geography or employment were in shaping certain themes. But I consider the most important personal factor something less obvious, namely that these essays were written by a reader of poetry. I was attracted to poetry long before I ever thought of writing it (and eons before I had any notion of writing about it). Whatever my other affiliations with the art, I still think of myself primarily as a reader—one passionately grateful for the pleasure, enlightenment, and consolation that poetry affords. Perhaps when I claimed to have written these pieces for a mixed audience of writers, critics, and readers, I meant I wrote them largely for myself. I enjoyed the intensity of attention they required. I hope other readers will share that pleasure.

Dana Gioia

Can Poetry Matter?

—

AMERICAN POETRY now belongs to a subculture. No longer part of the mainstream of artistic and intellectual life, it has become the specialized occupation of a relatively small and isolated group. Little of the frenetic activity it generates ever reaches outside that closed group. As a class, poets are not without cultural status. Like priests in a town of agnostics, they still command a certain residual prestige. But as individual artists they are almost invisible.

What makes the situation of contemporary poetry particularly surprising is that it comes at a moment of unprecedented expansion for the art. There have never before been so many new books of poetry published, so many anthologies or literary magazines. Never has it been so easy to earn a living as a poet. There are now several thousand college-level jobs in teaching creative writing, and many more at the primary and secondary levels. Congress has even instituted the position of poet laureate, as have twenty-five states. One also finds a complex network of public subvention for poets, funded by federal, state, and local agencies, augmented by private support in the form of foundation fellowships, prizes, and subsidized retreats. There has also never before been so much published criticism about contemporary poetry; it fills dozens of literary newsletters and scholarly journals.

The proliferation of new poetry and poetry programs is astounding by any historical measure. Just under a thousand new collections of verse are published each year, in addition to a myriad of new poems printed in magazines both small and large. No one knows how many poetry readings take place each year, but surely the total must run into the tens of thousands. And there are now about 200 graduate creative-writing programs in the United States, and more than 1,000 undergraduate ones. With an average of 10 poetry students in each graduate section, these programs alone will produce about 20,000 accredited professional poets over the next decade. From such statistics an observer might easily conclude that we live in the golden age of American poetry.

But the poetry boom has been a distressingly confined phenomenon. Decades of public and private funding have created a large professional class for the production and reception of new poetry, comprising legions of teachers, graduate students, editors, publishers, and administrators. Based mostly in universities, these groups have gradually become the primary audience for contemporary verse. Consequently, the energy of American poetry, which was once directed outward, is now increasingly focused inward. Reputations are made and rewards distributed within the poetry subculture. To adapt Russell Jacoby's definition of contemporary academic renown from *The Last Intellectuals,* a "famous" poet now means someone famous only to other poets. But there are enough poets to make that local fame relatively meaningful. Not long ago, "only poets read poetry" was meant as damning criticism. Now it is a proven marketing strategy.

The situation has become a paradox, a Zen riddle of cultural sociology. Over the past half century, as American poetry's specialist audience has steadily expanded, its general readership has declined. Moreover, the engines that have driven poetry's institutional success—the explosion of academic writing programs, the proliferation of subsidized magazines and presses, the emergence of a creative-writing career track, and the migration of American literary culture to the university—have unwittingly contributed to its disappearance from public view.

To THE AVERAGE READER, the proposition that poetry's audience has declined may seem self-evident. It is symptomatic of the art's current isolation that within the subculture such notions are often rejected. Like chamber-of-commerce representatives from Parnassus, poetry boosters offer impressive recitations of the numerical growth of publications, programs, and professorships. Given the bullish statistics on poetry's material expansion, how does one demonstrate that its intellectual and spiritual influence has eroded? One cannot easily marshal numbers, but to any candid observer the evidence throughout the world of ideas and letters seems inescapable.

Daily newspapers no longer review poetry. There is, in fact, little coverage of poetry or poets in the general press. From 1984 until this year

[1992] the National Book Awards dropped poetry as a category. Leading critics rarely review it. In fact, virtually no one reviews it except other poets. Almost no popular collections of contemporary poetry are available except those, like the *Norton Anthology,* targeting an academic audience. It seems, in short, as if the large audience that still exists for quality fiction hardly notices poetry. A reader familiar with the novels of Joyce Carol Oates, John Updike, or John Barth may not even recognize the names of Gwendolyn Brooks, Gary Snyder, or W. D. Snodgrass.

One can see a microcosm of poetry's current position by studying its coverage in the *New York Times.* Virtually never reviewed in the daily edition, new poetry is intermittently discussed in the Sunday *Book Review,* but almost always in group reviews where three books are briefly considered together. Whereas a new novel or biography is reviewed on or around its publication date, a new collection by an important poet like Donald Hall or David Ignatow might wait up to a year for a notice. Or it might never be reviewed at all. Henry Taylor's *The Flying Change* was reviewed only after it had won the Pulitzer Prize. Rodney Jones's *Transparent Gestures* was reviewed months after it had won the National Book Critics Circle Award. Rita Dove's Pulitzer Prize–winning *Thomas and Beulah* was not reviewed by the *Times* at all.

Poetry reviewing is no better anywhere else, and generally it is much worse. The *New York Times* only reflects the opinion that although there is a great deal of poetry around, none of it matters very much to readers, publishers, or advertisers—to anyone, that is, except other poets. For most newspapers and magazines, poetry has become a literary commodity intended less to be read than to be noted with approval. Most editors run poems and poetry reviews the way a prosperous Montana rancher might keep a few buffalo around—not to eat the endangered creatures but to display them for tradition's sake.

ARGUMENTS ABOUT THE DECLINE of poetry's cultural importance are not new. In American letters they date back to the nineteenth century. But the modern debate might be said to have begun in 1934, when Edmund Wilson published the first version of his controversial essay "Is Verse a Dying Technique?" Surveying literary history, Wilson noted that verse's role had grown increasingly narrow since the eighteenth century. In particular, Romanticism's emphasis on intensity made poetry seem so "fleeting and quintessential" that eventually it dwindled into a mainly lyric medium. As verse—which had previously been a popular medium for narrative, satire, drama, even history and scientific speculation—retreated into lyric, prose usurped much of its cultural territory. Truly ambitious writers eventually had no choice but to write in prose. The future of great literature, Wilson speculated, belonged almost entirely to prose.

Wilson was a capable analyst of literary trends. His skeptical assessment of poetry's place in modern letters has been frequently attacked and qualified over the past half century, but it has never been convincingly dismissed. His argument set the ground rules for all subsequent defenders of contemporary poetry. It also provided the starting point for later iconoclasts, such as Delmore Schwartz, Leslie Fiedler, and Christopher Clausen. The most recent and celebrated of these revisionists is Joseph Epstein, whose mordant 1988 critique "Who Killed Poetry?" first appeared in *Commentary* and was reprinted in an extravagantly acrimonious symposium in *AWP Chronicle* (the journal of the Associated Writing Programs). Not coincidentally, Epstein's title pays a double homage to Wilson's essay—first by mimicking the interrogative form of the original title, second by employing its metaphor of death.

Epstein essentially updated Wilson's argument, but with important differences. Whereas Wilson looked on the decline of poetry's cultural position as a gradual process spanning three centuries, Epstein focused on the past few decades. He contrasted the major achievements of the Modernists—the generation of Eliot and Stevens, which led poetry from moribund Romanticism into the twentieth century—with what he felt were the minor accomplishments of the present practitioners. The Modernists, Epstein maintained, were artists who worked from a broad cultural vision. Contemporary writers were "poetry professionals," who operated within the closed world of the university. Wilson blamed poetry's plight on historical forces; Epstein indicted the poets themselves and the institutions they had helped create, especially creative-writing programs. A brilliant polemicist, Epstein intended his essay to be incendiary, and it did ignite an explosion of criticism. No recent essay on American poetry has generated so many immediate responses in literary journals. And certainly none has drawn so much violently negative criticism from poets themselves. To date at least thirty writers have responded in print. Henry Taylor published two rebuttals.

Poets are justifiably sensitive to arguments that poetry has declined in cultural importance, because journalists and reviewers have used such arguments simplistically to declare all contemporary verse irrelevant. Usually the less a critic knows about verse the more readily he or she dismisses it. It is no coincidence, I think, that the two most persuasive essays on poetry's presumed demise were written by outstanding critics of fiction, neither of whom has written extensively about contemporary poetry. It is too soon to judge the accuracy of Epstein's essay, but a literary historian would find Wilson's timing ironic. As Wilson finished his famous essay, Robert Frost, Wallace Stevens, T. S. Eliot, Ezra Pound, Marianne Moore, E. E. Cummings, Robinson Jeffers, H. D. (Hilda Doolittle), Robert Graves, W. H. Auden, Archibald MacLeish, Basil Bunting, and others were writing some of their finest poems, which, encompassing history, politics, economics, religion, and philosophy, are among the most culturally inclusive in the history of the language. At the same time, a new generation, which would include Robert Lowell, Elizabeth Bishop, Philip Larkin, Randall Jarrell, Dylan Thomas, A. D. Hope, and others, was just breaking into print. Wilson himself later admitted that the emergence of a versatile and ambitious poet like Auden contradicted several points of his argument. But if Wilson's prophecies were sometimes inaccurate, his sense of poetry's overall situation was depressingly astute. Even if great poetry continues to be written, it has retreated from the center of literary life. Though supported by a loyal coterie, poetry has lost the confidence that it speaks to and for the general culture.

ONE SEES EVIDENCE of poetry's diminished stature even within the thriving subculture. The established rituals of the poetry world—the readings, small magazines, workshops, and conferences—exhibit a surprising number of self-imposed limitations. Why, for example, does poetry mix so seldom with music, dance, or theater? At most readings the program consists of verse only—and usually only verse by that night's author. Forty years ago, when Dylan Thomas read, he spent half the program reciting other poets' work. Hardly a self-effacing man, he was nevertheless humble before his art. Today most readings are celebrations less of poetry than of the author's ego. No wonder the audience for such events usually consists entirely of poets, would-be poets, and friends of the author.

Several dozen journals now exist that print only verse. They don't publish literary reviews, just page after page of freshly minted poems. The heart sinks to see so many poems crammed so tightly together, like downcast immigrants in steerage. One can easily miss a radiant poem amid the many lackluster ones. It takes tremendous effort to read these small magazines with openness and attention. Few people bother, generally not even the magazines' contributors. The indifference to poetry in the mass media has created a monster of the opposite kind—journals that love poetry not wisely but too well.

Until about thirty years ago most poetry appeared in magazines that addressed a nonspecialist audience on a range of subjects. Poetry vied for the reader's interest along with political journalism, humor, fiction, and reviews—a competition that proved healthy for all the genres. A poem that didn't command the reader's attention wasn't considered much of a poem. Editors chose verse that they felt would appeal to their particular audiences, and the diversity of magazines assured that a variety of poetry appeared. The early *Kenyon Review* published Robert Lowell's poems next to critical essays and literary reviews. The old *New Yorker* showcased Ogden Nash between cartoons and short stories.

A few general-interest magazines, such as the *New Republic* and the *New Yorker,* still publish poetry in every issue, but, significantly, none except the *Nation* still reviews it regularly. Some poetry appears in the handful of small magazines and quarterlies that consistently discuss a broad cultural agenda with nonspecialist readers, such as the *Threepenny Review,* the *New Criterion,* and the *Hudson Review.* But most poetry is published in journals that address an insular audience of literary professionals, mainly teachers of creative writing and their students. A few of these, such as *American Poetry Review* and *AWP Chronicle,* have moderately large circulations. Many more have negligible readerships. But size is not the problem. The problem is their complacency or resignation about existing only in and for a subculture.

What are the characteristics of a poetry-subculture publication? First, the one subject it addresses is current American literature (supplemented perhaps by a few translations of poets who have already been widely translated). Second, if it prints anything other than poetry, that is usually short fiction. Third, if it runs discursive prose, the essays and reviews are overwhelmingly positive. If it publishes an interview, the tone will be unabashedly reverent toward the author. For these journals critical prose exists not to provide a disinterested perspective on new books but to publicize them. Quite often there are manifest personal connections between the reviewers and the authors they discuss. If occasionally a negative review is published, it will be openly sectarian, rejecting an aesthetic that the magazine has already condemned. The unspoken editorial rule seems to be, Never surprise or annoy the readers; they are, after all, mainly our friends and colleagues.

By abandoning the hard work of evaluation, the poetry subculture demeans its own art. Since there are too many new poetry collections appearing each year for anyone to evaluate, the reader must rely on the candor and discernment of reviewers to recommend the best books. But the general press has largely abandoned this task, and the specialized press has grown so overprotective of poetry that it is reluctant to make harsh judgments. In his book *American Poetry: Wilderness and Domesticity,* Robert Bly has accurately described the corrosive effect of this critical boosterism:

> We have an odd situation: although more bad poetry is being published now than ever before in American history, most of the reviews are positive. Critics say, "I never attack what is bad, all that will take care of itself," . . . but the country is full of young poets and readers who are confused by seeing mediocre poetry praised, or never attacked, and who end up doubting their own critical perceptions.

A clubby feeling also typifies most recent anthologies of contemporary poetry. Although these collections represent themselves as trustworthy guides to the best new poetry, they are not compiled for readers outside the academy. More than one editor has discovered that the best way to get an anthology assigned is to include work by the poets who teach the courses. Compiled in the spirit of congenial opportunism, many of these anthologies give the impression that literary quality is a concept that neither an editor nor a reader should take too seriously.

The 1985 *Morrow Anthology of Younger American Poets,* for example, is not so much a selective literary collection as a comprehensive directory of creative-writing teachers (it even offers a photo of each author). Running nearly 800 pages, the volume presents no fewer than 104 important young poets, virtually all of whom teach creative writing. The editorial principle governing selection seems to have been the fear of leaving out some influential colleague. The book does contain a few strong and original poems, but they are surrounded by so many undistinguished exercises that one wonders if the good work got there by design or simply by random sampling. In the drearier patches one suspects that perhaps the book was never truly meant to be read, only assigned.

And that is the real issue. The poetry subculture no longer assumes that all published poems will be read. Like their colleagues in other academic departments, poetry professionals must publish, for purposes of both job security and career advancement. The more they publish, the faster they progress. If they do not publish, or wait too long, their economic futures are in grave jeopardy.

In art, of course, everyone agrees that quality and not quantity matters. Some authors survive on the basis of a single unforgettable poem— Edmund Waller's "Go, lovely rose," for example, or Edwin Markham's "The Man With the Hoe," which was made famous by being reprinted in hundreds of newspapers—an unthinkable occurrence today. But bureaucracies, by their very nature, have difficulty measuring something as intangible as literary quality. When institutions evaluate creative artists for employment or promotion, they still must find some seemingly objective means to do so. As the critic Bruce Bawer has observed,

> A poem is, after all, a fragile thing, and its intrinsic worth, or lack thereof, is a frighteningly subjective consideration; but fellowships, grants, degrees, appointments, and publications are objective facts. They are quantifiable; they can be listed on a résumé.

Poets serious about making careers in institutions understand that the criteria for success are primarily quantitative. They must publish as much as possible as quickly as possible. The slow maturation of genuine creativity looks like laziness to a committee. Wallace Stevens was forty-three when his first book appeared. Robert Frost was thirty-nine. Today these sluggards would be unemployable.

The proliferation of literary journals and presses over the past thirty years has been a response less to an increased appetite for poetry among the public than to the desperate need of writing teachers for professional validation. Like subsidized farming that grows food no one wants, a poetry industry has been created to serve the interests of the producers and not the consumers. And in the process the integrity of the art has been betrayed. Of course, no poet is allowed to admit this in public. The cultural credibility of the professional poetry establishment depends on maintaining a polite hypocrisy. Millions of dollars in public and private funding are at stake. Luckily, no one outside the subculture cares enough to press the point very far. No Woodward and Bernstein will ever investigate a cover-up by members of the Associated Writing Programs.

The new poet makes a living not by publishing literary work but by providing specialized educational services. Most likely he or she either works for or aspires to work for a large institution—usually a state-run enterprise, such as a school district, a college, or a university (or lately even a hospital or prison)—teaching others how to write poetry or, at the highest levels, how to teach others how to write poetry.

To look at the issue in strictly economic terms, most contemporary poets have been alienated from their original cultural function. As Marx maintained and few economists have disputed, changes in a class's economic function eventually transform its values and behavior. In poetry's case, the socioeconomic changes have led to a divided literary culture: the superabundance of poetry within a small class and the impoverishment outside it. One might even say that outside the classroom—where society demands that the two groups interact—poets and the common reader are no longer on speaking terms.

The divorce of poetry from the educated reader has had another, more pernicious result. Seeing so much mediocre verse not only published but praised, slogging through so many dull anthologies and small magazines, most readers—even sophisticated ones like Joseph Epstein—now assume that no significant new poetry is being written. This public skepticism represents the final isolation of verse as an art form in contemporary society.

The irony is that this skepticism comes in a period of genuine achievement. Gresham's Law, that bad coinage drives out good, only half applies to current poetry. The sheer mass of mediocrity may have frightened away most readers, but it has not yet driven talented writers from the field. Anyone patient enough to weed through the tangle of contemporary work finds an impressive and diverse range of new poetry. Adrienne Rich, for example, despite her often overbearing polemics, is a major poet by any standard. The best work of Donald Justice, Anthony Hecht, Donald Hall, James Merrill, Louis Simpson, William Stafford, and Richard Wilbur—to mention only writers of the older generation—can hold its own against anything in the national literature. One might also add Sylvia Plath and James Wright, two strong poets of the same generation who died early. America is also a country rich in émigré poetry, as major writers like Czeslaw Milosz, Nina Cassian, Derek Walcott, Joseph Brodsky, and Thom Gunn demonstrate.

Without a role in the broader culture, however, talented poets lack the confidence to create public speech. Occasionally a writer links up rewardingly to a social or political movement. Rich, for example, has used feminism to expand the vision of her work. Robert Bly wrote his finest poetry to protest the Vietnam War. His sense of addressing a large and diverse audience added humor, breadth, and humanity to his previously minimalist verse. But it is a difficult task to marry the Muse happily to politics. Consequently, most contemporary poets, knowing that they are virtually invisible in the larger culture, focus on the more intimate forms of lyric and meditative verse. (And a few loners, like X. J. Kennedy and John Updike, turn their genius to the critically disreputable demimonde of light verse and children's poetry.) Therefore, although current American poetry has not often excelled in public forms like political or satiric verse, it has nonetheless produced personal poems of unsurpassed beauty and power. Despite its manifest excellence, this new work has not found a public beyond the poetry subculture, because the traditional machinery of transmission—the reliable reviewing, honest criticism, and selective anthologies—has broken down. The audience that once made Frost and Eliot, Cummings and Millay, part of its cultural vision remains out of reach. Today Walt Whitman's challenge "To have great poets, there must be great audiences, too" reads like an indictment.

To MAINTAIN their activities, subcultures usually require institutions, since the general society does not share their interests. Nudists flock to "nature camps" to express their unfettered lifestyle. Monks remain in monasteries to protect their austere ideals. As long as poets belonged to a broader class of artists and intellectuals, they centered their lives in urban bohemias, where they maintained a distrustful independence from institutions. Once poets began moving into universities, they abandoned the working-class heterogeneity of Greenwich Village and North Beach for the professional homogeneity of academia.

At first they existed on the fringes of English departments, which was probably healthy. Without advanced degrees or formal career paths, poets were recognized as special creatures. They were allowed—like aboriginal chieftains visiting an anthropologist's campsite—to behave according to their own laws. But as the demand for creative writing grew, the poet's job expanded from merely literary to administrative duties. At the university's urging, these self-trained young writers designed history's first institutional curricula for young poets. Creative writing evolved from occasional courses taught within the English department into its own undergraduate major or graduate-degree program. Writers fashioned their academic specialty in the image of other university studies. As the new writing departments multiplied, the new professionals patterned their infrastructure—job titles, journals, annual conventions, organizations—according to standards not of urban bohemia but of educational institutions. Out of the professional networks this educational expansion created, the subculture of poetry was born.

Initially, the multiplication of creative-writing programs must have been a dizzyingly happy affair. Poets who had scraped by in bohemia or had spent their early adulthood fighting the Second World War suddenly secured stable, well-paying jobs. Writers who had never earned much public attention found themselves surrounded by eager students. Poets who had been too poor to travel flew from campus to campus and from conference to conference, to speak before audiences of their peers. As Wilfrid Sheed once described a moment in John Berryman's career, "Through the burgeoning university network, it was suddenly possible to think of oneself as a national poet, even if the nation turned out to consist entirely of English Departments." The bright postwar world promised a renaissance for American poetry.

In material terms that promise has been fulfilled beyond the dreams of anyone in Berryman's Depression-scarred generation. Poets now occupy niches at every level of academia, from a few sumptuously endowed chairs with six-figure salaries to the more numerous part-time stints that pay roughly the same as Burger King. But even at minimum wage, teaching poetry earns more than writing it ever did. Before the creative-writing boom, being a poet usually meant living in genteel poverty or worse. While the sacrifices poetry demanded caused much individual suffering, the rigors of serving Milton's "thankless Muse" also delivered the collective cultural benefit of frightening away all but committed artists.

Today poetry is a modestly upwardly mobile, middle-class profession—not as lucrative as waste management or dermatology but several big steps above the squalor of bohemia. Only a philistine would romanticize the blissfully banished artistic poverty of yesteryear. But a clear-eyed observer must also recognize that by opening the poet's trade to all applicants and by employing writers to do something other than write, institutions have changed the social and economic identity of the poet from artist to educator. In social terms the identification of poet with teacher is now complete. The first question one poet now asks another upon being introduced is "Where do you teach?" The problem is not that poets teach. The campus is not a bad place for a poet to work. It's just a bad place for all poets to work. Society suffers by losing the imagination and vitality that poets brought to public culture. Poetry suffers when literary standards are forced to conform to institutional ones.

Even within the university contemporary poetry now exists as a subculture. The teaching poet finds that he or she has little in common with academic colleagues. The academic study of literature over the past twenty-five years has veered off in a theoretical direction with which most imaginative writers have little sympathy or familiarity. Thirty years ago detractors of creative-writing programs predicted that poets in universities would become enmeshed in literary criticism and scholarship. This prophecy has proved spectacularly wrong. Poets have created enclaves in the academy almost entirely separate from their critical colleagues. They write less criticism than they did before entering the academy. Pressed to keep up with the plethora of new poetry, small magazines, professional journals, and anthologies, they are frequently also less well read in the literature of the past. Their peers in the English department generally read less contemporary poetry and more literary theory. In many departments writers and literary theorists are openly at war. Bringing the two groups under one roof has paradoxically made each more territorial. Isolated even within the university, the poet, whose true subject is the whole of human existence, has reluctantly become an educational specialist.

To UNDERSTAND how radically the social situation of the American poet has changed, one need only compare today with fifty years ago. In 1940, with the notable exception of Robert Frost, few poets were working in colleges unless, like Mark Van Doren and Yvor Winters, they taught traditional academic subjects. The only creative-writing program was an experiment begun a few years earlier at the University of Iowa. The Modernists exemplified the options that poets had for making a living. They could enter middle-class professions, as had T. S. Eliot (a banker turned publisher), Wallace Stevens (a corporate insurance lawyer), and William Carlos Williams (a pediatrician). Or they could live in bohemia supporting themselves as artists, as, in different ways, did Ezra Pound, E. E. Cummings, and Marianne Moore. If the city proved unattractive, they could, like Robinson Jeffers, scrape by in a rural arts colony like Carmel, California. Or they might become farmers, like the young Robert Frost.

Most often poets supported themselves as editors or reviewers, actively taking part in the artistic and intellectual life of their time. Archibald MacLeish was an editor and writer at *Fortune.* James Agee reviewed movies for *Time* and the *Nation,* and eventually wrote screenplays for Hollywood. Randall Jarrell reviewed books. Weldon Kees wrote about jazz and modern art. Delmore Schwartz reviewed everything. Even poets who eventually took up academic careers spent intellectually broadening apprenticeships in literary journalism. The young Robert Hayden covered music and theater for Michigan's black press. R. P. Blackmur, who never completed high school, reviewed books for *Hound & Horn* before teaching at Princeton. Occasionally a poet might supplement his or her income by giving a reading or lecture, but these occasions were rare. Robinson Jeffers, for example, was fifty-four when he gave his first public reading. For most poets, the sustaining medium was not the classroom or the podium but the written word.

If poets supported themselves by writing, it was mainly by writing prose. Paying outlets for poetry were limited. Beyond a few national magazines, which generally preferred light verse or political satire, there were at any one time only a few dozen journals that published a significant amount of poetry. The emergence of a serious new quarterly like *Partisan Review* or *Furioso* was an event of real importance, and a small but dedicated audience eagerly looked forward to each issue. If people could not afford to buy copies, they borrowed them or visited public libraries. As for books of poetry, if one excludes vanity-press editions, fewer than a hundred new titles were published each year. But the books that did appear were reviewed in daily newspapers as well as magazines and quarterlies. A focused monthly like *Poetry* could cover virtually the entire field.

Reviewers fifty years ago were by today's standards extraordinarily tough. They said exactly what they thought, even about their most influential contemporaries. Listen, for example, to Randall Jarrell's description of a book by the famous anthologist Oscar Williams: it "gave the impression of having been written on a typewriter by a typewriter." That remark kept Jarrell out of subsequent Williams anthologies, but he did

[handwritten margin note: tough reviewers · mention Logan]

not hesitate to publish it. Or consider Jarrell's assessment of Archibald MacLeish's public poem *America Was Promises:* it "might have been devised by a YMCA secretary at a home for the mentally deficient." Or read Weldon Kees's one-sentence review of Muriel Rukeyser's *Wake Island*— "There's one thing you can say about Muriel: she's not lazy." But these same reviewers could write generously about poets they admired, as Jarrell did about Elizabeth Bishop, and Kees about Wallace Stevens. Their praise mattered, because readers knew it did not come lightly.

The reviewers of fifty years ago knew that their primary loyalty must lie not with their fellow poets or publishers but with the reader. Consequently they reported their reactions with scrupulous honesty, even when their opinions might lose them literary allies and writing assignments. In discussing new poetry they addressed a wide community of educated readers. Without talking down to their audience, they cultivated a public idiom. Prizing clarity and accessibility, they avoided specialist jargon and pedantic displays of scholarship. They also tried, as serious intellectuals should but specialists often do not, to relate what was happening in poetry to social, political, and artistic trends. They charged modern poetry with cultural importance and made it the focal point of their intellectual discourse.

Ill-paid, overworked, and underappreciated, this argumentative group of "practical" critics, all of them poets, accomplished remarkable things. They defined the canon of Modernist poetry, established methods to analyze verse of extraordinary difficulty, and identified the new mid-century generation of American poets (Lowell, Roethke, Bishop, Berryman, and others) that still dominates our literary consciousness. Whatever one thinks of their literary canon or critical principles, one must admire the intellectual energy and sheer determination of these critics, who developed as writers without grants or permanent faculty positions, often while working precariously on freelance assignments. They represent a high point in American intellectual life. Even fifty years later their names still command more authority than those of all but a few contemporary critics. A short roll call would include John Berryman, R. P. Blackmur, Louise Bogan, John Ciardi, Horace Gregory, Langston Hughes, Randall Jarrell, Weldon Kees, Kenneth Rexroth, Delmore Schwartz, Karl Shapiro, Allen Tate, and Yvor Winters. Although contemporary poetry has its boosters and publicists, it has no group of comparable dedication and talent able to address the general literary community.

Like all genuine intellectuals, these critics were visionary. They believed that if modern poets did not have an audience, they could create one. And gradually they did. It was not a mass audience; few American poets of any period have enjoyed a direct relationship with the general public. It was a cross section of artists and intellectuals, including scientists, clergymen, educators, lawyers, and, of course, writers. This group constituted a literary intelligentsia, made up mainly of nonspecialists, who took poetry as seriously as fiction and drama. Recently Donald Hall and other critics have questioned the size of this audience by citing the low average sales of a volume of new verse by an established poet during the period (usually under a thousand copies). But these skeptics do not understand how poetry was read then.

America was a smaller, less affluent country in 1940, with about half its current population and one sixth its current real GNP. In those pre-paperback days of the late Depression neither readers nor libraries could afford to buy as many books as they do today. Nor was there a large captive audience of creative-writing students who bought books of contemporary poetry for classroom use. Readers usually bought poetry in two forms—in an occasional *Collected Poems* by a leading author, or in anthologies. The comprehensive collections of writers like Frost, Eliot, Auden, Jeffers, Wylie, and Millay sold very well, were frequently reprinted, and stayed perpetually in print. (Today most *Collected Poems* disappear after one printing.) Occasionally a book of new poems would capture the public's fancy. Edwin Arlington Robinson's *Tristram* (1927) became a Literary Guild selection. Frost's *A Further Range* sold 50,000 copies as a 1936 Book-of-the-Month Club selection. But people knew poetry mainly from anthologies, which they not only bought but also read, with curiosity and attention.

Louis Untermeyer's *Modern American Poetry,* first published in 1919, was frequently revised to keep it up to date and was a perennial best-seller. My 1942 edition, for example, had been reprinted five times by 1945. My edition of Oscar Williams's *A Pocket Book of Modern Poetry* had been reprinted nineteen times in fourteen years. Untermeyer and Williams prided themselves on keeping their anthologies broad-based and timely. They tried to represent the best of what was being published. Each edition added new poems and poets and dropped older ones. The public appreciated their efforts. Poetry anthologies were an indispensable part of any serious reader's library. Random House's popular Modern Library series, for example, included not one but two anthologies—Selden Rodman's *A New Anthology of Modern Poetry* and Conrad Aiken's *Twentieth-Century American Poetry*. All these collections were read and reread by a diverse public. Favorite poems were memorized. Difficult authors like Eliot and Thomas were actively discussed and debated. Poetry mattered outside the classroom.

Today these general readers constitute the audience that poetry has lost. United by intelligence and curiosity, this heterogeneous group cuts across lines of race, class, age, and occupation. Representing our cultural intelligentsia, they are the people who support the arts—who buy classical and jazz records; who attend foreign films, serious theater, opera, symphony, and dance; who read quality fiction and biographies; who listen to public radio and subscribe to the best journals. (They are also often the parents who read poetry to their children and remember, once upon a time in college or high school or kindergarten, liking it themselves.) No one knows the size of this community, but even if one accepts the conservative estimate that it accounts for only 2 percent of the U.S. population, it still represents a potential audience of almost five million readers. However healthy poetry may appear within its professional subculture, it has lost this larger audience, who represent poetry's bridge to the general culture.

BUT WHY SHOULD ANYONE but a poet care about the problems of American poetry? What possible relevance does this archaic art form have to contemporary society? In a better world, poetry would need no justification beyond the sheer splendor of its own existence. As Wallace Stevens once observed, "The purpose of poetry is to contribute to man's happiness." Children know this essential truth when they ask to hear their favorite nursery rhymes again and again. Aesthetic pleasure needs no justification, because a life without such pleasure is one not worth living.

But the rest of society has mostly forgotten the value of poetry. To the general reader, discussions about the state of poetry sound like the debating of foreign politics by émigrés in a seedy café. Or, as Cyril Connolly more bitterly described it, "Poets arguing about modern poetry: jackals snarling over a dried-up well." Anyone who hopes to broaden poetry's audience—critic, teacher, librarian, poet, or lonely literary amateur—faces a daunting challenge. How does one persuade justly skeptical readers, in terms they can understand and appreciate, that poetry still matters?

A passage in William Carlos Williams's "Asphodel, That Greeny Flower" provides a possible starting point. Written toward the end of the author's life, after he had been partly paralyzed by a stroke, the lines sum up the hard lessons about poetry and audience that Williams had learned over years of dedication to both poetry and medicine. He wrote,

> My heart rouses
>   thinking to bring you news
>   of something
> that concerns you
>   and concerns many men. Look at
>   what passes for the new.
> You will not find it there but in
>   despised poems.
>   It is difficult
> to get the news from poems
>   yet men die miserably every day
>   for lack
> of what is found there.

Williams understood poetry's human value but had no illusions about the difficulties his contemporaries faced in trying to engage the audience that needed the art most desperately. To regain poetry's readership one must begin by meeting Williams's challenge to find what "concerns many men," not simply what concerns poets.

There are at least two reasons why the situation of poetry matters to the entire intellectual community. The first involves the role of language in a free society. Poetry is the art of using words charged with their utmost meaning. A society whose intellectual leaders lose the skill to shape, appreciate, and understand the power of language will become the slaves of those who retain it—be they politicians, preachers, copywriters, or newscasters. The public responsibility of poetry has been pointed out repeatedly by modern writers. Even the arch-symbolist Stéphane Mallarmé praised the poet's central mission to "purify the words of the tribe." And Ezra Pound warned that,

> Good writers are those who keep the language efficient. That is to say, keep it accurate, keep it clear. It doesn't matter whether a good

writer wants to be useful or whether the bad writer wants to do harm. . . .

If a nation's literature declines, the nation atrophies and decays.

Or, as George Orwell wrote after the Second World War, "One ought to recognize that the present political chaos is connected with the decay of language. . . ." Poetry is not the entire solution to keeping the nation's language clear and honest, but one is hard pressed to imagine a country's citizens improving the health of its language while abandoning poetry.

The second reason why the situation of poetry matters to all intellectuals is that poetry is not alone among the arts in its marginal position. If the audience for poetry has declined into a subculture of specialists, so too have the audiences for most contemporary art forms, from serious drama to jazz. The unprecedented fragmentation of American high culture during the past half century has left most arts in isolation from one another as well as from the general audience. Contemporary classical music scarcely exists as a living art outside university departments and conservatories. Jazz, which once commanded a broad popular audience, has become the semi-private domain of aficionados and musicians. (Today even influential jazz innovators cannot find places to perform in many metropolitan centers—and for an improvisatory art the inability to perform is a crippling liability.) Much serious drama is now confined to the margins of American theater, where it is seen only by actors, aspiring actors, playwrights, and a few diehard fans. Only the visual arts, perhaps because of their financial glamour and upper-class support, have largely escaped the decline in public attention.

THE MOST SERIOUS QUESTION for the future of American culture is whether the arts will continue to exist in isolation and decline into subsidized academic specialties or whether some possibility of rapprochement with the educated public remains. Each of the arts must face the challenge separately, and no art faces more towering obstacles than poetry. Given the decline of literacy, the proliferation of other media, the crisis in humanities education, the collapse of critical standards, and the sheer weight of past failures, how can poets possibly succeed in being heard? Wouldn't it take a miracle?

Toward the end of her life Marianne Moore wrote a short poem called "O To Be a Dragon." This poem recalled the biblical dream in which the

Lord appeared to King Solomon and said, "Ask what I shall give thee."
Solomon wished for a wise and understanding heart. Moore's wish is
harder to summarize. Her poem reads,

> If I, like Solomon, . . .
> could have my wish—
>
> my wish . . . O to be a dragon,
> a symbol of the power of Heaven—of silkworm
> size or immense; at times invisible.
> Felicitous phenomenon!

Moore got her wish. She became, as all genuine poets do, "a symbol
of the power of Heaven." She succeeded in what Robert Frost called "the
utmost of ambition"—namely, "to lodge a few poems where they will be
hard to get rid of." She is permanently part of the "felicitous phenomenon" of American literature.

So wishes can come true—even extravagant ones. If I, like Marianne
Moore, could have my wish, and I, like Solomon, could have the self-
control not to wish for myself, I would wish that poetry could again become a part of American public culture. I don't think this is impossible.
All it would require is that poets and poetry teachers take more responsibility for bringing their art to the public. I will close with six modest pro-
posals for how this dream might come true.

1. *When poets give public readings, they should spend part of every program
   reciting other people's work*—preferably poems they admire by writers
   they do not know personally. Readings should be celebrations of
   poetry in general, not merely of the featured author's work.
2. *When arts administrators plan public readings, they should avoid the standard subculture format of poetry only.* Mix poetry with the other arts,
   especially music. Plan evenings honoring dead or foreign writers. Combine short critical lectures with poetry performances. Such combina-
   tions would attract an audience from beyond the poetry world without
   compromising quality.
3. *Poets need to write prose about poetry more often, more candidly, and more
   effectively.* Poets must recapture the attention of the broader intellectual community by writing for nonspecialist publications. They must

also avoid the jargon of contemporary academic criticism and write in a public idiom. Finally, poets must regain the reader's trust by candidly admitting what they don't like as well as promoting what they like. Professional courtesy has no place in literary journalism.

4. *Poets who compile anthologies—or even reading lists—should be scrupulously honest in including only poems they genuinely admire.* Anthologies are poetry's gateway to the general culture. They should not be used as pork barrels for the creative-writing trade. An art expands its audience by presenting masterpieces, not mediocrity. Anthologies should be compiled to move, delight, and instruct readers, not to flatter the writing teachers who assign books. Poet-anthologists must never trade the Muse's property for professional favors.

5. *Poetry teachers, especially at the high-school and undergraduate levels, should spend less time on analysis and more on performance.* Poetry needs to be liberated from literary criticism. Poems should be memorized, recited, and performed. The sheer joy of the art must be emphasized. The pleasure of performance is what first attracts children to poetry, the sensual excitement of speaking and hearing the words of the poem. Performance was also the teaching technique that kept poetry vital for centuries. Maybe it also holds the key to poetry's future.

6. *Finally, poets and arts administrators should use radio to expand the art's audience.* Poetry is an aural medium, and thus ideally suited to radio. A little imaginative programming at the hundreds of college and public-supported radio stations could bring poetry to millions of listeners. Some programming exists, but it is stuck mostly in the standard subculture format of living poets reading their own work. Mixing poetry with music on classical and jazz stations or creating innovative talk-radio formats could reestablish a direct relationship between poetry and the general audience.

The history of art tells the same story over and over. As art forms develop, they establish conventions that guide creation, performance, instruction, even analysis. But eventually these conventions grow stale. They begin to stand between the art and its audience. Although much wonderful poetry is being written, the American poetry establishment is locked into a series of exhausted conventions—outmoded ways of presenting, discussing, editing, and teaching poetry. Educational institutions have codified them into a stifling bureaucratic etiquette that enervates the art. These conventions may once have made sense, but today they imprison poetry in an intellectual ghetto.

It is time to experiment, time to leave the well-ordered but stuffy classroom, time to restore a vulgar vitality to poetry and unleash the energy now trapped in the subculture. There is nothing to lose. Society has already told us that poetry is dead. Let's build a funeral pyre out of the desiccated conventions piled around us and watch the ancient, spangle-feathered, unkillable phoenix rise from the ashes.

The Dilemma of
the Long Poem

—

AMERICAN POETRY prides itself on its great scope and diversity, but one wonders if an outsider might not come away with a very different notion. Imagine what an intelligent eighteenth-century reader would conclude if he surveyed the several hundred books of poetry published in America in an average year. (For simplicity's sake, let us keep this long-suffering gentleman's conclusions descriptive rather than evaluative. There is no way of know what, if anything, he would actually enjoy amid this poetic avalanche.) His overall reaction, I suspect, would be a deep disappointment over the predictable sameness, the conspicuous lack of diversity in what he read. Where are the narrative poems, he would ask, the verse romances, ballads, hymns, verse dramas, didactic tracts, burlesques, satires, the songs actually meant to be sung, and even the pastoral eclogues? Are stories no longer told in poetry? Important ideas no longer discussed at length? The panoply of available genres would seem reduced to a few hardy perennials that poets worked over and over again with dreary regularity—the short lyric, the ode, the familiar verse epistle, perhaps the epigram, and one new-fangled form called the "sequence," which often seemed to be either just a group of short lyrics stuck together or an ode in the process of falling apart. Amid this myriad of shorter work he would see only a few poems longer than six or seven pages—most of them massive and complex undertakings running many times the length of the average thin volume. These, he would ascertain, are the epics of this age, but he would probably not be able to classify them further since they were mostly difficult, allusive works not governed by a narrative or expository structure. They undoubtedly belonged to a genre whose rules he didn't understand.

This hypothetical gentleman would also be perplexed by the paucity of technical means he saw employed. Most of what he read would be in free verse (some of which he would recognize as such from his familiarity with Milton, Smart, and, of course, the Old Testament) balanced by a little irregular pentameter, an occasional sestina, and virtually nothing else. What happened to rhyme, he would ask, and all the meters ancient and modern plus all the familiar stanza forms of English? These new poets, he might conclude, are a very monotonous bunch indeed who can manage only the shorter forms and even those only within the slenderest range of technical means. Poems longer than a half a dozen pages seem to be beyond their powers altogether. Yes, American poetry would seem to be a very limited enterprise. It not only lacks great poets of the stature of Shakespeare, Spenser, Milton, Dryden, and Pope, it also lacks estimable lesser writers of scope and versatility, like Dyer, Thomson, Collins, Cowper, Young, Shenstone, and Gay.

Such judgments would infuriate our poets and critics alike, but are they so inaccurate? American poetry may be bold and expansive in its moods and subject matter, but it remains timorous and short-winded in its range. Despite its enormous volume, the poetry published each year tends to be conceived almost exclusively in shorter forms. It does not take a university professor to notice this bias. Any reader familiar with at least one other period of literature in English would have to ask why the tremendous talent of contemporary poets has been so narrowly focused.

The orthodox academic reply is that the intensity and concentration of modern poetry have made the long poem impossible. An extended work in verse would perforce break up into shorter fragments. This explanation sounds plausible at first, and indeed it may even have some limited applicability to certain early modern schools such as Imagism, but careful observation proves it untrue in any general case. Contemporary poetry is not particularly intense or concentrated on either an absolute or relative basis. Certainly concentration and intensity are characteristics of good short poetry in any age, but the twentieth century has little special claim on them. Compare half a dozen widely anthologized contemporary poems with a lyric by George Herbert or a sonnet by Milton, and one will usually find the modern work relaxed and casual in comparison. Why then could a poet like Milton, an unquestioned master of the short, concentrated poem, also manage brilliant longer poems whereas our contemporaries cannot? The answer is complex and encompasses several acknowledged factors, such as the increasing identification of all poetry with the lyric mode, the subsequent rejection of narrative and didacticism as available poetic strategies, and the neglect of precisely those metrical resources in English that have traditionally provided long poems with an underlying structure. There is another factor, however, which I have never heard discussed but which has had a crucial impact on our literature.

The major problem facing the long poem today is that contemporary theory allows the poet almost no middle ground between the concentration of the short lyric and the vast breadth of the epic (the modern epic, that is, in its distinctive form as the historical culture poem). Of course, our theoreticians have not banned all other kinds of poetry, but the critical emphases on lyric and epic have been so strong over the past seventy years that to poets and teachers alike they have become the distinctive forms of both the Modern and so-called Postmodern periods. The long poem has nearly died as a result. It has become an all-or-nothing proposition, an obsessive, lifelong undertaking. The poet must confront his entire culture and prepare some vast synthesis of its history and values. There may be one or two poets in any age who are capable of bringing off so ambitious an enterprise, but how many geniuses have botched their careers trying it? To take the most conspicuous example in our century, consider Ezra Pound, who stopped writing other poetry at the height of his powers to concentrate on his never completed *Cantos*. Ultimately the *Cantos* may well be the most interesting poem in American literature, but it is surely not a success (if the word *success* has any meaning left in describing a form that has relinquished the conventional standards of literary performance and intends only to re-create an author's private sensibility without any concessions to his audience). Or consider Conrad Aiken, who spent his entire career trying repeatedly, but in vain, to write the definitive long poem of his age.

Indeed the long modern poem is virtually doomed to failure by its own ground rules. Any extended work needs a strong overall form to guide both the poet in creating it and the reader in understanding it. By rejecting the traditional epic structures of narrative (as in Virgil) and didactic exposition (as in Lucretius), the modern author has been thrown almost entirely on his own resources. He must not only try to synthesize the complexity of his culture into one poem, he must also create the form of his discourse as he goes along. It is as if a physicist were asked to make a major new discovery in quantum mechanics but prevented from using any of the established methodologies in arriving at it. Even genius cannot accomplish such a task. Could Milton have succeeded so brilliantly with

Paradise Lost without the examples of Homer, Virgil, Dante, Tasso, and Spenser behind him? Given that the structure of the modern epic has become an elaborate nonce form, it is not surprising that one finds no incontestable masterpieces among the major long poems of this century but only a group of more or less interesting failures, none widely read in its entirety by the literary public, though all jealously guarded by some particular faction (with no group quite so rabidly partisan as those professors who have staked their academic careers on researching and explicating a particular poem): Williams's *Paterson,* Jones's *The Anathemata,* Olson's *Maximus Poems,* Zukofsky's *A,* Berryman's *Dream Songs,* Dorn's *Gunslinger,* and so forth.

Given the immensity of the commitment and the high odds of failure involved in writing the modern epic, it is hardly surprising that most poets have chosen to concentrate single-mindedly on shorter forms, especially the lyric (both in its simple and conglomerate form, the sequence). Here at least the talented poet can make a lasting place for himself. It is instructive to consider how many contemporary poets have achieved important reputations almost solely on short poems: Elizabeth Bishop, Randall Jarrell, Weldon Kees, James Wright, Sylvia Plath, Robert Graves, Richard Wilbur, Howard Nemerov, Adrienne Rich, Howard Moss, Louis Simpson, J. V. Cunningham, Philip Larkin, Charles Tomlinson, W. S. Merwin, William Stafford. The list could go on and on. Most of these writers have done extended imaginative work, but significantly they avoided poetry as the medium for it. Poets like Graves or Nemerov turned to the novel, while others like Bishop or Kees chose the short story. Some, like Wilbur and Merwin, concentrated on verse translation or, like Rich, on polemical prose. Even drama, as in Moss's case, or autobiographical prose, as in Simpson's, served as the natural conduit for their most expansive work. The diverse extended work of these poets has only one thing in common—the avoidance of verse as its medium.

American literature needs a more modest aesthetic of the long poem, a less chauvinistic theory that does not vainly seek the great at the expense of the good and genuine. It needs to free poets from the burden of writing the definitive long poem and allow them to work in more manageable, albeit limited, genres like satire, comedy, unheroic autobiography, discursive writing, pure narrative—be it fictional or historic—and even perhaps such unlikely narrative subgenres as science fiction, detective, or adventure stories—wherever, in short, their imagination takes them. It also needs to foster poems of "middle length," extended pieces not long enough to fill up an entire volume. Such poems have played an important role in English from Chaucer's *Canterbury Tales* to Browning's major dramatic monologues, but today they are shunned by editors, publishers, and critics alike (a sad situation that parallels the almost total extinction of the novella by the novel and short story in contemporary fiction). Poems of middle length allow a poet to explore a particular theme without overextending it, and they do not require the Herculean effort necessary to complete an epic. Some poets work best in longer forms—Byron, Crabbe, Morris, Pope, and Dryden are a few historical examples—but their talents may not necessarily be suited for the straight epic. They need an array of possible forms as broad and various as their talents, an array that unfortunately does not seem widely available at present.

Notes on the
New Formalism

~

TWENTY YEARS AGO it was a truth universally acknowledged that a young poet in possession of a good ear would want to write free verse. Today one faces more complex and problematic choices. While the overwhelming majority of new poetry published in the United States continues to be in "open" forms, for the first time in two generations there is a major revival of formal verse among young poets. The first signs of this revival emerged at the tail end of the seventies, long after the more knowing critics had declared rhyme and meter permanently defunct. First a few good formal books by young poets like Charles Martin's *Room for Error* (1978) and Timothy Steele's *Uncertainties and Rest* (1979) appeared but went almost completely unreviewed. Then magazines like *Paris Review,* which hadn't published a rhyming poem in anyone's memory, suddenly began featuring sonnets, villanelles, and syllabics. Changes in literary taste make good copy, and the sharper reviewers quickly took note. Soon some of the most lavishly praised debuts like Brad Leithauser's *Hundreds of Fireflies* (1982) and Vikram Seth's *The Golden Gate* (1986) were by poets working entirely in form.

Literature not only changes; it must change to keep its force and vitality. There will always be groups advocating new types of poetry, some of it genuine, just as there will always be conservative opposing forces trying to maintain the conventional methods. But the revival of rhyme and meter among some young poets creates an unprecedented situation in American poetry. The New Formalists put free-verse poets in the ironic and unprepared position of being the status quo. Free verse, the creation of an older literary revolution, is now the long-established, ruling orthodoxy, formal poetry the unexpected challenge.

There is currently a great deal of private controversy about these New Formalists, some of which occasionally spills over into print. Significantly, these discussions often contain many odd misconceptions about poetic form, most of them threadbare clichés that somehow still survive from the sixties. Form, we are told authoritatively, is artificial, elitist, retrogressive, right-wing, and (my favorite) un-American. None of these arguments can withstand critical scrutiny, but nevertheless, they continue to be made so regularly that one can only assume they provide some emotional comfort to their advocates. Obviously, for many writers the discussion of formal and free verse has become an encoded political debate.

When the language of poetic criticism has become so distorted, one needs to make some fundamental distinctions. Formal verse, like free verse, is neither intrinsically bad nor good. The terms are strictly descriptive not evaluative. They define distinct sets of metrical technique rather than rank the quality or nature of poetic performance. Nor do these techniques automatically carry with them social, political, or even, in most cases, aesthetic values. (It would, for example, be very easy for a poet to do automatic writing in meter. One might even argue that surrealism is best realized in formal verse since the regular rhythms of the words in meter hypnotically release the unconscious.) However obvious these distinctions should be, few poets or critics seem to be making them. Is it any wonder then that so much current writing on poetry is either opaque or irrelevant? What serious discussion can develop when such primary critical definitions fail to be made with accuracy?

2

METER IS AN ANCIENT, indeed primitive, technique that marks the beginning of literature in virtually every culture. It dates back to a time, so different from our specialized modern era, when there was little, if any, distinction among poetry, religion, history, music, and magic. All were performed in a sacred, ritual language separated from everyday speech by its incantatory metrical form. Meter is also essentially a preliterate technology, a way of making language memorable before the invention of writing. Trained poet-singers took the events and ideas a culture wanted to preserve—tribal histories, magic ceremonies—formulated them in meter, and committed these formulas to memory. Before writing, the poet and the poem were inseparable, and both represented the collective memory of their culture.

Meter is therefore an aural technique. It assumes a speaker and a listener, who for the duration of the poem are intertwined. Even in later literary cultures meter has always insisted on the primacy of the physical sound of language. Unlike prose, which can be read silently with full enjoyment, poetry demands to be recited, heard, even memorized for its true appreciation. Shaping the words in one's mouth is as much a part of the pleasure as hearing the sound in the air. Until recently education in poetry always emphasized memorization and recitation. This traditional method stressed the immediately communicable and communal pleasures of the art. Certainly a major reason for the decline in poetry's popular audience stems directly from the abandonment of this aural education for the joylessly intellectual approach of critical analysis.

Free verse is a much more modern technique that presupposes the existence of written texts. While it does not abandon the aural imagination—no real poetry can—most free verse plays with the way poetic language is arranged on a page and articulates the visual rhythm of a poem in a way earlier method verse rarely bothered to. Even the earliest known free verse, the Hebrew Psalms (which actually inhabit a middle ground between free and formal verse since they follow a principle of syntactic but not metrical symmetry) were created by "the people of the Book" in a culture uniquely concerned with limiting the improvisatory freedom of the bard for the fixed message of the text.

Most often one first notices the visual orientation of free verse in trivial ways (the lack of initial capitals at the beginning of lines, the use of typographical symbols like "&" and "7," the arbitrary use of upper- or lower-case letters). E. E. Cummings spent his life exploiting these tricks trying to create a visual vocabulary for modern poetry. Eventually, however, one sees how the visual field of the page is essential to the organization of sound in free verse. Rearranged in prose lines, a free-verse poem usually changes radically. Its rhythms move differently from their original printed form (whereas most metrical verse would still retain its basic rhythmic design and symmetry). This visual artifice separates free verse from speech. Technological innovation affects art, and it is probably not accidental that the broad-scale development of free verse came from the first generation of writers trained from childhood on the shift-key typewriter introduced in 1878. This new device allowed writers to predict accurately for the first time the *look* of their words on the printed page rather than just their sound.

All free verse deals with the fundamental question of how and when to end lines of poetry when there is no regular meter to measure them out. The earliest free verse matched the line with some syntactic unit of sense (in Hebrew poetry, for instance, the line was most often a double unit of parallel syntactic sense):

1   Except the Lord build the house, they labor in vain that build it:
    Except the Lord keep the city, the watchman waketh but in vain.
2   It is vain for you to rise up early, to sit up late,
    To eat the bread of sorrows: for so he giveth his beloved sleep.
                                                              PSALM 127

Once free verse leaves the strict symmetry of sacred Hebrew poetry, there is no way for the ear to judge accurately from the sounds alone the metrical structure of a poem (unless the reader exaggerates the line breaks). Sometimes one wonders if even the poet hears the purely aural pattern of his words. Most critics do not. For instance, it has never been noted that the most famous American free-verse poem of the twentieth century, William Carlos Williams's "The Red Wheelbarrow," is not only free verse but also two rather undistinguished lines of blank verse:

so much depends upon a red wheel barrow
glazed with rain water beside the white chickens

One reason that these lines have proved so memorable is that they are familiarly metrical—very similar in rhythm to another famous passage of blank verse, even down to the "feminine" endings of the lines:

To be or not to be that is the question
Whether 'tis nobler in the mind to suffer . . .

That Williams wrote blank verse while thinking he was pioneering new trails in prosody doesn't necessarily invalidate his theories (though it may lead one to examine them with a certain skepticism). This discrepancy, however, does suggest two points. First, even among its adversaries, metrical language exercises a primitive power, even if it is frequently an unconscious one. Second, the organizing principle of Williams's free verse is visual. What makes "The Red Wheelbarrow" free verse is not the sound alone, which is highly regular, but the visual placement of those sounds on the page.

so much depends
upon

a red wheel
barrow

glazed with rain
water

beside the white
chickens.

Here the words achieve a new symmetry, alien to the ear, but no less genuine. The way Williams arranges the poem into brief lines and stanzas slows the language until every word acquires an unusual weight. This deliberate visual placement twists a lackluster blank-verse couplet into a provocatively original free-verse lyric that challenges the reader's definition of what constitutes a poem. Much of the poem's impact comes from catching the reader off guard and forcing him to reread it in search of what he has missed because nothing of what Williams has said constitutes a satisfactory poem in a conventional sense. The element of surprise makes this type of poem a difficult trick to repeat and may explain why so much of the minimalist poetry written in the Williams tradition is so dull. The poetic experience comes in the rereading as the reader consciously revises his own superficial first impression and sees the real importance of Williams's seemingly mundane images. Just as Williams's imagery works by challenging the reader to see the despoiled modern world as charged with a new kind of beauty, so too does his prosody operate by making everyday words acquire a new weight by their unexpectedly bold placement on the page. No aural poem could work in this way.

3

THE CURRENT MOMENT is a fortunate one for poets interested in traditional or experimental form. Two generations now of younger writers have largely ignored rhyme and meter, and most of the older poets who worked originally in form (such as Louis Simpson and Adrienne Rich) have abandoned it entirely for more than a quarter of a century. Literary journalism has long declared it defunct, and most current anthologies present no work in traditional forms by Americans written after 1960. The British may have continued using rhyme and meter in their quaint, old-fashioned way and the Irish in their primitive, bardic manner, but for up-to-date Americans it became the province of the old, the eccentric, and the Anglophilic. It was a style that dared not speak its name, except in light verse. Even the trinominate, blue-haired state laureates now wrote in free verse.[1] By 1980 there had been such a decisive break with the literary past that in America for the first time in the history of modern English most published young poets could not write with minimal competence in traditional meters (not that this failing bothered anyone). Whether this was an unprecedented cultural catastrophe or a glorious revolution is immaterial to this discussion. What matters is that most of the craft of traditional English versification had been forgotten.

Since 1960 there has also been relatively little formal innovation done by the mainstream either in metrical or free verse. Radical experimentation like concrete poetry or language poetry has been pushed off to the fringes of the literary culture where it either has been ignored by the mainstream or declared irrelevant. At the same time most mainstream poets have done little of the more focused (and less radical) experimentation with meters or verse forms that open up new possibilities for poetic language. Since 1960 the only new verse forms to have entered the mainstream of American poetry have been two miniatures: the double dactyl and the ghazal, the latter usually in a dilute unrhymed version of the Persian original.

Indeed, the most influential form in American poetry over this quarter century has been the prose poem, which strictly speaking is not a verse form at all but a stylistic alternative to verse as the medium for poetry. In theory the prose poem is the most protean form of free verse in which all line breaks disappear as a highly charged lyric poem achieves the ultimate organic form. In recent American practice, however, it has mostly be-

---

[1] The editors of the *Hudson Review* ask, as they should, if this statement is a sexist stereotype. I offer it rather as investigative journalism based on firsthand knowledge of the work of such contemporary poets as Sudie Stuart Hager, Winifred Hamrick Farrar, Maggie Culver Fry, Helen von Kolnitz Hyer, and the late Peggy Simson Curry (the official poets laureate of Idaho, Mississippi, Oklahoma, South Carolina, and Wyoming, respectively). When such rear-guard, middle-class poets write in free verse, how can that style not be said to belong to the establishment?

come a kind of absurdist parable having more to do with the prose tradition of Kafka and Borges than the poetic tradition of Baudelaire and Rimbaud. As poetry literally became written in prose, was it any wonder that verse technique suffered?

Likewise, although the past quarter century has witnessed an explosion of poetic translation, this boom has almost exclusively produced work that is formally vague and colorless. Compared to most earlier translation, these contemporary American versions make no effort whatsoever to reproduce the prosodic features of their originals. One can now read most of Dante or Villon, Rilke or Mandelstam, Lorca or even Petrarch in English without any sense of the poem's original form. Sometimes these versions brilliantly convey the theme or tone of the originals, but more often they sound stylistically impoverished and anonymous. All of the past blurs together into a familiar tune. Unrhymed, unmetered, and unshaped, Petrarch and Rilke sound misleadingly alike.

This method of translating foreign poetry into an already available contemporary style also brings less to the language than the more difficult attempt to re-create a foreign form in English (as Sir Thomas Wyatt did for the Italian sonnet or the anonymous translators of the King James Bible did for the Hebrew Psalms). New verse forms and meters can have a liberating effect on poetry. They allow writers to say things that have never worked in poetry before or else to restate familiar things in original ways. Many of the most important forms in our language were once exotic imports—the sonnet, sestina, ballade, villanelle, triolet, terza rima, pantoum, rubaiyat, haiku, ottava rima, free verse, even the prose poem. Recent translation has done little to expand the formal resources of American poetry. Ironically it may have done more to deaden the native ear by translating all poetry of all ages into the same homogeneous style. Studying great poetry in such neutralized versions, one gets little sense of how the forms adopted or invented by great writers are inseparable from their art. Not only the subtleties are lost but even the general scheme.

This assessment does not maintain that metrical innovation is necessary to write good poetry, that successful poetic translation must always follow the verse forms of the original, or that prose is an impossible medium for poetry. It merely examines some current literary trends and speculates on both their origins and consequences. It also suggests that the recent dearth of formal poetry opens interesting possibilities for young poets to match an unexploited contemporary idiom with traditional or experimental forms. Indeed, the current moment may even offer poets an opportunity for formal innovation and expansion unprecedented in the language since the end of the eighteenth century, for no age since then has been so metrically narrow or formally orthodox as our own.

4

FOR THE ARTS at least there truly is a Zeitgeist, especially at moments of decisive change when they move together with amazing synchronization. We are now living at one such moment to which critics have applied the epithet "Postmodern," an attractive term the meaning of which no two writers can agree on precisely because it does not yet have one. The dialectic of history is still moving too fast, and events still unforeseen will probably define this moment in ways equally unexpected. One day cultural historians will elucidate the connections between the current revival of formal and narrative poetry and this broader shift of sensibility in the arts. The return to tonality in serious music, to representation in painting, to decorative detail and nonfunctional design in architecture will link with poetry's reaffirmation of song and story as the most pervasive development of the American arts toward the end of this century.

No one today can accurately judge all of the deeper social, economic, and cultural forces driving this revival, but at least one central motivation seems clear. All these revivals of traditional technique (whether linked or not to traditional aesthetics) both reject the specialization and intellectualization of the arts in the academy over the past forty years and affirm the need for a broader popular audience. The modern movement, which began this century in bohemia, is now ending it in the university, an institution dedicated at least as much to the specialization of knowledge as to its propagation. Ultimately the mission of the university has little to do with the mission of the arts, and this long cohabitation has had an enervating effect on all the arts but especially on poetry and music. With the best of intentions the university has intellectualized the arts to a point where they have been cut off from the vulgar vitality of popular traditions and, as a result, their public has shrunk to groups of academic specialists and a captive audience of students, both of which refer to everything beyond the university as "the real world." Mainly poets read contemporary poetry, and only professional musicians and composers attend concerts of new music.

Like the new tonal composers, the young poets now working in form reject the split between their art and its traditional audience. They seek to reaffirm poetry's broader cultural role and restore its parity with fiction and drama. The poet Wade Newman has already linked the revival of form with the return to narrative and grouped these new writers as an "expansive movement" dedicated to reversing poetry's declining importance to the culture. These young poets, Newman claims, seek to engage their audience not by simplifying their work but by making it more relevant and accessible. They are also "expansive" in that they have expanded their technical and thematic concerns beyond the confines of the short, autobiographical free-verse lyric that so dominates contemporary poetry. Obviously, the return to form and narrative is not the only possible way of establishing the connection between the poet and the broader public, but it does represent one means of renewal, and if this particular "expansive movement" continues to develop successfully, American poetry will end this, its most distinguished century, with more promise to its future than one sees today.

5

ONE OF THE MORE interesting developments of the 1980s has been the emergence of pseudo-formal verse. This sort of writing began appearing broadly a few years ago shortly after critics started advertising the revival of form. Pseudo-formal verse bears the same relationship to formal poetry as the storefronts on a Hollywood back lot do to a real city street. They both look vaguely similar from a distance. In pseudo-formal verse the lines run to more or less the same length on the page. Stanzas are neatly symmetrical. The syllable count is roughly regular line by line, and there may even be a few rhymes thrown in, usually in an irregular pattern.

Trying to open the window on a Hollywood façade, one soon discovers it won't budge. The architectural design has no structural function. Pseudo-formal verse operates on the same principle. It displays no comprehension of how meters operate in English to shape the rhythm of a poem. Though arranged in neat visual patterns, the words jump between incompatible rhythmic systems from line to line. The rhythms lack the spontaneity of free verse without ever achieving the focused energy of formal poetry. They grope toward a regular rhythmic shape but never reach it. Ultimately, there is little, if any, structural connection between the look and the sound of the poem.

There are two kinds of pseudo-formal poem. The first type is the more sophisticated. It tries to be regularly metrical. The first line usually scans according to some common meter, but thereafter problems occur. The poet cannot sustain the pattern of sounds he or she has chosen and soon begins to make substitutions line by line, which may look consistent with the underlying form but actually organize the rhythms in incompatible ways. What results technically is usually neither good free verse nor formal verse. Here, for example, is the opening of a poem by a young writer widely praised as an accomplished formalist. (Most poetry reviewers call any poem that looks vaguely regular "formal.") This passage wants to be blank verse, but despite a few regular lines, it never sustains a consistent rhythm long enough to establish a metrical base:

> From this unpardoned perch, a kitchen table
> In a sunless walk-up in a city
> Of tangled boulevards, he tested
> The old, unwieldy nemesis—namelessness.
> Forgetting (he knew) couldn't be remedied
> But these gestures of identity (he liked to think)
> Rankled the equanimities of time:
> A conceit, of course, but preferable to
> The quarrels of the ego, the canter of
> Description or discoveries of the avant-garde.

At first glance this passage appears to be in blank verse. The poem's first line unfolds as regular iambic pentameter (with a feminine ending). The second line has ten syllables, too, but it scans metrically either as awkward trochees or pure syllabics. A regular iambic rhythm appears again in line three, but now it falls decisively one foot short. Line four begins as regular blank verse but then abruptly loses its rhythm in wordplay between "nemesis" and "namelessness." Line five can only be construed as free verse. After a vague start line six plays with a regular iambic movement but dissipates itself over thirteen syllables. And so it continues awkwardly till the end. Good blank verse can be full of substitutions, but the variations always play off a clearly established pattern. Here the poem never establishes a clear rhythmic direction. The lines never quite become blank verse. They only allude to it.

The second type of pseudo-formal poem is more common because it is easier to write. It doesn't even try to make a regular pattern of sound, however awkwardly. It only wants to look regular. The lines have no auditory integrity, as free or formal verse. Their integrity is merely visual—in a gross and uninteresting sense. The same issue of the *Agni Review,* which published the previous example, also contains a poem in quatrains that has these representative stanzas:

> When at odd moments, business and pleasure
> pale, and I think I'm staring into space,
> I catch myself gazing at a notecard propped
> on my desk, "The Waves at Matsushima."
>
> . . .
>
> and wider than the impossible journey
> from island to island so sheerly
> undercut by waves that no boot could find
> a landing, nor a shipwrecked couple
>
> rest beneath those scrubby pines at the top
> that could be overgrown heads of broccoli,
> even if they could survive the surf, tall
> combers, more like a field plowed by a maniac . . .

These line lengths seem determined mainly by their typographic width. Why else does the author break the lines between "pleasure" and "pale" or "tall" and "combers"? The apparently regular line breaks fall without any real rhythmic relation either to the meter or the syntax. As Truman Capote once said, "That's not writing—it's typing." There is no rhythmic integrity, only incompatible, provisional judgments shifting pointlessly line by line. The resulting poems remind me of a standard gag in improvisational comedy where the performers pretend to speak a foreign language by imitating its approximate sound. Making noises that resemble Swedish, Russian, Italian, or French, they hold impassioned conversations on the stage. What makes it all so funny is that the actors, as everyone in the audience knows, are only mouthing nonsense.

The metrical incompetence of pseudo-formal verse is the most cogent evidence of our literature's break with tradition and the lingering consequences. These poets are not without talent. Aside from its rhythmic ineptitude, their verse often exhibits many of the qualities that distinguish good poetry. Even their desire to try traditional forms speaks well for their ambition and artistic curiosity. How then do these promising authors, most of whom not only have graduate training in writing or literature but also work as professional teachers of writing, not hear the confusing rhythms of their own verse? How can they believe their expertise in a style whose basic principles they so obviously misunderstand? That these writers by virtue of their training and position represent America's poetic intelligentsia makes their performance deeply unnerving—rather like hearing a conservatory-trained pianist rapturously play the notes of a Chopin waltz in 2/4 time.

These young poets have grown up in a literary culture so removed from the predominantly oral traditions of metrical verse that they can no longer hear it accurately. Their training in reading and writing has been overwhelmingly visual not aural, and they have never learned to hear the musical design a poem executes. For them poems exist as words on a page rather than sounds in the mouth and ear. While they have often analyzed poems, they have rarely memorized and recited them. Nor have they studied and learned by heart poems in foreign languages where sound patterns are more obvious to non-native speakers. Their often extensive critical training in textual analysis never included scansion, and their knowledge of even the fundamentals of prosody is haphazard (though theory is less important than practice in mastering the craft of versification). Consequently, they have neither much practical nor theoretical training in the way sounds are organized in poetry. Ironically, this very lack of training makes them deaf to their own ineptitude. Full of confidence, they rely on instincts they have never developed. Magisterially they take liberties with forms whose rudimentary principles they misconstrue. Every poem reveals some basic confusion about its own medium. Some misconceptions ultimately prove profitable for art. Not this one.

6

IN MY OWN POETRY I have always worked in both fixed and open forms. Each mode offered possibilities of style, subject, music, and development the other did not suggest, at least at that moment. Likewise, experience in each mode provided an illuminating perspective on the other. Working in free verse helped keep the language of my formal poems varied and contemporary, just as writing in form helped keep my free verse more focused and precise. I find it puzzling therefore that so many poets see these modes as opposing aesthetics rather than as complementary techniques. Why shouldn't a poet explore the full resources the English language offers?

I suspect that ten years from now the real debate among poets and concerned critics will not be about poetic form in the narrow technical sense of metrical versus nonmetrical verse. That is already a tired argument, and only the uninformed or biased can fail to recognize that genuine poetry can be created in both modes. How obvious it should be that no technique precludes poetic achievement, just as none automatically assures it (though admittedly some techniques may be more difficult to use at certain moments in history). Soon, I believe, the central debate will focus on form in the wider, more elusive sense of poetic structure. How does a poet best shape words, images, and ideas into meaning? How much compression is needed to transform versified lines—be they metrical or free—into genuine poetry? The important arguments will not be about technique in isolation but about the fundamental aesthetic assumptions of writing and judging poetry.

At that point the real issues presented by recent American poetry will become clearer: the debasement of poetic language; the prolixity of the lyric; the bankruptcy of the confessional mode; the inability to establish a meaningful aesthetic for new poetic narrative; and the denial of musical texture in the contemporary poem. The revival of traditional forms will be seen then as only one response to this troubling situation. There will undoubtedly be others. Only time will prove which answer is the most persuasive.

Strong Counsel

—

NO MAJOR AMERICAN POET has been treated worse by posterity than Robinson Jeffers. Twenty-five years after his death, he has still not received either a collected poems or a responsible biography. The only comprehensive bibliography of his work appeared in 1933—shortly after Jeffers's sudden rise to fame—and was never updated to cover the remaining three quarters of his prolific career. His critical and autobiographical prose remains scattered. Although the poet lived and wrote until 1962, the only substantial gathering of his voluminous work appeared half a century ago in Random House's 1938 *Selected Poems of Robinson Jeffers*.

In 1955 Horace Gregory called Jeffers the "poet without critics." In 1987, the centennial of the poet's birth, one would hardly revise that verdict. Academic interest in Jeffers remains negligible. No longer considered by critics prominent enough to attack, he is now ignored. Not only is there little first-rate academic commentary on his poetry; compared with the massive scholarship on his most significant contemporaries— Eliot, Pound, Williams, Moore, Stevens, Frost, Crane, and Cummings— there isn't even much second-rate writing. What little scholarship appears originates mainly in California, where Jeffers spent virtually all his adult life. Half a century ago he towered as an international literary figure. Now he survives as a regional figure studied mainly by specialists in West Coast authors.

Although no representative historical anthology can exclude Jeffers's verse, few general collections of poetry consider him worth notice. The three widely used, nonhistorical college textbooks on my shelf—X. J. Kennedy's *An Introduction to Poetry,* John Ciardi and Miller Williams's *How Does a Poem Mean?* and John Frederick Nims's *Western Wind: An Introduction to Poetry*—include only one short poem by Jeffers in their collective 1,300-plus pages. Poor Jeffers! Even Rod McKuen gets two poems.

As these anthologies suggest, Jeffers is not much taught. An informal poll of friends who teach college-level English revealed that not one was ever assigned a Jeffers poem from high school through graduate study. Nor, it seems important to add, are any of them currently teaching him in their classes. His verse, especially the wild, expansive narratives that made him famous in the 1920s, does not fit into the conventional definitions of modern American poetry. His work is not essentially lyric, elliptical, stylistically innovative, or self-referential. Likewise, his preoccupations with sexuality, violence, intergenerational conflict, and the extremes of mental and physical disease bear little relation to the thematics of his poetic contemporaries. (One can't imagine Wallace Stevens writing on incest or Marianne Moore on patricide.) Instead, Jeffers's poems ask to be compared to the work of novelists and dramatists like Lawrence, Faulkner, Hemingway, and O'Neill—a difficult request for academic specialists who usually study these genres in isolation.

The academy's neglect is particularly interesting because Jeffers, unlike most Modernist poets, still commands a general readership. Compared with the usual audience for twentieth-century poetry (which is made up mainly of poets, would-be poets, academic specialists, and students), Jeffers's readers form an unusual group. Few of them inhabit English departments. If they are at the university at all, they will most likely be found in the sciences. In the author's lifetime they were so numerous that he became one of the best-selling serious poets in American history. Even now enough fans remain to keep fourteen books of his verse in print without the subsidy of a captive student market. His 622-page *Selected Poems* has been reprinted so many times (with progressively cheaper paper and binding) that Random House has lost count of its sales. Even the meager paperback selection of 58 short poems issued after his death sold more than 80,000 copies before it went out of print in 1987.

In a culture where most intellectuals agree that "poetry makes nothing happen," Jeffers also remains strangely influential. He is the unchallenged laureate of environmentalists. The Sierra Club's lavish folio *Not Man Apart: Photographs of the Big Sur Coast* (poems by Jeffers accompanied by the stunning landscape images of Ansel Adams, Edward Weston, and others) helped focus political efforts to preserve that spectacular stretch of California coast the poet celebrated in his verse. It also turned a passage from his 1937 poem "The Answer" into a credo for Western conservationists:

> A severed hand
> Is an ugly thing, and man dissevered from the earth and stars
>   and his history . . . for contemplation or in fact . . .
> Often appears atrociously ugly. Integrity is wholeness, the
>   greatest beauty is
> Organic wholeness, the wholeness of life and things, the
>   divine beauty of the universe. Love that, not man
> Apart from that, or else you will share man's pitiful
>   confusions, or drown in despair when his days darken.

Perhaps what makes Jeffers's poetry so important to environmentalists is exactly what repels academics. More than any other American Modernist Jeffers wrote about ideas—not teasing epistemologies, learned allusions, or fictive paradoxes—but big, naked, howling ideas that no reader can miss. The directness and clarity of Jeffers's style reflects the priority he put on communicating his worldview. Many interesting studies have been written on the styles of Eliot and Stevens, for indeed one needs to understand *how* most Modernist poems mean (to use Ciardi's famous formulation) before one can understand *what* they mean. Jeffers's verse, however, presents no such barriers to an intelligent reader. It states its propositions so lucidly that the critic has no choice but to confront its content. The discussion can no longer be confined within the safe literary categories of formal analysis—internal structure, consistency, thematics, tone, and symbolism—that still constitute the overwhelming majority of all academic studies. Instead, he or she must deal with the difficult and disagreeable primary issues of religious belief and morality.

Jeffers's worldview certainly never makes it easy for his critics. His self-proclaimed philosophy of "inhumanism" contains something to offend everyone—Christian, Jew, Marxist, or humanist—who assumes man's central position in the cosmos. He resolutely refused to be bound by any of the usual allegiances of human society—not merely those of race, class, religion, or nation. (Voltaire and Nietzsche had already questioned those pieties.) Jeffers's originality came from going beyond social loyalties to the more fundamental ones of species, time, and even—no, I'm not kidding—planet. No poet ever wrote more consistently *sub specie aeternitatis.* For Jeffers, humanity was ultimately only one species, which happened to gain biological ascendancy (like the bison or the passenger pigeon) over a particular range in a certain epoch. Mankind may be more intelligent or adaptable than other species, but these gifts hardly compensate for its cruelty, greed, and arrogance. Before any other imaginative writer, Jeffers articulated the immense evil inherent in humanity's assumption that it stands above and apart from the world. He saw the pollution of the environment, the destruction of other species, the squandering of natural resources, the recurrent urge to war, the violent squalor of the cities as the inevitable result of a race out of harmony with its own world.

Attempting this cosmic scope, carrying the weight of his harsh message, Jeffers took as great a risk as any more stylistically innovative Modernist. He not only risked being pompous and banal with his grave philosophizing. Stating his uncomfortable ideas strongly and lucidly, he risked being *wrong.* Alone among the Modernist poets, he challenged scientists on their own territory. Unlike most writers, he had studied science seriously in college and graduate school. His break with tradition was intellectual, not stylistic. He accepted the destruction of anthropocentric values explicit in current biology, geology, and physics, which humanists had struggled against since the Victorian age. Instead, Jeffers concentrated on articulating the moral, philosophical, and, indeed, imaginative implications of those discoveries. He struggled to answer the questions science had been able only to ask: What are man's responsibilities in a world not made solely for him? How does humankind lead a good and meaningful life without God? Jeffers's great triumph is that now—sixty years after he began his radical redefinition of human values—his answers still seem disturbingly fresh and cogent, while the political and social theories of Pound, Yeats, Eliot, and others have become musty period pieces.

But Jeffers's poetic independence came at the price of being banished from the academic canon, where the merits of a Modernist are still mostly determined by distinctiveness of stylistic innovation and self-referential consistency of vision. In this environment Robert Hass's *Rock and Hawk: A Selection of Shorter Poems by Robinson Jeffers* constitutes a major act of restitution. This medium-sized anthology represents, difficult as it is to believe, the first representative selection from Jeffers's life work ever assembled. There are criticisms to be made of the collection, but one must first credit the seriousness and quality of effort displayed here. The book is well conceived, intelligently edited, suavely introduced, and beautifully designed. It also contains some of the best poetry ever written by an American.

The critical language we have inherited from Modernism makes it difficult to discuss the qualities that distinguish Jeffers's poetry without sounding hopelessly out of touch with contemporary literary taste. To say that his chief imaginative gifts were scope, simplicity, narrative poise, and moral seriousness makes him seem closer to a distinguished jurist than a great poet. But there was something of the judge—particularly the Old Testament variety—about Jeffers. Standing apart from the world, he passed dispassionate judgment on his race and civilization, and he found them wanting. Pointing out some grievous contradictions at the core of Western industrial society earned Jeffers a reputation as a bitter misanthrope (he sometimes was) but this verdict hardly invalidates the essential accuracy of his message. As clearly as any Marxist, he saw the interdependence of economic and moral ideologies. His genius lay in translating these complex sociopolitical situations into a few stunning images. In "Ave Caesar," for instance, he portrays a crippling contradiction at the heart of America's vision of its destiny:

No bitterness: our ancestors did it.
They were only ignorant and hopeful, they wanted freedom but
    wealth too.
Their children will learn to hope for a Caesar.
Or rather—for we are not aquiline Romans but soft mixed colonists—
Some kindly Sicilian tyrant who'll keep
Poverty and Carthage off until the Romans arrive.
We are easy to manage, a gregarious people,
Full of sentiment, clever at mechanics, and we love our luxuries.

This short poem shows Jeffers's unique style. His language is direct and conversational without ever being dull or simplistic. The subject unfolds as clearly as in expository prose. A listener can follow the story perfectly, even on first hearing. The language, while strong and concise, never calls so much momentary attention to itself that it overwhelms the narrative line. The images and metaphors are subordinated to a paraphrasable argument. One notices what Jeffers is saying, not how he says it. His subject also has a public importance one rarely sees in modern poetry.

On rereading the poem, however, one notices how much Jeffers has packed into these eight lines. He sets up three temporal planes—the past of the ancestors, the present of the speaker, and the future of the children—and outlines the political choices each must make. He manages to condemn American values without bitterness, through a clever rhetorical trick. He begins the poem by discussing contemporary America, but just as the message becomes harsh (at the end of line three), the narrator relocates it metaphorically to the ancient Mediterranean world. Without ever being difficult, this metaphor is complex. It shifts twice, each time becoming slightly crueler. First the children will "learn to hope" (through unpleasant experience) for a Caesar (notice they don't get the heroic original but some latter-day autocrat). No sooner has this insult registered, however, than Jeffers qualifies it. His fellow Americans don't even deserve to be called decadent Romans. The Romans (like, by implication, the British) at least once built a great imperial civilization. Americans are merely soft colonials like the Sicilians and a petty tyrant is enough to keep them in order.

Even by today's hyperbolic standards Jeffers's public career was remarkable for the speed both of his rise to literary fame and his plunge to critical dismissal. His public breakthrough resembled a young writer's daydream. Having published two volumes of elegantly dull juvenilia, Jeffers was unable to place any of his mature poetry. After years of quiet work he decided in 1924 to publish *Tamar and Other Poems* with a vanity press. For a year after it appeared nothing happened. Then James Rorty and George Sterling decided to use one of Jeffers's new poems as the title piece for *Continent's End,* a 1925 anthology of California verse, and the grateful poet sent both of them copies of *Tamar.* (After all, the 37-year-old author had nearly all the original printed copies still stuffed in his tiny attic.) Suddenly Jeffers's luck changed. Not only did Rorty review the book ecstatically in March 1925 for the *New York Herald Tribune,* but he also passed on copies to Mark Van Doren, who lauded it a few days later in the *Nation,* and Babette Deutsch, who told readers in the *New Republic* that she "felt somewhat as Keats professed to feel, on looking into Chapman's Homer."

Jeffers shipped a coffin-sized crate of books to New York City, where they immediately sold out. By November an expanded trade edition containing Jeffers's most famous poem, "Roan Stallion," was issued by Boni and Liveright. The critical reception was tumultuous. Dozens of excited articles and reviews appeared hailing Jeffers as a great tragic poet. Critics compared him to Sophocles and Shakespeare, and *Roan Stallion, Tamar and Other Poems* went into multiple reprintings. Leonard and Virginia Woolf published a British edition. Even a French translation was reprinted five times. By the end of the decade, Alfred Kreymborg felt obliged to devote the final chapter of his now forgotten but still engaging *Our Singing Strength: A History of American Poetry 1620–1930* solely to Jeffers, declaring him the heir to Whitman. When Boni and Liveright went bankrupt, in 1933, thirteen publishers scrambled to sign up Jeffers, who had recently appeared on the cover of *Time.* The wily Bennett Cerf flew out to Carmel to court him personally. He knew Jeffers's name would add prestige to his fledgling Random House. As Cerf later commented, "There are always a few poets that people think it's smart to have around." Indeed, by then Jeffers was such a celebrity that Carmel real estate brokers used his name in their ads to sell property.

Meanwhile, Jeffers remained in Carmel where he and his beloved, domineering wife, Una, had lived since fall 1914. Carmel then was not the chic resting place for retired financiers and real estate moguls it is today but an isolated rural area with a touch of bohemianism. Writers since Robert Louis Stevenson and Jack London had found its breathtaking scenery and its privacy invigorating. But it was more than Carmel's natural magnificence that first drove the couple there. They also needed to escape their past—the long, scandalous breakup of Una's first marriage in Los Angeles and the death of the newlyweds' first daughter at birth. They had hoped to move to England (as Frost, H. D., Eliot, and Pound already had), but the outbreak of World War I prevented them. They came instead to Big Sur, their "inevitable place," where they would remain the rest of their lives.

The couple lived simply, without electricity or indoor plumbing, in Tor House, a small stone cottage that Robin, as his few friends called him, had constructed on a headland overlooking the Pacific at Carmel Point. He wrote in the morning, quarried stone for further building in the afternoon, and read to his wife and twin sons by lamplight each evening. Little changed for them after he achieved fame, except for the pestering of visitors. But Jeffers's austere, colorful life and patrician good looks made him a favorite subject for the press, and, as with Frost, a popular myth soon began forming around this quiet, private man.

To his credit Jeffers ignored his celebrity. He wanted nothing to do

with literary society or worshipful fans. What the forty-year-old author
now wanted was to work. Inspired by his sudden if late success, he made
up for lost time by embarking on the most remarkable, ambitious, and
bizarre series of narrative poems in American literature. In the ten years
following the acclaim of *Roan Stallion,* Jeffers published eight major collections of poetry: *The Women at Point Sur, Cawdor and Other Poems, Dear
Judas and Other Poems, Descent to the Dead, Thurso's Landing, Give Your
Heart to the Hawks, Solstice and Other Poems,* and *Such Counsels You Gave to
Me and Other Poems*—nearly a book a year, almost a thousand pages of
verse in all. These poems, which have never been adequately assessed by
literary criticism, constitute an American realist and regionalist alternative to the mandarin aestheticism of international Modernism. Largely
ignored by poets in the two generations after Jeffers, curiously, they are
just beginning to have an impact on American literature through the
young poets currently reviving narrative verse.

Nearly every volume centers on one or more long narrative poems,
usually set in Big Sur. Violent, sexy, subversive, these compelling verse
novellas are impossible to describe briefly. Sometimes hard to stomach,
they are always difficult to put down. Their tragic stories of family rivalry
and primal emotion usually move at lightning pace toward their bloody
finales. There is nothing quite like them in American poetry. In sheer narrative energy and visual scope they frequently remind one of movies. Not
real films but wild, imaginary ones where high and low art collide—
Bergman's *Cries and Whispers* reshot as a Peckinpah western or Kurosawa's
Rashomon reset as a California thriller by De Palma. In these poems
Jeffers's central human obsessions emerge as the suffocating burden of
the past on human freedom, the harsh interdependence of power and sexuality, and the impossibility of human salvation. At their worst they become ponderously philosophic and psychologically hyperbolic. At their
best, however, as in "Cawdor," they remain among the few successful
long poems in modern American literature.

From the beginning these narratives divided Jeffers's audience. Many
of his early supporters could not accept the sprawling energy, the lurid
violence, the sheer weirdness of *The Women at Point Sur.* What critics had
judged as a young poet's momentary nightmare in "Tamar" or "Roan
Stallion" now emerged as Jeffers's considered view of humanity. Each
book fueled new controversy. Conservative readers bridled at Jeffers's explicit sexuality, his strident anti-Christianity and antinationalism. Leftists

found his distrust of all political programs for human improvement repugnant. His use of free verse and Freudian psychology likewise alienated literary reactionaries. Meanwhile, the New Critics rightly perceived Jeffers's commitment to a poetry of direct statement and linear narrative as a challenge to the high Modernist mode they had championed. To the degree they acknowledged Jeffers at all, the New Critics attacked him savagely. Yvor Winters suggested that if Jeffers truly believed his own philosophy, he should kill himself. Randall Jarrell mocked him as "Old Rocky Face, perched on his sea crag . . . who must prefer a hawk to a man, a stone to a hawk." All factions agreed Jeffers had no place in textbooks or anthologies.

The controversial long poems caused Jeffers another problem as well: they overshadowed his shorter work. Reviewers treated him like a novelist. As his collections appeared, they focused on the central narrative and ignored the many stunning short poems that were tucked away in the back pages of each book. The critical agenda was to debate the psychological realism and moral impetus of each histrionic story, not listen carefully to the sad, quiet music of Jeffers's lyric poems. Complaining in the *New Yorker* about "Robinson Jeffers's latest set-piece of human savagery," Louise Bogan was so busy damning the title poem of *Such Counsels You Gave to Me* that she missed "The Purse-Seine," "The Answer," and "The Beaks of Eagles" in the same volume, all of them, I believe, permanent additions to American literature.

Though Jeffers's books continued to sell well, by the end of the 1930s his critical reputation had collapsed, never to rise again. The Depression had made his cosmic pessimism less palatable to intellectuals caught up in international politics. Jeffers still commanded a small but devoted group of serious readers, but the literary establishment had deserted him. The orthodoxy of Eliot and Joyce had banished all other variants of Modernism. Finally, Pearl Harbor did what little damage to his reputation there was left to deliver. For years Jeffers had warned that America's entry into a new world war would drag the country into the temptations of imperialism. Now his refusal to endorse the American war effort as an absolute good fighting absolute evil disgusted many of his remaining readers.

Surely not only international but literary politics contributed to Jeffers's fall from public grace. He had no interest in the literary world, and once the initially receptive literati realized his indifference, they gradually returned it. Even then the American poetry world was a

buzzing network of personal loyalties, interests, and obligations that collectively shaped literary fashion. Unlike a Pound or Frost, Jeffers never
developed the relationships that sustain a writer's reputation through
the vacillations of opinion. Hating big cities, he scarcely stirred from
Carmel. (Eleven years once passed between visits to San Francisco, only
a hundred miles up the coast.) He would not teach or lecture. He
scarcely answered his mail, and even then he was more likely to respond
to a serviceman than a fellow writer. He declined all invitations to read
from his work. The one reading tour of his career—at the age of fifty-
four, in 1941—was undertaken only to pay his property taxes in a Carmel
growing too expensive for him. Worst of all for his reputation, Jeffers
stayed in California, which the literary establishments of London and
New York have never taken seriously. Has any American author ever
been able to build and sustain a major literary presence from the West
Coast? As writers from Allen Ginsberg to Joan Didion know, if one lives
out West, one must also keep an apartment in Manhattan.

By 1948 even Random House had grown impatient with its former
prestige author. Reading the manuscript of *The Double Axe,* Jeffers's editor, Saxe Commins, declared it "proof of early senility" to his colleagues and forcefully persuaded the author to tone down its political
language. Jeffers eventually dropped ten short poems from the manuscript and made changes in eight more, mostly removing insulting
comments about Roosevelt and Truman. But Commins convinced Cerf
to print an embarrassing disclaimer on the dust jacket and front section
of the volume to annouce that "Random House feels compelled to go
on record with its disagreement over some of the political views pro-
nounced by the poet." Meanwhile, Cerf, always the businessman, commented hopefully that this "footnote" would "attract added space and
attention from reviewers." Thus high principle and low commercialism
combined to reduce the public reception of one of Jeffers's most powerful volumes to a political squabble. By the time the reviewers began
their attack, Jeffers probably didn't care. He now lived almost totally in
the quiet isolation of his family. When Una died two years later, he sank
gradually into an alcoholic loneliness waiting for his own death. The end
of his last long poem, "Hungerfield," written in 1954, is heartbreaking.
The violent story finishes, and suddenly Jeffers breaks into an unexpected lyric coda:

Here is the poem, dearest; you will
never read it nor hear it. You were more beautiful
Than a hawk flying; you were faithful and a lion heart like
this rough hero Hungerfield. But the ashes have fallen
And the flame has gone up; nothing human remains. You are
earth and air; you are in the beauty of the ocean
And the great streaming triumphs of sundown; you are alive
and well in the tender young grass rejoicing
When soft rain falls all night, and little rosy-fleeced clouds
float on the dawn. — I shall be with you presently.

A few years later Jeffers joined his wife in the nonhuman world. His ashes were buried with hers in the Tor House garden. "Posthumous long before his death," as Robert Zaller put it, Jeffers received obituaries that displayed "chiefly the surprise that he had still been living." He had never won a major literary award, but the bulk of his work was still in print.

In attempting to rehabilitate Jeffers's reputation, Robert Hass has sidestepped the central issue in evaluating the poet's legacy by limiting his selections for *Rock and Hawk* to Jeffers's shorter work. Fortunately, he cheats a little by stretching the definition of "shorter" to include two fiery medium-length narratives—the early "Roan Stallion" and the late "Hungerfield" (twenty-one and twenty-two tightly packed pages, respectively). But beyond these Hass offers only two unpersuasive excerpts from *The Tower Beyond Tragedy* (Jeffers's reworking of *The Oresteia*) and *The Women at Point Sur* as well as the two lyric set-pieces from "Cawdor" that Jeffers himself chose for his 1938 *Selected Poems*. One can understand, if not totally sympathize with, Hass's conservatism. He wants to present Jeffers at his most accessible and uncontroversial best. Certainly the case he makes for Jeffers in this volume is irresistible, if incomplete.

No reader ever entirely approves of someone else's selections from a favorite poet. But the usual grumbling aside, Hass does an excellent job. Even in his short work Jeffers wrote obsessively about a few subjects, and Hass displays exemplary taste in presenting just enough of the best poems of each sort to register the author's fixations without wearying the reader. Hass's choices also reflect some interesting biases beyond the omission of any long narratives. He generally favors the earlier work over the later. Most of the poems I would wish to add come from the second half of the canon. Poems like "Hellenistics," "Cassandra," "The Eye," and "Why Do You Still Make War?" seem conspicuous in their absence. Hass also reprints virtually all of *Descent to the Dead* (an atypical collection written after Jeffers visited Britain and Ireland), presumably to highlight the unacknowledged debt Ted Hughes and Seamus Heaney owe the elder poet.

Knowledgeable and sympathetic though Hass is, however, he does make a few curious mistakes. Organizing his selections according to the original volumes from which they are drawn, he places Jeffers's famous "Shine, Perishing Republic" in the wrong book. Meanwhile, going to the length of presenting the poems from *American Poetry 1927: A Miscellany* as a separate group (which Jeffers himself did not do in his *Selected Poems*), Hass conflates the title as *An American Miscellany*. He also misconstrues the lineation of "Hungerfield" at one point to give the poem a bizarre visual leap on the page at odds with Jeffers's intention. (This, unfortunately, is a common problem in reprinting long-lined free verse, about which Jeffers himself frequently complained.) These are small mistakes but annoying ones. The book also lacks an index of poems by title and, worse yet, an index by first line. Publishers today assume that readers no longer search out a poem because a particular line has been buzzing around in their heads. And the publishers are almost right. Most contemporary poetry is eminently forgettable.

But Jeffers is a distractingly memorable writer. Rereading his poems in *Rock and Hawk,* I found an astonishing number of his lines tumbling around in my head. But hearing them there, I noticed it wasn't only their strong music I savored but the hard edge of their wisdom. They held their own against experience. It was good to live with these poems again. Jeffers has entered his second century quite splendidly.

Postscript: This essay was written in December 1987 to mark the end of the Jeffers centenary, an occasion that had gone virtually unnoticed in the literary world. Little has changed for Jeffers since this article appeared. He remains invisible to most critics. California, however, has not forgotten its greatest poet. Stanford University, once home to Jeffers's harshest critic Yvor Winters, has begun the publication of *The Collected Poetry of Robinson Jeffers,* edited by Tim Hunt, in four elegant, oversized volumes.

The Loneliness
of Weldon Kees

—

I

When we think of the masterpieces that nobody praised and nobody read, back there in the past, we feel an impatient superiority to the readers of the past. If we had been there, we can't help feeling, *we'd* have known that *Moby-Dick* was a good book—why, how could anyone help knowing?

—RANDALL JARRELL, *An Unread Book*

ON JULY 18, 1955, an abandoned car was found on the approach to the Golden Gate Bridge. It belonged to Weldon Kees, a poet who had been living in and around San Francisco for five years. The circumstances suggested suicide, but there was also speculation that Kees had faked his death and disappeared to Mexico, where he had often talked of going to start a new life. He certainly had enough talent and energy to embark on a new career. In the twenty years since he had finished college, he had distinguished himself in half a dozen professions—poet, journalist, painter, musician, fiction writer, photographer, and filmmaker. But, despite enough accomplishments for several men, Kees had been deeply unhappy. His marriage had broken up the previous July. He had aggravated his already severe mood swings with drugs and alcohol. He had begun researching a book on famous suicides. Yet no one saw him jump, and no body was ever found. Kees was forty-one years old.

Five years later two young printers in Iowa put together a complete collection of Kees's poems in an expensive hand-set edition of two hundred copies, edited by Donald Justice. Two years after that, John Kees, the poet's devoted father, persuaded the University of Nebraska Press to issue a paperback edition of the book to honor its missing native son

(Kees had been born in Nebraska). Both editions received good reviews, but at that time most critics were too busy debating the merits of the Beats and Confessional poetry to give an outdated figure like Kees serious attention. He belonged to the poetry of the forties, with its supple formalism and inauthentic irony, and that sort of verse must have seemed slightly remote to anyone immersed in *Howl* or *Life Studies.* Kees's work soon drifted out of print and out of mind. More than a decade passed before the *Collected Poems* was reprinted in 1975, this time in a slightly revised edition, which in its turn received a few enthusiastic reviews, but had little impact. While it was certainly something for a poet's complete work to remain in print for more than twenty years after his death, Kees's poetry seemed destined for what Vladimir Nabokov once called the "Lethean Library."

Perhaps obscurity is the fate of most modern poets. By the standards of the mass media few of them are known at all. Moreover, when a genuine poet like Ezra Pound or Robert Lowell, Sylvia Plath or Anne Sexton acquires public notoriety, it is usually for reasons other than writing. Perhaps fame in the old sense is now meaningless when discussing literature. Poetry has its own audience, which, though small, is also enduring, miraculously managing to renew itself each generation. While poets lack the wide-reaching fame that the mass media can bestow, they can win, however slowly, a lasting place within a smaller, more discerning circle. The fame or obscurity of a contemporary poet can therefore be judged only in relation to this specialized audience.

The proper standards of such literary fame are easy to discover. How much of the poet's work is in print? How much appears in anthologies? Is the work discussed by reviewers? Is it studied in schools and universities? Has it received careful attention from critics? Has it exercised an influence on other writers? And, more difficult to estimate, is it read and reread by those people for whom poetry is an essential part of their lives?

By most of these standards Kees is a forgotten writer. His work was ignored by anthologists during his life and even now is usually represented only by two or three poems, if at all. Most anthologists still ignore him altogether. (There have been a few notable exceptions, such as Conrad Aiken's *Twentieth-Century American Poetry,* which reprinted nine poems by Kees, more than any other poet after Eliot and Pound.) It may seem petty to bicker about his representation in anthologies until one remembers that the total printings of Kees's three books of poetry during his

lifetime did not greatly exceed one thousand copies and subsequent printings of his *Collected Poems* have not been much larger. If he were to have
reached a larger audience, it would have been through anthologies. Even
the one collection of his work currently in print has never been widely
distributed.

In San Francisco Kees's name is occasionally mentioned in the litanies
of undervalued West Coast writers, but the plaintiffs remark at most on a
few details of his unhappy life, which is perhaps all they know about. His
work itself is largely unread and undiscussed. Kenneth Rexroth, San
Francisco's leading man of letters, stubbornly insisted on Kees's importance, but in "the City" Rexroth was always famous for his store of recon-
dite knowledge. No one felt obliged to take the brainy old magus too
seriously. After all, as one San Franciscan writer complained, "Rexroth
wants us to read everything." In a town where poetry is one of the performing arts, it is hard to read anything but a newspaper.

Kees is no better known in New York, the city where he spent his most
productive years supporting himself first as a writer for *Time* (like so
many other poets of his generation, such as Robert Fitzgerald, James
Agee, and Kenneth Fearing), then as a writer for Paramount Newsreel,
and finally as art editor for the *Nation*. Here his obscurity is harder to
understand, for New Yorkers do read, and they are even more fervent
than San Franciscans in publicizing their own. Perhaps neglect was
Kees's punishment for having committed the New York literary establishment's one unforgivable sin—moving to California. What is especially
strange about Kees's obscurity in New York is that he was an early figure
in two of its most influential postwar movements in the arts, the rise of
abstract expressionist painting in the 1940s, and the slightly later collection of poets whose interest in the aesthetics of abstract expressionism
earned them the title of the "New York School of Poets." As a critic, Kees
was an early champion of abstract expressionism. He also painted, and on
at least one occasion exhibited his work with paintings by Hans Hofmann
and Willem de Kooning. As a poet, he was an important precursor of the
supple, contemporary, and prosy verse style later exploited by the New
York School. Although Kees's poetry has a direct, emotional intensity
unlike most later New York School poetry, its rhythm and diction are
clearly cut from the same cloth. Nevertheless, Kees appears nowhere in
the dozen or so books and anthologies dedicated to that movement.

Most important, Kees's work is just not part of the invisible anthology poetry readers carry in their heads. All other measures of Kees's fame would be of secondary importance if his work had found a real audience, however small. Instead he has fallen into a twofold obscurity: he has not only been more or less forgotten by his original readers, but he has also never been discovered by the young, that generation of poets and critics now in their twenties and early thirties. A few young poets may recognize his name and vaguely recall seeing a poem or two in some anthology. Older readers may remember a newspaper blurb on his disappearance. But his work remains largely unknown and unappreciated except by a few scattered admirers.

This neglect would not be so surprising except that, as a poet, Kees was one of the four or five most talented members of his generation. And this is the great postmodern generation of American poets that includes Robert Lowell, Elizabeth Bishop, John Berryman, Delmore Schwartz, Randall Jarrell, and Theodore Roethke. That these other writers are so widely known and discussed while Kees is so forgotten seems strange indeed.

Kees's poetry is not obscure or difficult, especially when compared to the work of Berryman or Lowell. He speaks with a startling clarity. Indeed, his best work has an immediacy not found in the early work of any of his contemporaries, except Bishop and Roethke. Possibly it was this simplicity that made him uninteresting to academic critics. For while there are critical problems in Kees's work—mysteries so deep and painful that the reader cries instinctively for answers—they are not the sort of problems to be clarified by an unimaginative reading or seminar discussion. Kees's work demands a critic who shares his belief in the desperate importance of poetry, and most critics—both in and outside of the universities—don't believe that poetry matters all that much to anyone's life. In their eyes it has become just another profession where the important inside issues are jobs, reputations, classroom hours, and promotions. Here a writer's worth is best measured in the number of dissertations or books it has already supported. It would have taken a passionate and articulate poet-critic like Jarrell to have explored Kees's work twenty years ago with sufficient tact and understanding to have won him an audience. It simply didn't happen, and he was never admitted to the canon of important contemporary poets. Since most academic work is based on previous academic work and most anthologists simply redigest other anthologies, Kees's work has remained unknown, while that of more chic poets has been discussed in numbing detail. Within such a system it is inevitable that first-rate poets, especially those outside the mainstream, will be ignored. (Witness the continuing obscurity of J. V. Cunningham, the crown prince of unpopularity but nonetheless a contrarian master.) Since Kees's work has never received serious critical attention, it is the unabashed purpose of this essay, the first extended consideration of his poetry, to make a bid for reappraisal.

2

While the train flashed through never-ending miles of ripe wheat, by country towns and bright-flowered pastures and oak groves wilting in the sun, we sat in the observation car, where the woodwork was hot to the touch and red dust lay deep over everything. The dust and heat, the burning wind, reminded us of many things. We were talking about what it is like to spend one's childhood in little towns like these, buried in wheat and corn, under stimulating extremes of climate: burning summers when the world lies green and billowy beneath a brilliant sky, when one is fairly stifled in vegetation, in the colour and smell of strong weeds and heavy harvests; blustery winters with little snow, when the whole country is stripped bare and grey as sheet-iron. We agreed that no one who had not grown up in a little prairie town could know anything about it. It was a kind of freemasonry, we said.
— WILLA CATHER, *My Ántonia*

HARRY WELDON KEES was born in Beatrice, Nebraska, on February 24, 1914, the son of John A. Kees, a prosperous local businessman. The family had been in Beatrice since 1874, when the poet's grandfather, Frederick Kees, a German locksmith and toolmaker, settled there and eventually opened a metal hardware factory. Kees attended several Midwestern colleges, graduating from the University of Nebraska in 1935. By then he had already published two short stories in *Prairie Schooner* and had seen two of his one-act plays performed at Doane College.

In 1935 Nebraska lay devastated by the Depression, and out of necessity Kees took an editorial job with the Federal Writers' Project in Lincoln on the recommendation of Lowry Charles Wimberly, an English professor at the University of Nebraska. (Wimberly also placed another of his protégés in the Nebraska Writers' Project—the young Loren Eiseley.) Kees disliked his editorial duties, however, and stayed with the job only a year before moving to Denver, where he worked as a research librarian. About the same time, Kees gradually shifted his attention from fiction to poetry. Although he had considerable success as a writer of short stories, within a few years his published literary work was almost exclusively poetry.

When the twenty-three-year-old Kees published his first poem in the obscure little magazine *Signatures,* he had already found a distinctly personal voice. While this poem, "Subtitle," does not rank among his best works, it already talks in a characteristic way about what will become Kees's pervasive themes. Placed at the beginning of his *Collected Poems,* it could easily have been written last to summarize the contents of the volume. The poem ends:

> We say again: there are
> No exits here, no guards to bribe,
> No washroom windows.
>
> No finis to the film unless
> The ending is your own.
> Turn off the lights, remind
> The operator of his union card:
> Sit forward, let the screen reveal
> Your heritage, the logic of your destiny.

This early piece already shows many of the characteristic techniques of Kees's mature poetry: the direct manner, the conversational style that operates at the edge of prose, the powerful contemporary images, the emotional intensity seething below the matter-of-fact surface.

In 1943, when the poet was twenty-nine, his first book, *The Last Man*, appeared from the Colt Press in San Francisco. The book contains many of Kees's best poems. Few American poets have made such a strong and enduring impression in their first book. Kees was one of those rare poets who produced no juvenilia. Almost every poem in *The Last Man* was unmistakably spoken in Kees's own voice and proper register. While it was easy to see his sources—Eliot, Baudelaire, and, above all, Auden—their tone and subject matter came so naturally to him that after a few poems it is impossible to see Kees as their imitator, but rather as some terrifying reincarnation, *un semblable, un frère*. He had Baudelaire's bitter experience with failure and felt Eliot's despair but without benefit of clergy. It is clearly a testimony to the authenticity of Kees's despair that he never had any hesitation in discovering his own poetic voice. From the first it was *ego clamavi de profundis*.

Probably it is only now after thirty-five years that it is possible to see how fine a book *The Last Man* really is. When it first appeared along with the premier volumes of Kees's contemporaries (most of whom were trying out their own variations of the same Eliotic Audenesque), what might have struck the reader was its similarity to the other poetry rather than its distinctiveness. Now that the prevailing styles of American poetry have moved in different directions, it is easier to read these books of the late thirties and early forties with more detachment. Most of those "stunning new voices" now sound like the lifeless imitations that they were, but Kees's book is still alive. Its best poems speak with a force and directness that seems absolutely contemporary. Is "For My Daughter" any less unsettling now than when it appeared thirty-five years ago?

For My Daughter

Looking into my daughter's eyes I read
Beneath the innocence of morning flesh
Concealed, hintings of death she does not heed.
Coldest of winds have blown this hair, and mesh
Of seaweed snarled these miniatures of hands;
The night's slow poison, tolerant and bland,
Has moved her blood. Parched years that I have seen
That may be hers appear: foul, lingering
Death in certain war, the slim legs green.
Or, fed on hate, she relishes the sting
Of others' agony; perhaps the cruel
Bride of a syphilitic or a fool.
These speculations sour in the sun.
I have no daughter. I desire none.

For Kees is not a comfortable poet to read. He is one of the bitterest poets in our literature. As Kenneth Rexroth said, Kees "lived in a permanent and hopeless apocalypse." Many American writers have lived in despair, but none more powerfully made that darkness visible. If Kees saw little beyond this despair, it is astonishing how keen his vision was within that range. Life for him was a meaningless exile from a country he could not recall, a punishment for a crime he did not understand. But unlike much poetry of despair, his poems are not monotonous and self-pitying complaints. (Whatever his literary faults, Kees is never dull.) They are often savagely funny. Like the best prose, his poems engage the attention. Perhaps for this reason, Donald Justice said they belong to "the Prose Tradition in poetry." They actively engage the intelligence as well as the emotions. Unlike most confessional poetry, his poems do not direct the reader's attention toward the writer. Rather they focus that attention on a world of common experience.

When one compares Kees's work to that of his contemporaries, one immediately notices its lack of any old-fashioned poetic subjects or stances. While many poets went to great lengths to develop styles that could successfully employ the Romantic tradition in some new way, Kees never longed for a glorious vanished past. To him, the past was as bleak and sordid as the present. In this regard he was the least "poetic" and most modern of twentieth-century American poets. Coming a full generation after the great experimental writers like Eliot, Joyce, Pound, and Williams, he felt no need to struggle with the nineteenth century in his verse, because unlike them he felt no dangerous attraction toward it. His verse does not teem unnecessarily with the Modernist stage business of twentieth-century poetry. Instinctively grasping the situation, images, and tone of his epoch, Kees did not have to display his modernity in the same way as so many of his contemporaries who busied themselves in disguising, subduing, denying, and at times transforming their innate Romanticism under some ferocious mask of modernity.

For this reason too Kees was not interested in technical innovation at the beginning of his career. The style he had inherited from Eliot, Auden, Joyce, and Baudelaire was adequate for the nasty business he had to perform. From the first he understood his mission in writing and did not need to engage in technical exercises to discover it. As he grew older he began experimenting boldly with musical and narrative forms, but these innovations came gradually only after the visionary center of his work had been established. He had already mapped out the territory of his vision. Now he would explore it more completely.

Kees, then, is a poet of narrow scope, but this is hardly a damning

criticism. Herbert, Hopkins, Housman, Larkin, not to mention conti-
nental writers like Trakl and Leopardi, are all poets who could be accused
of having narrow interests. It is not only the breadth of a poet's response
to life that matters, but also the depth and intensity of that vision. In this
regard Kees can scarcely be called to task. A single, intensely felt vision
unifies all of this work from the earliest published piece to the last, post-
humously printed poems. While vision alone does not make a poet, Kees
had the imagination, the ear, and the technical resources to convey this
vision superbly in poem after poem.

Kees began by writing fiction. He had a novelist's eye for his subject,
which, I suspect, is more dependable than that of most poets, simply because it is less concerned with exploiting its own idiosyncrasies and more
with registering perceptions that can be endorsed by other people. Kees
also had a fiction writer's eye for interesting subjects. Even his weakest
poems are seldom dull, a difficult claim to make for many other poets. In
its ability to grab the reader's attention, Kees's poetry resembles that of
our language's most accomplished novelist-poet, Thomas Hardy. As
in Hardy, Kees's poems often tell a story or describe a character with
such straightforwardness that the reader is swept along to the end. Like
Hardy, Kees made his bleak vision bearable by mixing it with black
humor. Their darkest poems are often very funny. And, as in Hardy, the
reader usually remembers the entire poem as much as particular lines in
it. The special quality of Kees's poetry can, therefore, be seen more
clearly in comparison to Hardy than to a writer like Eliot, despite the
debt Kees's work owes to the latter poet. It is lamentable that the handful of reviews Kees's work received in the author's lifetime fastened on its
similarities to Eliot and never made the attempt to understand it on its
own terms. The distinctions between Eliot and Kees are crucial.

There is a consistent landscape behind Kees's poetry, but it is not an
Eliotic wasteland because there is no hope, religious or otherwise, of renewal. Nor are the narrators the tired, world-weary figures that Eliot
adapted from Tennyson. Kees's figures are usually young men who want
to escape but cannot, and their despair vents itself in sardonic self-
contempt. The poems exhibit a tremendous energy, one that doesn't
work only at a deliberate, Eliotic pace, but often breaks out in single, passionate explosions. Listen, for example, to this early poem:

The Scene of the Crime

There should have been some witness there, accusing—
Women with angry mouths and burning eyes
To fill the house with unforgiving cries;
But there was only silence for abuse.

There should have been exposure—more than curtains
Drawn, the stairway coiling to the floor
Where no one walked, the sheeted furniture,
And one thin line of light beneath the door.

Walking the stairs to reach that room, a pool
Of blood swam in his thought, a hideous guide
That led him on and vanished in the hall.
There should have been damnation. But, inside,
Only an old man clawed the bed, and drooled,
Whispering, "Murderer!" before he died.

Poems like this show Kees's particular genius. He can present a scene of terrifying importance with a speed and fluency unmatched by anyone of his generation. Kees's best poems sweep the listener along with such unexpected smoothness that he has no time to defend himself against their shocking conclusions. Notice how the uncompleted rhyme between "accusing" and "abuse" refuses to allow the reader a rest at the end of the first stanza. Or observe how Kees's lineation plays with the reader by making the innocent "pool" at the end of line nine become a hideous "pool of blood" in the next line, only to qualify it away a few words later as a metaphor for the murderer's thoughts. Kees was a master of quick but subtle effects like these, worked into the lines so smoothly that a reader never notices them consciously until they are pointed out. This gift allowed him to build poems rapidly from mundane beginnings to almost apocalyptic conclusions. For example, in another poem, after only a dozen lines he can create a context strong enough to ask convincingly:

Where is the grave
Of Time? What would you picture for decay?
A horse's hoof, white bones, a lifeless tree,

Cold hemispheres, dried moss, and a blue wave
Breaking at noon on shores you will not see.

Yet Kees could also modulate this bitter voice into moments of tenderness:

Tired after love and silent in this house,
Your back turned to me, quite alone,
Standing with one hand raised to smooth your hair,
At a small window, green with rain.

Characteristically, this tenderness is touched by sadness. Consider the unexpected pang of "quite alone." Even in his gentlest poems one senses that the most Kees hoped for were brief moments of peace amid the great sadness of existence. The poems are hopeful only in their belief that the present moment is secure. There is no such faith in the past or the future. Nor is there any ultimate reconciliation with existence, even tentatively. Most often these peaceful poems are delicate explorations of grief, as in "Homage to Arthur Waley," a short poem that demonstrates the superb naturalness with which Kees could handle a literary subject (seamlessly weaving in a quotation from Waley's version of Po Chü-i's "Arriving at Hsün-Yang"). I quote it in its entirety:

Homage to Arthur Waley

Seattle weather: it has rained for weeks in this town,
The dampness breeding moths and a gray summer.
I sit in the smoky room reading your book again,
My eyes raw, hearing the trains steaming below me
In the wet yard, and I wonder if you are still alive.
Turning the worn pages, reading once more:
"By misty waters and rainy sands, while the yellow dusk thickens."

Despite the formal structure underlying most of his poems, Kees almost always spoke in a conversational tone—what Justice linked to the classical definition of a good prose style, "natural words in a natural order." This deceptive informality links Kees to other San Francisco writers and separates him from the formal literary tone of early Lowell and

Berryman. From his earliest poems Kees created both a believable speaking voice and a clear dramatic situation. This dramatic mode came naturally to this former playwright, and it is probably responsible for the uncanny speed and grace of his best work. He could create a character or a scene in a few words. Consider the opening lines from some of Kees's most characteristic poems:

> The smiles of the bathers fade as they leave the water

> . . .

> Memories as rich as Proust's or Baudelaire's are yours,
> You think

> . . .

> No eyes. No light. The one chilled and imperfect hand
> Claws at the spot where banisters had been

> . . .

> It must have been in March the rug wore through.

> . . .

> No butler, no second maid, no blood upon the stair.

The jagged rhythms, the compressed locutions, the stress-heavy meters, the conscious ambiguities, the closely worked-out symbolism, and the intertextual allusiveness that characterized American formalist poetry in the early forties are almost entirely absent from Kees's work. While his poems are often formal, their rhythms always stay true to contemporary American speech. Even his virtuoso pieces—the villanelles, sestinas, and sonnets—sound conversational. In an era when critics made a poet's style into his most important subject, Kees exhibited few of the mannerisms expected of a serious young poet—no typographic peculiarities, stylistic extremes, repetitious technical tricks, or narrow metrical assumptions. No predictable flourishes immediately signaled a Kees poem. His rich and fluent style was not so easily summarized, and the sheer flexibility of his talent, the clarity and precision of his language, made him untrustworthy to critics trained to explain the obscure and celebrate the idiosyncratic. Likewise, his assimilation of the idioms and images of popular culture trivialized his work in the eyes of critics immersed in the elite aesthetic of high Modernism. His poetry was intelligent, urbane, and allusive, but it did not reek of the university. An eclectic writer as much at home in jazz, journalism, and cinema as in the self-referential world of modern poetry, Kees was more likely to frame his poems in devices borrowed from popular culture than from serious literature. And, if he alluded to high culture, he was more likely to treat it in a savagely satirical way. Steeped in Modernism, he was not in awe of its totems. A middle-class Midwesterner, he was also rooted in the mainstream of American mass culture. A visionary of the contemporary apocalypse, he did not need to prop up his private obsessions with literary archetypes when he could so naturally merge his personal nightmares with public ones.

3

There is one story and one story only
That will prove worth your telling
Whether as learned bard or gifted child;
To it all lines and lesser gauds belong
That startle with their shining
Such common stories as they stray into.
　　　　—ROBERT GRAVES, "To Juan at Winter Solstice"

THE SCALE OF KEES'S achievement becomes clearer when one realizes that he died at forty-one, an age at which many of his contemporaries had yet to write their best or most distinctive work. (Compare his oeuvre to Berryman's before *77 Dream Songs,* Roethke's before *The Far Field,* Jarrell's before *The Woman at the Washington Zoo,* and Lowell's before *Life Studies* to put it in proper perspective.) In his lifetime he published only three proverbially thin books of verse that contain almost all of his poetry. There were only eleven years separating the appearance of the first book from the last. Kees's poetic career was one short journey toward self-discovery. It sounds cheaply clever to say that the price of this journey was self-destruction, but judging from the overriding despair of even his

earliest work, is it cruel to say that suicide might have been the only end
for Kees even if he had never written? Perhaps it was only by directing his
tremendous energy into poetry, fiction, painting, filmmaking, and music
that he was able to live as long and productively as he did.

The brevity of Kees's poetic career must be a central fact in any attempt
to assess his contribution to American literature. His oeuvre is small and
intensely unified. All of his best poems are interrelated. For this reason his
work must be approached as a whole before the full extent of its power becomes apparent. Images, situations, attitudes, ideas recur from poem to
poem and in ways that make them gain force and clarity. His work gradually creates a world of its own—one that is both fascinating and frighten-
ingly real. In many ways the modern poet whom Kees most closely
resembles is the Austrian expressionist Georg Trakl. Despite the drastic
differences in the styles of their poetry, both men shared an all-pervasive
cosmic pessimism that transcends their own suicidal obsessions. Both
poets could write only variations on a single theme. In Kees, as in Trakl,
the word *myth*—as recklessly as it has been tossed around—is the only
term that can be used to describe the vision informing their oeuvre. They
do not use discrete symbols designed to emphasize a particular point.
Instead they seem to draw images from a mysterious, preexisting world
behind their poetry, a world that appears obliquely but is never fully realized in any single poem. Even when the meaning of these symbols is not
totally apparent to the reader, they have a deep sense of purpose and ap-
propriateness because the vision from which they have been drawn is obsessively consistent. Therefore, what is crucial in understanding Kees's
poetry is not the individual symbols, however interesting they may be,
but instead the single, underlying vision that unifies it. One sees the consistency of this vision most clearly in three elements that reappear in his
poetry: a special landscape, a particular kind of antihero, and a recurring
human drama. While no single element in isolation reveals the complete
scope of his vision, together they constitute the myth that informs it.

The mythic landscape of Kees's poetry is the wasteland, a fallen world
where real time has stopped. An unexplained curse hangs over the land,
and it permeates everything. The season is frozen on the uneasy threshold
between late winter and early spring, but the spring either will not come
or arrives barren, bringing no rejuvenation. The atmosphere is oppres-
sive; the weather turbulent but without resolution. Since the dominant
feature of this world is its deathly barrenness, a season of real or meta-

phorical winter, it is not important whether the landscape appears as either urban or rural. Kees could use either setting successfully. What is critically important, however, is that it is always a peopled landscape, an inhabited or cultivated one. Most American poets are at their best writing about solitary confrontation with Nature in the virgin landscape. (Think of poets as dissimilar in other ways as Emerson, Jeffers, Stevens, Winters, Ammons, and Snyder.) The landscape of Kees's poetry is always a civilized one. If it is uninhabited, it is only because of some apocalyptic desolation or migration. In this sense Kees's sensibility is European. For him the people are an essential part of the landscape. The characteristics of his wasteland become apparent only in its inhabitants. They are as barren and lifeless as the landscape.

In mythic worlds there are patterns of action that demand completion, and a fallen world must have its redeemer, be it Christ or Parsifal, or even Hercule Poirot. Without its redeemer the landscape and its inhabitants exude a feeling of incompleteness and anxiety. Everything is tentative and temporary. Kees took his mythic landscape from Eliot (just as Eliot had taken it from Baudelaire, James Thomson, and the Grail romances), but Kees adapted it in a tellingly original way. Kees created his own redemption myth, a story as cyclical as an ancient legend. It was the vision of human destiny as an endless succession of heroes who try to redeem this fallen world and always fail.

The hero and the story usually appear in contemporary guise. "Crime Club" is an excellent example. The setting is a suburban house where a man has been murdered. The hero is the detective. But none of the clues come together. There was no reason for the murder. When finally the detective is unable to find a guilty party, his failure becomes symbolic of the unredeemable nature of his fallen world. For, if there is no individual guilt to be assigned, the guilt must somehow be general, and no human hero can change this condition. The poem ends:

> Small wonder that the case remains unsolved,
> Or that the sleuth, Le Roux, is now incurably insane,
> And sits alone in a white room in a white gown,
> Screaming that all the world is mad, that clues
> Lead nowhere, or to walls so high their tops cannot be seen;
> Screaming all day of war, screaming that nothing can be solved.

Published in 1943, this poem used the paraphernalia of popular culture to make a profound critique of the culture that produced it. In a way that prefigures Auden's influential 1948 essay "The Guilty Vicarage," Kees's poem explores the theological substructure in mysteries—those fascinating and almost interchangeable novels that allow the reader to admit how evil the world is but feel that such corruption is only a momentary deflection from an inevitable order. The detective is the savior who by entering the fallen world of the crime and exposing himself to danger from the guilty party can use reason to restore a just order. But in Kees there is no underlying order to restore, no inevitable triumph of reason or justice. The hero not only fails to save the world, he cannot even save his own sanity.

This story is retold throughout Kees's poetry in different ways for different effects, but it always ends in defeat. No matter how gifted or aggressive the hero, he eventually discovers that his quest is impossible. But the hero is no ordinary man. He is a fanatic or a saint and continues to struggle against the curse that blights the landscape. Therefore his end is always violent or bleak—death, imprisonment, madness, or pointless anticipation.

The role of this antihero becomes clearer when he appears in his purest form, as a blasphemous version of Christ. Parodies of Christ abound in Kees's poetry, and their role is always the same. They are potential redeemers of the wasteland, grotesque or ridiculous messiahs chosen to die for the salvation of a graceless world. Sometimes they go self-deluded to their deaths. More often they are involuntary victims, chosen as sacrificial lambs by their families or societies. Their deaths, however, are always pointless. Whatever god they are being offered to remains silent or unmoved. No new dispensation of grace results. The central importance of this myth in Kees's poetry explains the violence and pessimism that permeate his work. He is not gratuitously trying to shock the reader. Rather he is confronting what to him is the basic tragedy of human existence: Man leads a meaningless life in an indifferent, natural world, but longing for some higher purpose he pointlessly sacrifices himself or others to bring about a newer, better order. Kees offered tragedy without catharsis. This is no pleasant vision. As Geoffrey Hill once wrote, "There is no bloodless myth will hold."

The figure of Christ exercised a tremendous fascination on Kees, but his Jesus was not the sentimental moralist of American Protestantism or the Romantic idealist of Renan. He was Jesus the Apocalyptic who preached the imminent destruction of the world and the sudden coming of the Kingdom of God. Kees's views were influenced by Albert Schweitzer's comprehensive *The Quest of the Historical Jesus* (1906) and probably the German theologian's earlier *The Mystery of the Kingdom of God* (1901). Though Kees nowhere mentions Schweitzer, a student familiar with both authors will see striking resemblances. A conspicuous example of Schweitzer's influence is "A Distance from the Sea," one of Kees's best poems, which is based on the theories of Karl Friedrich Bahrdt, an obscure German philologist of the eighteenth century, who is discussed in Schweitzer's *Quest*. In fact, a five-line passage in the poem (lines 41–45) is an unacknowledged, word-for-word adaptation of a simile Schweitzer draws earlier in the book. One suspects that Kees's poems contain many similar secret homages to other authors, and here—as in so many other areas—the poet awaits the attention of a dedicated scholar.

For Kees, as for Schweitzer, Christ is a visionary tragically at odds with circumstance, and his crucifixion is more a gruesome and terrifying revelation of his mortality than a triumphant act of redemption. Although Schweitzer carefully skirts the issue in both books, a careful reading suggests that he would deny the Resurrection. His Christ is preeminently a man. And it is as a man tortured with a hopeless vocation of divinity rather than as a God-made-man that Kees uses his figure of Christ.

Sometimes Kees presents these Christ figures directly, more often indirectly. Their mission is always seen in the same way: their deaths will bring about a new age. In "Eight Variations" there is an episode that parodies Eliot's *The Waste Land*, in which the speaker talks about an eagerly awaited resurrection. Here the religious mystery has become a commodity:

> We welcomed one poor hackneyed Christ,
> Sad bastard, croaking of pestilence. The basement
> Holds him now. He has not as yet arisen.
> The tickets are ready; the line forms on the right.

Likewise, in "River Song," a small sardonic masterpiece, Kees describes the crucial moment of all redemption myths, the sacrificial death of the hero, in a form that recalls a nursery rhyme. It ends:

The bands were playing when they cut me down
By the dirty river where the children cried,
And a man made a speech in a long black gown.

He called me a hero. I didn't care.
The river ran blood and the children died.
And I wanted to die, but they left me there.

Since the Romantic movement the hero and the poet have often become the same figure, and in poems like "River Song" and "Crime Club"
it is correct, I think, to see Kees implicitly describing his own condition.
His art can ultimately redeem nothing—not the world, not even his own
troubled life. "All a poet can do today is warn," so Kees quoted Wilfred
Owen in the epigraph to an early poem. Warning others was the only role
Kees allowed himself in art.

Rexroth's claim that Kees lived in "a permanent and hopeless apocalypse" employed the appropriate metaphor. The vision unifying all of
Kees's poetry is of a desperate, never-ending wait for an apocalypse that
will not come, just as all Christian belief centers on the redeeming apocalypse of Christ's second coming. That is why the Christian vision of redemption provided Kees so naturally with a symbolic structure for his
poetry. Christ preached that the world was coming to an end, that existence as people knew it—evil and transitory—was about to perish and
that a new order would appear. The Christian vision is therefore essentially eschatological. Until the new order arrives, mankind is in the period
of waiting and preparation for the final apocalypse. That vision explains
why the eschatological elements in Kees's poetry are so powerful. His vi-
sions of civilization coming to an end are not stage properties borrowed
from Eliot or Auden; they are his central subject matter.

In "A Distance from the Sea," Kees retells the historical Christ story.
The poem is a monologue spoken presumably by Saint John toward the
end of the Evangelist's life. Beginning with a splendid description of
Jesus walking on the waves, John carefully recounts how each of Christ's
miracles was faked by the Apostles. But the trickery of John and the
Apostles was not undertaken for any gain on their part. Their mission
was utterly altruistic. Every deceit was done for mankind's benefit. They
labored to give others the faith, which they themselves knew was impossible. In a brilliant touch, Kees has John ridicule the liberal theologians of

his day who underestimate the importance of miracles in the scheme of Christ's message:

> —And now there are those who have come saying
> That miracles were not what we were after. But what else
> Is there? What other hope does life hold out
> But the miraculous . . . ?

For Kees there was no other hope, and, as his version of John makes clear, he knew it to be a false one. Yet like his nihilistic Apostle, Kees could not help working against the void by trying to create at least the illusion of hope—a hope against death, against the fear that this painful life led nowhere but to extinction. In John's summary of the Apostles' accomplishment, one can also hear Kees talking, toward the end of his life, on his vocation as a poet:

> . . . It was our making. Yet sometimes
> When the torrent of that time
> Comes pouring back, I wonder at our courage
> And our enterprise. It was as though the world
> Had been one darkening, abandoned hall
> Where rows of unlit candles stood; and we
> Not out of love, so much, or hope, or even worship, but
> Out of the fear of death, came with our lights
> And watched the candles, one by one, take fire, flames
> Against the long night of our fear. We thought
> That we could never die.

4

> All visions are of death.
>
> —Theodore Roethke

So far in this essay I have described the general course of Kees's career and what I consider the fundamental qualities of his poetry. So little has been written about his life and work that it seemed necessary to approach him in this foursquare fashion. But there are obvious shortcomings in such an approach. Dealing with the lives of suicidal poets will always be dangerous for a literary critic. The biographical stories are so fascinating that they threaten to overwhelm the poetry, especially in the case of a poet like Kees where so much is speculated and so little known for sure. One has only to read the few pieces published about Kees since his disappearance to discover how completely the legend has eclipsed the poetry. Still it is hardly easier to talk about the nature of Kees's work from a strictly literary viewpoint with so little of it available for examination. His excellent short stories have never been collected. His essays and reviews on art, literature, film, and music remain still scattered among the magazines that printed them. His plays and novel have never been published. Nor has criticism supplied many helpful insights on how to consider what is available, his poetry. Since there are no accepted ways of looking at his poetry (except as the work of a *poète maudit*), I have tried to suggest at least one possible viewpoint. If Kees is to be remembered as anything beyond an extraordinarily talented period figure, it will be through his poetry. It is time then to turn our complete attention to it.

Now that the reader has at least some familiarity with the nature of Kees's poetry, I would like to conclude by examining two of his poems in detail. This examination will not be a conscientious delving for deeper meaning. Rather it will be an appreciation of their masterful surfaces. It will concentrate on the main characteristics of Kees's style—the smooth syntax, the rapid succession of images, the cinematic and narrative structure, and the sudden, startling conclusions—and demonstrate how these features combine with his personal vision to create the resonance and integrity associated with the best poetry. I have purposely chosen two poems dissimilar in style, tone, and subject to emphasize both the depth and range of his talent while underlining the common quality of his best work. It is on the basis of poems like these that I believe Weldon Kees deserves a place among the best American poets of the past half century.

"1926" is one of Kees's finest short poems. It reveals a quiet tenderness that one doesn't often associate with him. The language is conversational; the diction and prosody never call attention to themselves. The poem is so simple that even after a single reading one might wonder what can be said about it.

1926

The porchlight coming on again,
Early November, the dead leaves

Raked in piles, the wicker swing
Creaking. Across the lots
A phonograph is playing *Ja-Da*.

An orange moon. I see the lives
Of neighbors, mapped and marred
Like all the wars ahead, and R.
Insane, B. with his throat cut,
Fifteen years from now, in Omaha.

I did not know them then.
My airedale scratches at the door.
And I am back from seeing Milton Sills
And Doris Kenyon. Twelve years old.
The porchlight coming on again.

The poem's title is merely a date, but one which has more than the purely personal significance of setting the scene in Kees's youth. It also places the poem in a particularly peaceful and prosperous period of American history. The scene is Nebraska in November, 1926. The First World War is only a memory; the next war has not yet come. Nor has the Great Depression arrived, which will ravage the state. The setting is a small, old-fashioned town, the kind that Americans, even those raised in huge cities, look on as their national Garden of Eden, that original innocence from which all later development has been a Fall. For Hollywood this sort of town became an idyllic American archetype. For Kees it was the real world of his childhood. Here once again national and personal myths came together in his work.

The poem unfolds in three stanzas and takes the form of one memory being interrupted by another. It begins with a small detail remembered from the past that suddenly propels the poet back into the world of his childhood. He is twelve years old again early one evening in his old neighborhood, where houses still have porches, the yards have wicker swings, and there are empty lots for children to play in. He is walking home from the movies (Doris Kenyon and Milton Stills were a famous silent-film couple), and he sees the light on his home porch coming on. One by one the sights and sounds of his old home come back to him. There is even a jazzy old dance tune to provide background music. The stern November weather notwithstanding, the scene is the sober, wholesome world of the American pastoral. The memory is an unexpected moment of grace, the innocence of childhood returned. The narrator then looks up, however, and sees the moon, an orange moon, lying low on the horizon. Perhaps because the moon has a more specific association for him than simply those of his childhood, or perhaps because of some other unspoken reason, the sight of it brings his thoughts back to the present. Returned to adulthood, he recalls what has happened to these people. Knowing what he does now, he sees their lives as doomed. Their destinies are mapped out ahead of them, and nothing they do will save them. The imagery of the orange moon and the "mapped" wars ahead is violent, as are the two horrifying cases he mentions. One neighbor has gone insane. Another has either been murdered or killed himself.

The final stanza returns to the world of innocence and eventually to the same image of home that began the poem. A superficial reader might wish to hear the poem as a reaffirmation of the pastoral vision of the child's world, as a comforting and quiet circle of images. But this would be to miss the ironic nature of the ending. The final stanza begins with the only ambiguous line of the poem, "I did not know them then." Here the reader must pause to interpret what it means. The line cannot be taken on a literal level. The child obviously knew, or at least knew of, his neighbors. What the line implies is that the speaker did not understand his neighbors then, specifically the two who met frightening ends, as deeply as he does now. From his bitter present knowledge, he now can see the past clearly. Most important, he also sees his past self clearly. In retrospect, his own life is no less "mapped and marred" than those of his childhood neighbors. He can change nothing in either their lives or his own.

Once this subtle turn of consciousness in the poem has been understood, the final lines have an underlying poignancy unlike the opening. They now describe a past that he is powerless to change. To remember this past is no longer a moment of innocence regained but a punishment. In the final stanza the narrator reexperiences the same scene as in the opening lines, but now on two levels simultaneously, both as an ignorant child and as a doomed adult. Now when the poem ends with the same line with which it began, the effect is quite different. The poem has quietly led the reader to a terrifying discovery.

"Aspects of Robinson" is probably Kees's best-known poem, which is to say it has been anthologized a few times since it first appeared in the *New Yorker* in 1948. It is, I propose, one of the finest short American poems of its period.

Aspects of Robinson

Robinson at cards at the Algonquin; a thin
Blue light comes down once more outside the blinds.
Gray men in overcoats are ghosts blown past the door.
The taxis streak the avenues with yellow, orange, and red.
This is Grand Central, Mr. Robinson.

Robinson on a roof above the Heights; the boats
Mourn like the lost. Water is slate, far down.
Through sounds of ice cubes dropped in glass, an osteopath,
Dressed for the links, describes an old Intourist tour.
—Here's where old Gibbons jumped from, Robinson.

Robinson walking in the Park, admiring the elephant.
Robinson buying the *Tribune,* Robinson buying the *Times.*
    Robinson
Saying, "Hello. Yes, this is Robinson. Sunday
At five? I'd love to. Pretty well. And you?"
Robinson alone at Longchamps, staring at the wall.

Robinson afraid, drunk, sobbing Robinson
In bed with a Mrs. Morse. Robinson at home;
Decisions: Toynbee or luminol? Where the sun
Shines, Robinson in flowered trunks, eyes toward
The breakers. Where the night ends, Robinson in East Side bars.

Robinson in Glen plaid jacket, Scotch-grain shoes,
Black four-in-hand and oxford button-down,
The jeweled and silent watch that winds itself, the brief-
Case, covert topcoat, clothes for spring, all covering
His sad and usual heart, dry as a winter leaf.

"Aspects of Robinson" demonstrates how Kees could take the material of the preceding literary generation and develop it into something distinctly personal. Robinson, a character who appears in four of Kees's poems, is a classic figure in modern poetry—the cultivated, self-conscious, lonely man lost in an impersonal, urban world. Robinson bears a family resemblance to Eliot's Prufrock and Aiken's Senlin. He also resembles Weldon Kees, and to deny that likeness is to ignore willfully the source of the poem's emotional intensity.

"Aspects of Robinson" is a formal poem of five stanzas, each stanza made up of five loose iambic lines. For the most part the lines are in either blank verse or unrhymed hexameter. They present a series of scenes with a quickening tempo throughout the poem and end in a slow tableau. Understanding this pacing is crucial to understanding the poem. This reading will try to delineate its characteristic structure while placing the details of the poem within it.

The poem begins with two discrete episodes, each filling one stanza. These scenes carefully establish Robinson and the "landscape" of the poem, both of which will be exploited brilliantly later. "Aspects of Robinson" opens at the Algonquin, Manhattan's famous literary hotel, where Robinson is playing cards, probably illegally. There is no nature in Manhattan, everything is an artifact. Even the light from outside is an unnatural blue. People are hardly more real. From inside the hotel, men on the street seem like insubstantial ghosts blown out of the Underworld. New York is, by implication, an urban hell, Baudelaire's *"Fourmillante cité, cité pleine de rêves."* Taxis streak through the rainy streets in violent colors— yellow, orange, red. Suddenly another voice interrupts the poem, "This is Grand Central, Mr. Robinson." With the abruptness of a cinematic cut the reader is now in one of those speeding taxis. A driver's voice is speaking to Robinson, but the reader has no sense of the context. This deliberate sense of dislocation will be repeated through the poem. The reader is forced to look between the lines to supply the context. Grand Central Station is only a few blocks from the Algonquin. Why does Robinson need a cab to get there? Why does Robinson need the station pointed out to him? Is he drunk, dreaming, lost in thought? Where is Robinson going? The reader hears only the macabre interruption.

The next stanza opens on a rooftop party in Brooklyn Heights, the beautiful nineteenth-century neighborhood built on the cliffs above the East River and Brooklyn docks. But for the moment it could be any cliff above any river. Robinson stares down at the water and hears the foghorns calling from the freighters below. The ominous imagery of the cold gray water far below is immediately trivialized by the sound of ice cubes being dropped into a cocktail glass. An osteopath in golf clothes begins chatting about vacations. The poem seems directed at social satire when suddenly there is another macabre interruption. Unexpectedly, somebody unnoticed until now is standing beside the protagonist pointing out, "Here's where old Gibbons jumped from, Robinson." Some common acquaintance committed suicide by jumping from the point where Robinson was staring down. The water below once again seems ominous.

Each of the two opening stanzas presented a single episode that began and ended with Robinson's name. Now using a similar technique but a faster tempo, the next two stanzas present a series of scenes, each depicting Robinson in one definitive flash. They are almost photographs, a yearlong series of snapshots capturing a man's life: Robinson at Central Park admiring a caged animal; Robinson buying one or another of two morning newspapers as if the petty choices of a consumer represented real freedom. And Robinson is overheard speaking his only lines in the poem, polite but ontologically eerie chitchat on the phone. He affirms that he is there and changes the subject. He is observed alone in an expensive restaurant. He is almost always alone.

Using this quickened tempo, the third stanza begins a brilliant counterpoint of proper nouns. Robinson's name is set against a catalogue of things to buy, possess, or use. Count the proper nouns and brand names in the next eleven lines: Central Park, the *Tribune,* the *Times,* Sunday, Longchamps, Mrs. Morse, Toynbee, luminol, the East Side, Glen plaid, Scotch grain, oxford button downs, and the name of Robinson itself twelve times. The repetition of his name alone could easily become irritating. But Kees controls the rhythms of the poem so well that, set against these other names, Robinson becomes an insistent and solitary ground bass for despair.

The fragmentary pageant of Robinson's life continues in the fourth stanza. He is afraid. He is drunk and sobbing in bed with a married woman. He is at home, an insomniac deciding between a book and a drug, as if they were equal choices. He is at the beach in summer staring out at the waves. As in all the other episodes, Robinson is largely a passive spectator. He observes the ominous world around him silently.

Up until now the poem has stayed true to its title. It has presented a man through fragments, exterior aspects of an unarticulated interior life. A jumbled collection of superficial observations that should not add up to a total person, and yet somehow do. Sadly, they give some sense of an achingly human being underneath. It is as if a man were no more than the sum of his pastimes and possessions.

The poem ends in one long sentence fragment that provides a chilling anatomy of a contemporary man. Robinson is seen in an East Side bar late at night dressed as meticulously as a model in a spring fashion advertisement. In every detail he appears the successful, well-dressed man. The quick, cumulative technique of the earlier stanzas is now adapted to building one slow final tableau. Robinson is described at length but only in terms of the clothes he wears, one item after another, "all covering / His sad and usual heart, dry as a winter leaf." The final line is stunning, but what makes it so effective? The contrast could easily have been too sharp and sudden. The answer, I believe, is that the final twist not merely rejects the fashionable exterior but qualifies it on every important level. Robinson's secret despair is located by the poet literally in his heart, the one natural organ in this sardonic anatomy. This "sad and usual" organ is literally covered by his clothes in the same way that the sadness it represents is covered by the outer show of success. The new clothes he dons for spring don't change his usual, inescapable despair.

"Usual" is the key word here. His heart is not reborn with the spring as his wardrobe is. It persists "dry as a winter leaf." Everything around Robinson renews itself, even his self-winding watch, but he himself is not renewed. His possessions mock him. His fresh public attire is not merely superficial; it is, quite literally, a travesty. Even the sounds of the poem link the exterior Robinson with his sad interior. Notice two musical effects, the run-on rhyme of "brief" and "leaf" (the poem's only end rhymes) and the subtle transformation of "covert" into "covering." These musical correspondences strike harmonies on a deeper level. The violent lineation of "brief- / Case" creates a subliminal reminder of mortality and a preparation for the final image. Likewise, Robinson's fashionable waterproof woolen coat, which is specifically what a "covert topcoat" is, connotes the deception of his outer appearance, also prefiguring the final image. Kees works with such speed that the reader does not initially have time to register the sheer accuracy of these effects while listening to the poem, but the details all contribute to the powerful total effect of the poem. On an almost unconscious level they prepare the reader for the startling final image.

The challenge for a young poet is to reconcile the world with the imagination. These two poems demonstrate how Kees transformed the alienation and vacuity of contemporary life into lyric poetry. He does not offer readers comfort or escape. He did not transcend the problems of his century with a religious or political faith. He did not elude the vulgarization of public culture by immigrating to an aesthetic realm. What he offered was uncompromising honesty, the transforming shock of recognition. "All a poet can do today is warn." Kees used the detritus of a spiritually bankrupt society—the ephemera of slang, popular songs, brand names, advertising, fashion, journalism, movies—to provide a backdrop stark enough to dramatize the human situation. He practiced a realism so bitter it borders on prophecy. He presented only the choices history offered his generation, and none of them were attractive. There are contemporary poets more modern than Kees, but none of them seems truer to modern life. He wrote about the noisy world we are trapped in, about the spoiled landscapes that surround us, using the sordid images that confront us every day. Many writers tried to fuse these fragments into art, but few had the necessary imaginative energy. Kees did. He is the poet our age deserves—whether it wants him or not.

POSTSCRIPT: Since this essay first appeared, the state of Weldon Kees's literary reputation has changed most interestingly. His work has acquired a significant reputation among poets, especially younger ones, but it remains virtually unknown to academic critics. The bulk of Kees's work is now in print. Although no biography has yet been published, his life and mysterious disappearance have achieved legendary status among poets both in America and England, many of whom consider him a major influence. This growing Kees cult has already produced enough poems and essays to fill several sizable volumes. Meanwhile his name remains conspicuously absent in recent academic anthologies and literary histories. I will not belabor this paradox. It is merely one more example of the growing split between the taste of imaginative writers and university critics that characterizes our current literary culture.

The Anonymity of the Regional Poet

1. The Predicament of Popular Poetry

Ordinary thoughts and feelings are not necessarily shallow, any more than subtle or unusual ones are necessarily profound.

— EDWIN MUIR

TED KOOSER is a popular poet. This is not to say that he commands a mass public. No contemporary poet does — at least in America. Kooser is popular in that unlike most of his peers he writes naturally for a nonliterary public. His style is accomplished but extremely simple — his diction drawn from common speech, his syntax conversational. His subjects are chosen from the everyday world of the Great Plains, and his sensibility, though more subtle and articulate, is that of the average Midwesterner. Kooser never makes an allusion that an intelligent but unbookish reader will not immediately grasp. There is to my knowledge no poet of equal stature who writes so convincingly in a manner the average American can understand and appreciate.

But to describe Kooser merely as a poet who writes plainly about the ordinary world is misleading insofar as it makes his work sound dull. For here, too, the comparison with popular art holds true. Kooser is uncommonly entertaining. His poems are usually short and perfectly paced, his subjects relevant and engaging. Finishing one poem, the reader instinctively wants to proceed to another. It has been Kooser's particular genius to develop a genuine poetic style that accommodates the average reader and portrays a vision that provides unexpected moments of illumination from the seemingly threadbare details of everyday life.

If Kooser's work is visionary, however, it is on a decidedly human scale. He offers no blinding flashes of inspiration, no mystic moments of transcendence. He creates no private mythologies or fantasy worlds. Instead he provides small but genuine insights into the world of everyday experience. His work strikes the difficult balance between profundity and accessibility, just as his style manages to be personal without being idiosyncratic. It is simple without becoming shallow, striking without going to extremes. He has achieved the most difficult kind of originality. He has transformed the common idiom and experience into fresh and distinctive poetry.

But what does an instinctively popular poet do in contemporary America, where serious poetry is no longer a popular art? The public whose values and sensibility he celebrates is unaware of his existence. Indeed, even if they were aware of his poetry, they would feel no need to approach it. Cut off from his proper audience, this poet feels little sympathy with the specialized minority readership that now sustains poetry either as a highly sophisticated verbal game or secular religion. His sensibility shows little similarity to theirs except for the common interest in poetry. And so the popular poet usually leads a marginal existence in literary life. His fellow poets look on him as an anomaly or an anachronism. Reviewers find him eminently unnewsworthy. Publishers see little prestige attached to printing his work. Critics, who have been trained to celebrate complexity, consider him an amiable simpleton.

It is not surprising then that Kooser's work has not received sustained attention from academic critics. In an age when serious critics have begun to look on themselves either as creative personalities hardly less important than the authors they discuss or at the very least as great interpretive artists—the Van Cliburns of poetry—without whose skilled touch literature would remain as mute as an unopened score, there is little in Kooser's work that would summon forth a great performance. There are no problems to solve, no ambiguities to unravel, no dizzying bravado passages to master for the dexterous critic eager to earn an extra curtain call.

What can a critic meaningfully add to the attentive reader's appreciation of this poem, for instance, which is one of Kooser's more complex pieces:

The Blind Always Come as Such a Surprise

The blind always come as such a surprise,
suddenly filling an elevator

with a great white porcupine of canes,
or coming down upon us in a noisy crowd
like the eye of a hurricane.
The dashboards of cars stopped at crosswalks
and the shoes of commuters on trains
are covered with sentences
struck down in mid-flight by the canes of the blind.
Each of them changes our lives,
tapping across the bright circles of our ambitions
like cracks traversing the favorite china.

One can enumerate its small beauties—the opening image of a blind person (or persons) entering an elevator to the slight alarm of other passengers, the unexpectedly surreal equation of a porcupine's quills and the white-tipped canes, the sharp observations of how "normal" people pause uncomfortably when they notice the blind or disabled, the rhetorical trick of referring to the blind collectively, which gives them a mysterious, sexless, ageless composite identity, or the haunting final simile. But aside from cataloguing these moments, there is little a critic can provide that the average reader cannot, because the difficulties this poem provokes are experiential rather than textual. It poses none of the verbal problems critical methodologies have been so skillfully designed to unravel. Rather it quietly raises certain moral and psychological issues that the professional critic by training is not prepared to engage or resolve.

Paradoxically, the simpler poetry is, the more difficult it becomes for a critic to discuss intelligently. Trained to explicate, the critic often loses the ability to evaluate literature outside the critical act. A work is good only in proportion to the richness and complexity of interpretations it provokes. Finding little challenge in Kooser's poetry, the enterprising critic is tempted to dismiss it. Surely poetry so simple must lack depth. While admitting to a certain superficial fascination, the critic qualifies his admiration by exploring the author's limitations, which in itself becomes a compelling critical activity. While defining a poet's limitations is a legitimate critical pursuit, limitations in themselves are not necessarily shortcomings. Even the greatest authors have blind spots; Milton had little gift for comedy; Wordsworth a relatively narrow technical range. To find a limitation does not necessarily invalidate an author's achievement. Criticism should make meaningful distinctions, not apply irrelevant standards.

Kooser does have significant limitations as a poet. Looking across all his mature work, one sees a narrow range of technical means, an avoidance of stylistic or thematic complexity, little interest in ideas, and an unwillingness to work in longer forms. In his weaker poems one also notices a tendency to sentimentalize his subjects and too strong a need to be liked by his readers, which expresses itself in a self-deprecatory attitude toward himself and his poetry. In short, Kooser's major limitation is a deep-set conservatism that keeps him working in areas he knows he can master to please his audience.

Significantly, however, Kooser's limitations derive directly from his strengths. His narrow technical range reflects his insistence on perfecting the forms he uses. If Kooser has concentrated on a few types of poems, he has made each of these forms unmistakably his own. If he has avoided longer forms, what member of his generation has written so many unforgettable short poems? If he has not cultivated complexity in his work, he has also developed a highly charged kind of simplicity. What his poems lack in intellectuality they make up for in concrete detail. If he occasionally lapses into sentimentality, it is because he invests his poems with real emotion. Even Kooser's self-deprecatory manner betrays a consistent concern for the communal role of the poet. He will not strike superior poses to bully or impress his audience.

Limitations, however, are not necessarily weaknesses. Having catalogued Kooser's conspicuous limitations, one cannot help noticing that they are more often sins of omission than commission. Discussing them may be an interesting critical exercise, but it is useful only insofar as it sharpens one's understanding of Kooser's particular strengths. It may seem obvious to say, but it is surprising how often some otherwise intelligent critics forget, that a writer is better judged by how successfully he works with the material he includes than by what he omits. Kooser's achievement is in the consummate skill with which he handles the self-imposed limits of the short imagistic poem, the universal significance he projects from his local subject matter.

If Kooser's particular achievements as a poet don't fit comfortably into current critical standards, how then is one to judge the extent of the achievement? Here I would submit four simple criteria. After reading carefully through Kooser's work, one should consider the following questions. First, there is the question of quality. Has the author written any perfect poems, not just good poems but perfect ones—on whatever subject, in whatever style, of whatever length—which use the resources of the language so definitively that one cannot change a single phrase without diminishing the poem's effect? And if there are perfect poems, how many? Second, there is the question of originality. Are the author's best poems different from those of any preceding poet? Can one hear a distinctive personality or sensibility behind them that is either saying something new about the world or speaking in such an original way that it makes one see familiar parts of the world as if for the first time? Third, there is a question of scope. How many things can an author do well in his poetry? How many styles or subjects, moods or voices can he master? Fourth, and finally, there is the question of integrity. Do the author's poems hold together to provide a unique and truthful vision of the world, or do they remain isolated moments of illumination?

There are other criteria one might use, but, at the very least, this test helps distinguish a superb poet from one who is merely good. And it is a test that highlights some important ways in which Kooser surpasses some of his more highly praised contemporaries. Kooser has written more perfect poems than any poet of his generation. In a quiet way, he is also one of its most original poets. His technical and intellectual interest may be narrow (indeed, in terms of limited techniques, he shares a common fault of his generation), but his work shows an impressive emotional range always handled in a distinctively personal way. Finally, his work does coalesce into an impressive whole. Read individually, his poems sparkle with insight. Read together, they provide a broad and believable portrait of contemporary America.

2. Popular Poetry and Regional Identity

> All events and experiences are
> local, somewhere.
>
> —WILLIAM STAFFORD

POPULAR POETS always reflect the general taste and values of a particular time and place, even when those values are at odds with the high culture of the age. Robert Burns's folkish simplicity stands in sharp contrast to the cosmopolitan polish of his eighteenth-century contemporaries, just as Kipling's dance-hall exuberance sounds jarringly unlike the subtle orchestrations of the *fin de siècle* versifiers around him. Popular poetry draws its distinguishing vitality from the particular milieu it shares with its audience. It presents a more relevant world to this constituency than do the traditional *topoi* of high culture. Rooted in specifics ignored or excluded from mainstream culture, popular poetry therefore often assumes a regional identity. It represents the values and aspirations of a body culturally, politically, and often geographically separate from the ruling class of a nation.

Not surprisingly, therefore, Kooser's popular sensibility expresses itself most clearly in its regional loyalties. Kooser writes about the countryside, weather, towns, and people of the Great Plains. His regional perspective determines not only the subject matter of his poetry but also its texture and thematics. His language, imagery, ideas, attitudes, even his characteristic range of emotions reflect the landscapes, climate, and culture in which he has spent his entire life. To many critics such regionalism still equals provincialism, especially when the region in question is the Middle West. As it also becomes apparent that his work deals more with prosaic small towns and agricultural countryside than the conventionally poetic urban or natural landscapes, his parochialism simply becomes too much for most critics to bear.

Regionalism is ultimately a political term, a dismissive label applied to literature produced in and concerned with areas outside the dominant cultural and economic centers of a society. Classifying a work as "regional" implies that it cannot be judged by "national" standards. It suggests that certain subjects will be of only local interest. Where there are politics, however, there are also coups and revolutions. Sometimes a type of regional writing attains prominence because a new regime has come into power in the literary capital. The rising reputation of Southern literature in America, for example, neatly matches the influx of Southern writers and critics in the late forties into New York and the Ivy League universities.

In most industrialized countries there is also a pervasive urban bias against agricultural areas. In America that prejudice is focused on the Midwest, especially the Great Plains states, which are seen as flat, characterless, and provincial. Unlike the South, an older rural society that defiantly clings to its traditions, or the Southwest, which boasts a continuity of Spanish and Indian culture that has remained relatively intact amid its recent development, the Great Plains was settled later than most other areas of the country. Its economy is also less diversified, its population more widely scattered, and its people less ethnically heterogeneous, consisting largely of assimilated Northern Europeans (Kooser is of German descent). To the outsider there is less obvious local color—no accents, no dramatic social problems, less various scenery—although ironically it is this same uniformity that gives the Great Plains a distinctive cultural identity.

One would think that after Yeats and Faulkner, Joyce and Svevo, Verga and Cather, Cavafy and Hardy, regional writing would no longer be perceived as a second-class artistry practiced by those incapable of presenting the world at large. But although regionalism has become irresistibly attractive as an abstract concept in seminars studying "The Southern Literary Consciousness" or "Poetry and the Irish Revival," it meets with stern resistance when applied to uncanonized regions. The same professor who spent three years researching the facts of Yoknapatawpha County would usually never consider reading a novel by Wright Morris or Leonardo Sciascia. The regionalism celebrated in the universities usually centers on a few familiar territories, which have been described by such a long line of writers that they have been as thoroughly mythologized as Ilium or Rome, rather than the general notion that literature should be rooted in the reality of a particular place. In some cases, like rural Southern fiction or Los Angeles detective writing, one almost wonders if such writing can even still meaningfully be called regional. The local elements have become so thoroughly universalized through continual use that a skillful foreigner might be able to use them convincingly as purely literal patterns. After all, there is a point where the local becomes the universal. Parnassus was once only a small mountain near Delphi and Pan the local deity of impoverished rural Arcadia.

Midwestern critics have not helped the reputation of regional writing. Disenfranchised by a cultural establishment based largely in New York and New England, they have too often lost the objectivity that distance from the literary marketplace should allow. In retaliation to Eastern presumption they have adopted an unconvincing kind of regional boosterism, making extravagant claims for local writers of limited gifts. While one cannot excuse metropolitan critics for ignoring or undervaluing the work of important regional writers, neither can one sympathize with regional critics for applying looser standards to local writers than to those of national reputation. Regional favoritism is the worst kind of provincialism and eventually undermines the credibility of all local reputations.

Here, Midwestern critics could learn from Southerners. While there is no region in America second to the South in the intensity of its literary self-esteem, Southerners have had a long and distinguished tradition of native critics who judged regional writers without losing perspective. Southern critics like Allen Tate, Cleanth Brooks, Robert Penn Warren, Randall Jarrell, John Crowe Ransom, or, more recently, Henry Taylor, George Garrett, Fred Chappell, and William Jay Smith have often discussed their regional writers without lowering their standards.

To some degree, Kooser's reputation has suffered from all of these factors. Rather than viewing his regional roots as a source of authenticity and exactitude, some critics have seen them as parochialism. His local subject matter has been labeled quaint; his affection for the particulars of his native landscape declared sentimental. His insistence on creating a poetic language out of plain Midwestern speech has been construed as a lack of accomplished technique; his deliberate simplicity as folksy ignorance. In short, critics have considered his regional loyalties as limitations. Even more important, however, by labeling Kooser a regional rather than national poet, the majority of critics have missed his grand overriding theme—the gradual disappearance of American rural culture. Focusing on the Great Plains states, Kooser has captured one of the century's great changes, the shift from country to city, from farming to business, from traditional family life to ambiguous personal independence. In hundreds of precise vignettes Kooser has created a poignant mosaic of this cultural transition no less relevant to Abidjan or Osaka than to Omaha or Des Moines. But by stereotyping him as a regional artist, even his admirers have failed to recognize the breadth of his themes. He has been reduced to the product of their expectations.

3. The Development of a Regional Poet

> A poet's hope: to be
> like some valley cheese,
> local, but prized everywhere.
>
> —W. H. AUDEN

TED KOOSER'S poetic career reveals some of the problems faced by a regional writer who does not either immigrate to a major literary center or join the university network. Born in Ames, Iowa, in 1939, Kooser has spent his entire life in Iowa and Nebraska. He attended Iowa State

University, where he majored in English Education. Upon graduating in 1962, he taught high school for a year and then entered a graduate program in English at the University of Nebraska. After one year he stopped full-time study to begin a temporary job in insurance while finishing an M.A. at night. He has worked in insurance ever since and is currently a marketing executive at Lincoln Benefit Life. Thus, Kooser has been doubly alienated from the American literary establishment. First, he has lived only in two agricultural Midwestern states far removed from the centers of literary opinion. Second, he has spent the past twenty-five years working in business, cut off from the academic communities that support most regional writers and provide them with a professional network of colleagues, readers, and reviewers. This isolation would have destroyed most young writers' determination, but in Kooser it nourished an unusually strong sense of independence and self-sufficiency.

Kooser began his publishing career very conventionally, however, with *Official Entry Blank,* his wryly titled first book, which appeared in 1969 as part of the University of Nebraska's short-lived "Poetry from Nebraska" series. Not a precocious volume, *Official Entry Blank* showed a modestly talented young poet trying out a variety of contemporary models as he searched for his own characteristic style. Yet although the volume contained an example of almost every fashionable kind of workshop poem of the period, from heroic couplets to haiku, even those exercises usually gave glimpses of the author's smooth technique and engaging personality. It was an entertaining but curiously unfocused volume, which showed Kooser still writing under the influence of many older poets, most noticeably William Carlos Williams and Karl Shapiro, who had been Kooser's teacher.

Coming upon *Official Entry Blank* in 1969, one would have been hard-pressed either to predict Kooser's subsequent development or to define his individuality as a poet. Reading these poems today, however, one can occasionally hear Kooser's characteristic voice amidst the diversity of borrowed styles. Sometimes humorous, sometimes sober, it is never strained or sarcastic, for Kooser (unlike Whitman and his followers) is a truly democratic poet who addresses the reader as an equal. He never assumes the pose of prophet or professor instructing the unenlightened. He is intimate without being private, never obscure but also never public. He speaks as one would to an old friend. This tone of quiet trust, which characterizes Kooser's best poetry, may explain why the poet claims to dislike reading his work in public. His poems, he has commented, belong "on a page, not in an auditorium." Conceived in solitude, his poems are best encountered without the theatrical distractions of a public performance.

In *Official Entry Blank* one also notices Kooser's sharp eye for images. Again and again, he catches some tiny detail from everyday life that masterfully evokes a larger scene. He does not yet know how to frame these details for their full effect, but his observations often give these early poems, whatever their faults, an arresting freshness and immediacy. And in a few instances, like "Abandoned Farmhouse," he casts them in a form that foreshadows the best of his later work.

Official Entry Blank was the only immature or derivative book Kooser ever published, but, ironically, it was also the only one for the next eleven years with a university imprimatur. After its publication Kooser disappeared into the gulag of small regional presses. Printed in tiny editions, his books and pamphlets cultivated a small local audience—for some titles probably not more than a few dozen readers. Unnoticed in New York and Boston, they were sometimes reviewed by small and often ephemeral regional magazines like *Great Lakes Review, Raccoon,* and *Dacotah Territory.* More often they were not reviewed at all. But slowly Kooser's reputation grew in the Plains states, though readers and critics elsewhere were not generally aware of his work until the publication of his new and selected poems, *Sure Signs,* in 1980.

Two years after *Official Entry Blank,* Kooser issued a tiny pamphlet with his own illustrations. Self-published by his newly created Wildflower Press, *Grass Country* announced its intentions to combine "the author's illustrations with his poems in an attempt to more completely convey that vision of the great plains introduced in *Official Entry Blank.*" Those readers with eyesight sharp enough to decipher its microscopic typeface would have found that the pamphlet actually lived up to its blurb. In *Grass Country*'s eight short poems Kooser had found the proper subject and form for his poetry. Here, for example, is "Tom Ball's Barn":

> The loan that built the barn
> just wasn't big enough
> to buy the paint, so the barn
> went bare and fell apart
> at the mortgaged end of twelve
> nail-popping, splintering winters.

Besides the Januaries,
the barber says it was
five-and-a-half percent,
three dry years, seven wet,
and two indifferent,
the banker (dead five years)
and the bank (still open
but deaf, or *deef* as it were), *and*
poor iron in the nails that
were all to blame for the barn's collapse
on everything he owned, thus
leading poor Tom's good health
to diabetes and
the swollen leg that threw him
off the silo, probably
dead (the doctor said)
before he hit that board pile.

No single element in "Tom Ball's Barn" is new to American poetry, and yet the combination of these elements strikes a unique note. Without breaking from the past, Kooser had developed a new and personal way to describe the world of the Great Plains, especially the undramatic but tragic lives of its rural people. He had also found a way of universalizing its landscape and stories without losing their local character. He managed ordinary spoken language without making it sound dull and undistinguished.

"Tom Ball's Barn" has another importance in Kooser's career. It is the earliest successful example of the character poem—a kind of poem that would subsequently account for much of his best work. The model for Kooser's character studies were obviously Edwin Arlington Robinson's Tilbury Town portraits and Edgar Lee Masters's *Spoon River Anthology*—which remain the two touchstones of American regional poetry—but, as "Tom Ball's Barn" demonstrates, he handled his material very differently. Kooser's portraits have a relentless linearity in their exposition, which endows them with their peculiar speed and powerfully dramatic simplicity. This linearity, however, is balanced by the typically laconic and indirect presentation of the central character.

Syntax is the key to Kooser's expositions. Written in two long sentences,

"Tom Ball's Barn" moves quickly through a series of simple observations that the reader immediately understands but has no time to assimilate before his attention is pushed ahead to the next fact. This speed also gives each fact a certain inevitability, as if mere sequence were logic, so that at first glance the callous "thus" in line 17 really does seem to explain Ball's death. Likewise, the reader is immersed in the narrative situation so quickly that he has no time at first to notice the unusual way Ball's story is told. The poem is almost over before Ball is introduced. He is not shown directly; rather he is characterized by the things around him, especially the unpainted barn, whose decay and eventual collapse mirror his own fatal fall. Seen here explicitly for the first time, this equation between people and their property will become a major preoccupation of Kooser's poetry.

That Kooser was unaware of the possibilities he had uncovered in *Grass Country* is evident from his next collection, *Twenty Poems* (Best Cellar Press, 1973). This pamphlet shows Kooser uncertain of his direction. While in a few poems, especially the character sketches like "The Failed Suicide" and "Selecting a Reader" (a charming portrait of an ideal reader, who is sensible enough to reject him), Kooser develops the methods he had discovered in *Grass Country,* most of the new poems are facile exercises in conventional styles. Here Kooser sometimes explores his characteristic themes but in ways that dilute their effectiveness. There is also a series of macabre poems that matter-of-factly describe weird events—"Grating a Brain," "They Had Torn Off My Face at the Office," and "A Dead Man Driving a Car." Superficially effective, these poems trivialize Kooser's real talent. By affecting the blasé tone, the placeless setting, the surreal methods of San Francisco and New York poets, he lost the compassionate authenticity that characterizes his most vital work.

This lack of direction did not last long. The next year Kooser consolidated his achievement in *A Local Habitation & a Name* (Solo Press, 1974). Here, for the first time, he revealed the full range of his talent. Collecting about two dozen of his favorite earlier poems, he added fifty new pieces, including half a dozen perfect poems of unmistakable originality. This volume proved that the intermittent successes of his earlier books had been no fluke. Ranging in tone from comic to tragic, from gently nostalgic to savagely satiric, these new poems, which include such signature pieces as "Spring Plowing," "The Widow Lester," "The Blind Always Come as Such a Surprise," and "A Place in Kansas," showed Kooser capable of handling diverse material in a masterfully personal way. His mastery, however, was of a consciously modest variety. He had chosen the short poem as his medium. All of his poems were shorter than a page, most of them under ten lines. Seen together in bulk for the first time, however, they went beyond a series of dazzling miniatures and formed a memorable composite. All drawing their inspiration from the world of the Great Plains, they re-created that world as effectively in verse as any American poet had done before. Few people on either coast were paying attention (except the maverick William Cole, who in his chatty column in the *Saturday Review* called Kooser his "favorite young poet"), but the Great Plains had just produced a poet of national importance.

To show how far Kooser had developed in a few years, one need only compare two short poems that use similar material. First, here is "Haiku for Nebraskans" from *Official Entry Blank:*

> Telephone wires whine
> in the claws of red-tailed hawks—
> frightened mice screaming

In only seventeen syllables, this piece displays many of the conventions of the sixties' workshop poem. Technically competent but uninteresting, it is written in a notoriously easy foreign form that announces its fashionable independence from traditional English metrics. Having been scrupulously compressed to the point of small ellipses, the language is sharp but lackluster. The situation is conveyed visually, the structure of the poem being merely an equation between two images. The content is as unsurprising as the style. The poem begins with an easy contrast between nature and technology (though the technology has been animated—"whining" as it does). Although the ending pretends to be tough and elemental, it is actually cryptically sentimental. Although this poem is skillfully constructed, it ultimately shows no particular virtues to distinguish it from the work of a hundred other poets. Nor does Kooser use his tired images in any way that makes the reader see them with fresh eyes.

Now read "Spring Plowing" from *A Local Habitation & a Name:*

> West of Omaha the freshly plowed fields
> steam in the night like lakes.
> The smell of the earth floods over the roads.

> The field mice are moving their nests
> to the higher ground of fence rows,
> the old among them crying out to the owls
> to take them all. The paths in the grass
> are loud with the squeak of their carts.
> They keep their lanterns covered.

This perfect little poem has no exact precedent in American literature. Deceptively simple on first hearing, it bears sustained attention, and is ultimately satisfying on either a purely naturalistic or imaginative level. Not only is it more technically skilled than the earlier haiku (in the naturalness of the language, the complexity and originality of the imagery, and the structure of its development), but, more important, this poem opens the reader's eyes to the world—albeit some tiny part of a specifically Midwestern world. It enlarges our humanity in ways the earlier poem did not. It will be difficult to drive by a freshly plowed field without thinking of the vulnerable creatures it displaced.

The expository structure of "Spring Plowing" also shows how expert Kooser had become since *Official Entry Blank*. The poem's unexpected movement from ordinary observation to compassionate illumination illustrates Kooser's special achievement as a poet who can endow everyday subjects with a fresh and mysterious resonance. "Spring Plowing" begins conventionally with a description any competent poet might have written, but the first five lines don't prepare one for what will follow. As the poet adjusts his focus from an overview of the field to a close-up of the mice, the scene is suddenly transformed from a naturalistic description to a fantastic, humanized vision of the fleeing animals. Kooser compresses several implicit metaphors into the next four lines, and then ends with a sinister, enigmatic image. The language is highly charged but never clumsy or crowded. The metaphorical trick of transforming mice into threatened refugees is fresh and surprising. Only nine lines long, this poem accomplishes a complex but seamlessly executed shape.

Kooser's next book, *Not Coming to Be Barked At* (Pentagram Press, 1976), solidified his reputation as an important regional poet. (The strange title of this book comes from an incident in the Finnish national epic, the *Kalevala,* but it is also a typically self-deprecating Kooserian gesture to the reader.) By now Kooser was fully conscious—even if his critics were not—of the position he had created for himself in American poetry as the master of the short, colloquial, imagistic poem. Having perfected his technique, he began broadening his thematics, exploring more fully the world of the Great Plains. *Not Coming to Be Barked At* not only contained many of Kooser's best poems, such as "The Very Old," "Late February," "In a Country Cemetery," "Visiting Mountains," "So This Is Nebraska," and "Shooting a Farmhouse," it also demonstrated the consistent high quality that distinguishes his work. Virtually every poem has some particular virtue to recommend it, and page after page in poems like "Snowfence," "The Afterlife," "North of Alliance," "Old Soldier's Home," "Sitting All Alone in the Kitchen," "Living Near the Rehabilitation House," and many others, the reader feels the presence of a rich, naturally poetic imagination. The individual poems were short, but cumulatively they created a powerful picture of a real life in a particular time and place.

In his best poetry up to this time Kooser usually maintained a certain distance between himself and his subject. Most often he acted the part of a seemingly impartial observer who stamped his personality on the situation indirectly by choosing the details that he presented or omitted. Sometimes in more openly personal poems he put himself in the action of the poem, but he balanced his direct involvement by deliberately understating the emotional elements of the situation. In *Old Marriage and New* (Cold Mountain Press, 1978), Kooser tried to develop a more openly autobiographical kind of poetry. Writing about the failure of his first marriage and the promise of his second, he carefully established a series of thirteen short scenes that dramatized this difficult period in his life. Sharp and concisely written, these poems seem thin compared to Kooser's previous work. The final twist, with the kind of unexpected image that enlivened so many of his poems, often struck a flat or overly sentimental note here, as in "Driving to Work":

> Once in a while, when I'm driving to work
> in the morning, I see a schoolgirl
> walking slowly along, and something about her
> is you, and the way you must have been
> when you were a girl, still young
> and full of dreams; and seeing you there,
> oblivious to me, I feel as if
> a bird had darted out and struck the windshield.

This poem does not reveal a failure of technique but of sensibility. The final image is too embarrassingly obvious in its appeal to the emotions. One can understand Kooser's pain but cannot share it. *Old Marriage and New* was perhaps a necessary experiment for Kooser, but this chapbook ranks as the weakest of his mature collections.

Kooser remained little known outside the Midwest and undervalued even there until the publication of *Sure Signs: New and Selected Poems* from the University of Pittsburgh Press in 1980. His early career had been sustained by small regional presses and reviews that praised his work but did not distinguish it from that of dozens of other young Plains poets. *Sure Signs* not only brought Kooser national attention for the first time, it also established him as one of the few openly regional young poets whose work had broad appeal beyond the Midwest.

Sure Signs showed Kooser as a shrewd judge of his own poetry. He ruthlessly cut away his weaker work and presented the reader with only eighty-nine short poems from all of his earlier books. The careful editing gave *Sure Signs* a consistent quality that put most contemporary collections to shame. It also ensured that readers who came upon Kooser's work there for the first time were left impressed with the quality of his achievement. *Sure Signs* confirmed the poet's peculiar organization of his own work. Kooser has always resisted chronological arrangement of his poems. Instead he has done his best to disguise his own development as a poet by organizing his work in sequences that presumably heighten the particular strengths and variety of his poetry. One can assume from this choice that Kooser, with his characteristic modesty, finds the subjects and moods of his poems more interesting than their evidence of his personal development as a poet. One cannot dispute that decision, but it is important to note here how difficult it makes understanding his development, a difficulty intensified by his insistence on dropping unsuccessful poems from his canon. Only two poems in his confessional book, *Old Marriage and New,* for example, survive in *Sure Signs.*

Based on his first seven books and the considerable number of poems he has published in periodicals since *Sure Signs,* however, it seems appropriate now to attempt some overall conclusions about Kooser's development as a poet. In one way the achronological arrangement of *Sure Signs* testifies to Kooser's lack of dramatic growth. Once he discovered a mature personal voice in *Grass Country,* Kooser has demonstrated little substantial change. Although he has experimented with other styles such as the confessional or surreal, these experiments have not generally been successful, and he has returned to a few characteristic kinds of poems. On the other hand, while Kooser's poetry has not greatly changed since *Grass Country,* it has deepened. In poem after poem he has gradually populated a region of the imagination, a loving recreation of the Great Plains. As he has become increasingly conscious of his role in chronicling this region, so much of which is disappearing into history, his work has developed an intensity and integrity few of his contemporaries can match. He has slowly created a larger structure in which his short poems have acquired a new resonance. This regional allegiance has also helped unify his work, focusing the isolated brilliance of his individual poems into one overall vision. Therefore, without abandoning the short forms he has so carefully mastered, Kooser, through the consistency and authenticity of his concerns, has forged them into an ambitious larger work, a unified oeuvre that like an epic encompasses his world.

If Kooser's poetry has grown deeper with each book, it has also grown stronger. Unlike the writing of so many established poets entering middle age, his verse has suffered no drop-off in intensity or workmanship. Experience has only sharpened his skills. Moreover, in developing the overall vision of his work he has never sacrificed the quality and integrity of individual poems to the demands of the larger design. He has not sought refuge in grandiose imaginative schemes but has remained committed to realizing each poem fully in itself, for instinctively he knows that it is not the size of a poet's intentions that ensure survival but the quality of his individual poems. Whatever his other limitations, Kooser has succeeded in the poet's main task—bringing all the forces of language to bear in perfectly achieved poems. Few of his contemporaries have succeeded as often, and none of them in so accessible and engagingly humane a manner. Kooser is unsurpassed in articulating the subtle and complex sensibility of the common American.

Therefore, while one would not claim that Kooser is a major poet, one could well make the case that he will be an enduring one. His work is the genuine article—poetry concerned with themes of permanent value, written flawlessly in an original and distinctive way. However tightly one may draw the boundaries of his accomplishments, once one crosses the border into the territory of his imagination, one finds an unforgettable world of illumination and delight.

Business and Poetry

─

1. The Situation

> if you demand on the one hand,
> the raw material of poetry in
> all its rawness and
> that which is on the other hand
> genuine, then you are interested in poetry.
> —MARIANNE MOORE, "Poetry"

"MONEY IS A KIND OF POETRY," wrote Wallace Stevens, a vice president of Hartford Accident and Indemnity, a corporate lawyer, an expert on surety bonds, and, almost incidentally it might seem, one of America's greatest poets. It is a shame Stevens never expounded on this remark, for he certainly knew as much about both sides of the equation as any man of his time. But significantly, Stevens, who spent most of his life working in a corporate office, never made the slightest mention of business or finance in all of his poetry and criticism.

That so prolific a writer would have maintained half a century of silence on the world of his daily life seems strange at first. His personality must be partially responsible. Few men and fewer writers have proven as reticent as Stevens about their private affairs. But personality is only part of it. Stevens's silence was hardly unusual when seen in the context of American poetry. There have been many important American poets who supported themselves—either by necessity or choice—by working in business, but none of them has seen it as an experience fit to write about.

Another American poet, T. S. Eliot, spent the most productive decade of his life working in the international department of Lloyd's Bank of

London, but the closest he ever came to writing about that milieu was in these lines from *The Waste Land*:

> At the violet hour, when the eyes and back
> Turn upward from the desk, when the human engine waits
> Like a taxi throbbing waiting . . .

Hardly a major statement. But these lines summarize all that modern American poetry has had to say about the business world—its tedium, isolation, and impersonality.

American poetry has defined business mainly by excluding it. Business does not exist in the world of poetry, and therefore by implication it has become everything that poetry is not—a world without imagination, enlightenment, or perception. It is the universe from which poetry is trying to escape.

Modern American poets have written superbly of bicycles, of groundhogs, of laundry left out to dry, of baseball cards and telephone poles. One of Randall Jarrell's best poems depicts a supermarket. Elizabeth Bishop has written movingly about an atlas, and Robert Lowell about breaking in a pair of contact lenses. James Dickey found a way to put animals in heaven, and Ezra Pound put many of his London literary acquaintances in hell. Sodomy, incest, and pedophilia have been domesticated by our domineering national Muse as readily as have skunks, armadillos, hop toads, and at least one warthog. But somehow this same poetic tradition has never been able to look inside the walls of a corporate office and see with the same intensity what forty million Americans do during the working week. It often seems to be a poetry of the exception rather than the rule. Our poetry, in short, seldom deals directly with the public institutions that dominate American life, or with the situations that increasingly typify it. If our poetry recognizes business at all, it has reduced this enormous and diverse national enterprise into a few outdated images inherited from the movies—the factory smokestack belching fumes (circa 1870), the potbellied tycoon puffing his cigar (circa 1890), the Charlie Chaplin look-alike subverting the assembly line (circa 1920), and for the truly *au courant* the man in the gray flannel suit rushing to an expense account lunch on Madison Avenue (circa 1950). All images of a world seen only from the outside. For American poetry what happens on Wall Street or Wilshire Boulevard seems as remote as icebound Zembla. No, more remote, for even Zembla has had its recent admirers.

To say all this is not so much to criticize as to observe and, I believe, to observe fairly. The business world, including the huge corporate enterprises that for better and for worse have changed the structure of American life over the past fifty years, is generally and noticeably absent from the enormous body of poetry written in this century. While this omission is hardly a cause for alarm or even regret, it certainly deserves notice.

This exclusion is especially puzzling when one remembers that an important and recurring claim of contemporary American poetry has been its professed ability to deal with the full range of modern life. Everything, critics have insisted for decades, is the proper subject for modern poetry; unlike the art of the past, contemporary poetry excludes nothing. Our poets have often announced their indiscriminate openness to experiencing everything America encompasses. The most succinct of these avowals appeared in Louis Simpson's Pulitzer Prize–winning volume *At the End of the Open Road* (1963). Instructively, the poem is entitled "American Poetry." The entire poem runs:

> Whatever it is, is must have
> A stomach that can digest
> Rubber, coal, uranium, moons, poems.
>
> Like the shark, it contains a shoe.
> It must swim for miles through the desert
> Uttering cries that are almost human.

A brilliant short poem. But like most discussions of our native genius, it is prescriptive rather than descriptive. Like it or not, certain foods agree best with certain stomachs. American poetry has always had an easier time digesting other poems than rubber or coal, and it has found even the most seasoned executive unpalatable. Although American poetry sets out to talk about the world, it usually ends up talking about itself.

2. A Dilation of Money

> Give money me, take friendship whoso list.
> —BARNABE GOOGE

MONEY AND WEALTH are ancient subjects, as old as poetry. Although economic interpretations of culture hit their vogue mainly in the past

century, philosophers, moralists, theologians, and historians since Xeno-
phon have discussed the role of money. It has been from the beginning a
constantly interesting and perplexing subject. The Bible is full of maxims
and parables on earthly riches. Likewise, the mythology and folklore of
every Western culture contain cautionary tales on the pursuit and possession of wealth—from Midas to Dives and on to Rumpelstiltskin. Greed
and parsimony have always stood as standard subjects for comedy. In our
own tradition money has been a standard subject in verse since Chaucer's
pilgrims, and has remained important not only in major poets like Ben
Jonson and Alexander Pope but also in lesser ones like Barnabe Googe
and George Crabbe. Hence modern American poetry has never had any
difficulty in assimilating money as a subject. It has only had to look toward tradition.

Business, however, is in many ways a modern concept. Certainly the
ancients formed partnerships and corporations, but these were small
and personal affairs when contrasted to the enormous organizations of
today. Wealth can be personified in the wealthy, but how does one deal
with a business once the founder has passed away, the company has
merged into a conglomerate, and its real control has been divided between a dozen inconspicuous directors and a hundred thousand stock-
holders? Acquired, reorganized, and diversified, the company no longer
has any immediately comprehensible identity. It exists in a world of market forces and economic principles remote from the myths and symbols
of traditional poetry. Business, then, is an abstract collective noun as
difficult to deal with tangibly as *liberty, the people,* or any other political
buzzword.

Money has been a subject that has often interested American poets,
possibly because they usually have had so little of it. For many poets, it
must possess the irresistible lure of the unattainable. That the penurious
young Eliot made so little mention of money in his poetry testifies not
only to his patrician breeding; it may also be the best argument for considering him a British rather than an American poet. It is rather a writer
like Pound who typifies the real native attitude—money is the root of all
evil and all good. And who can deny its intrinsic appeal to a poet, for is
not money literally the one true metaphor, the one commodity that can
be translated into all else? Everything seems to have its price, and that
price is denominated in money. It is hardly a coincidence that Pound's
Cantos, whose unifying principle is metamorphosis, should eventually

have discovered money as its theme. It was only one step from Ovid to economics.

But while money itself was a subject very interesting to poets, few of them knew much about it. Not only the subtleties of the money markets but even the basics of economics, "the dismal science," were lost on them. Yet what they knew about money was important: it bestowed power. It was not money but the possession of it that interested them. Gradually in the forties and fifties American poets began exploiting the theme that novelists had discovered half a century before—namely, that while America has no kings or popes or princesses, it does have its millionaires and billionaires. The Rockefellers and Mellons are our Romanovs and Medicis, and the legends that surround men like Howard Hughes are hardly less amazing than those around King Vlad of Transylvania.

In most of the poems in which American writers seem to be discussing business, they are usually talking about wealth or, more specifically, about the wealthy. They deal with money in much the same way they deal with madness or genius. It is a gift or curse from the gods. When Robert Lowell, who came from one of Boston's most distinguished families, discusses the effect of money on his relatives, he sees wealth as a puzzling personal attribute, almost exactly analogous to his own poetic gift. As if in a pun, a fortune becomes a fate. Therefore, Lowell's presentations of the two businessmen in his immediate family—his grandfather, who made millions in hydraulic mining out West, and his father, who worked for Lever Brothers—are the stories of two individuals struggling with curses in the form of wealth. Likewise, Randall Jarrell's remarkable monologue for an imaginary multimillionaire, appropriately entitled "Money" (which, like Lowell, he based on a relative—an uncle who was a prosperous but hardly Croesean candy manufacturer), deals almost abstractly with power and personality. It could as easily be about a warlord as about an industrialist.

Stevens was right. Money *is* a kind of poetry: an epic as encyclopedic as the *Cantos*. Consider just a few variations. Money, the long green, cash, stash, rhino, jack, or just plain dough. Choke it up, fork it over, shell it out. To be made of it! To have it to burn! Put it on a barrelhead. Grease it on a palm. It feathers a nest, holds heads above water, burns holes in pockets, and makes both ends meet. Just one long shot can make a big killing. *Musae Americanae, canamus paulo maiora:* let's raise the bidding and up the ante. Who else is our national muse but lithe Miss Liberty, who has paraded in alluring deshabille across two hundred years of currency and graced our pocket change with her universally crowned head.[1] As any coin collector knows, latter-day Eisenhowers and Susan B. Anthonys are no true substitutes. If there is a native genius for language and metaphor, he will be found discussing money. In lump sums or loose change, greenbacks or double eagles, megabucks or buffalo heads, our national vision is most easily translated into dollars and cents. Though rates of exchange may fluctuate, the subject is always the same. But money, dear reader, is not business, and now let us return to the business of this essay.

3. Ways of Surviving

Reading over this account of a literary apprenticeship, I find that it often mentions very small sums of money. There is good reason for the mention, considering that money is the central problem of a young writer's life, or of his staying alive.

—MALCOLM COWLEY, *And I Worked at the Writer's Trade*

FEW CRITICS, I suspect, will be concerned about the absence of business from modern American poetry. They will probably feel that its omission is proper. The world of commerce will seem to them the territory of novelists rather than poets. It reflects a world of common experience, not the particular and private experiences supposedly at the center of poetry. If pressed, they might argue that its omission also comes from the personal backgrounds of our best poets. Few, they would assume, had much experience in the business world, so how could they write about it with any authority or interest?

We Americans have strong preconceptions about our poets. They must be people out of the ordinary; they must be strong, even eccentric individuals. Most often they are pictured either as scholars or vagabonds, Longfellows or Whitmans, Allen Tates or Allen Ginsbergs. The popular arts are full of such images. Consider dreamy-eyed Leslie Howard wan-

---

[1] One of her heads deserves special mention—that on the so-called Mercury dime, minted between 1916 and 1945, which was modeled after a young woman named Elsie Viola Kachel, also known as Mrs. Wallace Stevens.

dering through America with a knapsack in *The Petrified Forest.* To a surprising degree, even the more serious arts share these stereotypes—witness Bellow's *Humboldt's Gift,* Jarrell's *Pictures from an Institution,* Nabokov's *Pale Fire,* and the various Beat novels. Both academics and bohemians are perceived as living outside the economic and social systems that characterize our nation. They are cut off, usually by choice, from the daily lives of the American middle class. And we have been trained to respect them for this separation.

One anecdote will serve to summarize the conventional wisdom about business and poets. Allen Tate's brother, Benjamin Nathan Tate, was a self-made tycoon who had formed two coal companies in Cincinnati and sat on the board of directors of several large corporations including Western Union. When Allen left Vanderbilt in 1922, Benjamin decided to start his brother on a business career by securing him a job in one of his coal offices. "In one day I lost the company $700 by shipping some coal to Duluth that should have gone to Cleveland," Tate later explained. Benjamin soon agreed that Allen should seek a literary career. The moral is easily drawn. The poet is an impractical, dreamy sort of fellow incapable of holding down a real job. Too bored with business to pay attention to the most basic details of a job, a poet can be nothing but a poet.

But these stereotypes do not hold up to scrutiny. As often as not, American poets have emerged in the most unexpected places, including corporations. Stevens is not the inexplicable exception he is usually made out to be. Rather, he is the exemplary figure for a certain type of American poet, a type he did not even originate.

Although one now thinks of Stevens as the archetypal businessman-poet, Stevens himself would have looked back to Edmund Clarence Stedman as a role model. Stedman, a now forgotten poet, was probably the most influential critic and anthologist of poetry in turn-of-the-century America, and his work was still a powerful presence during Stevens's youth. Born in Stevens's adopted Hartford in 1833, Stedman entered Yale at sixteen only to be expelled before graduation (though in that sweet irony that follows poets' careers, twenty-two years later the University awarded him an honorary degree). After several unsuccessful attempts at journalism Stedman came in 1863 to Wall Street, where he soon opened up a brokerage firm. His financial and poetic careers prospered together. In his own poetry Stedman was a leading spokesman for the Genteel Tradition, but in his criticism he exhibited a broad appreciation for other poetry, which found its fullest expression in his once definitive collection *An American Anthology* (1900), which celebrated the nation's third century by defining the poetic achievement of its past. In town he presided over New York literary life, while out in his country manor in the newly established artists' colony of Bronxville he entertained obscure young poets like E. A. Robinson with his reminiscences of Whitman. He died at the height of his fame and prosperity in 1908.

Stedman has had many successors beyond Stevens and Eliot. Richard Eberhart was for many years one of the chief executives of the Butcher Polish Company in Boston and sat for years on its board of directors. The late L. E. Sissman was a director and eventually a vice president of Kenyon and Eckhart, a Boston advertising agency, where he worked on accounts in the financial and food industries. Even the late Archibald MacLeish, a lawyer by training, spent a decade as an editor of *Fortune,* the major American business magazine of the thirties and forties.

A. R. Ammons, who has won the Pulitzer Prize, the Bollingen Prize, the National Book Award, and the National Book Critics Circle Award in poetry, was a salesman for a scientific glass manufacturer in New Jersey when his first book appeared. He had left elementary-school teaching a few years earlier and joined the sales department of his father-in-law's company, Friedrich and Dimmock, Inc. "It was total isolation," he later recalled, but when making sales calls in the Paterson area he did manage to visit the invalid William Carlos Williams and take him out for an occasional drive. He spent ten years in business before leaving to teach at Cornell.

In his early thirties James Dickey also left teaching for a successful stint in business. He joined the McCann-Erickson advertising agency in New York in 1956 as a junior copywriter on its newly acquired Coca-Cola account. When the advertising agency moved the account to its Atlanta office, Dickey was promoted and transferred along with it. Three years later, having established himself in his new profession, he switched agencies to increase his salary and responsibilities, becoming copy chief at a small Atlanta agency. Two years later Dickey made another career jump, this time to become creative director at Burke Dowling Adams, Atlanta's largest agency. While making his career in advertising, Dickey also published his first book, *Into the Stone and Other Poems,* on the strength of which he won a Guggenheim fellowship, which inspired him to quit business for writing.

Robert Phillips also left academics for advertising. After six years of college teaching, Phillips joined the creative department of Benton & Bowles as a copywriter in 1964, then moved through McCann-Erickson and Grey Advertising before becoming a vice president for J. Walter Thompson, America's largest domestic agency, where he has had major responsibility for the enormous Ford Motor and Eastman Kodak accounts. In his early forties, David Ignatow spent eight years helping manage the Enterprise Bookbinding Company, a family business. After his father's death he briefly became president of the firm before liquidating it. Ignatow then took two other jobs in the printing industry before receiving a Guggenheim fellowship, which eventually led him into teaching.

There are many more examples. The late Richard Hugo spent thirteen years working for the Boeing Company in Seattle until the publication of his first book brought him the offer of a teaching position. In 1964 Ted Kooser left graduate school at the University of Nebraska and took a temporary job at Lincoln Benefit Life. He has worked there ever since, first as an insurance underwriter then as a marketing executive. William Bronk managed a family lumber and fuel company in upstate New York. R. M. Ryan works as a stockbroker in Milwaukee. Richard Grossman spent nearly ten years working for Gelco, a family-controlled leasing company in Minneapolis. James Weil also helped manage a family business for many years in addition to running a private literary press. Terry Kistler, a past chairman of Poets & Writers, manages an investment firm. James Autry, the president of Meredith Corporation's magazine group, is the author of two poetry collections. The late Ronald Perry was director of advertising and public relations for Outboard Marine International. Art Beck, the mysterious San Francisco poet, is the pseudonym of a local banker. If one also added poets who practiced law (a distinct profession that in some respects is more closely related to academics than to business), such as Melville Cane, Archibald MacLeish, and Lawrence Joseph, the list would be even longer. And there are undoubtedly many other businessmen-poets unknown to me.[2]

---

[2] Indeed there were. Since first publishing this essay I have received letters from numerous poets who work in business. Some of the more widely published writers include Miriam Goodman, Larry Rafferty, Michael Malinowitz, Charles Potts, Donald Axinn, Victor di Suvero, Richard Cole, Suzanne Noguere, John Barr, Suzanne Doyle, Daniel Rifenburgh, Timothy Murphy, and Chryss Yost.

There have also been some would-be poets among American business-men, most notably Hyman Sobiloff. A great philanthropist and mawk-ishly sentimental poet, Sobiloff sat on the board of half a dozen large companies and must have had a yearly income considerably greater than that of the top twenty American poets combined. He also bore the curi-ous distinction of being the only American poet to have been nominated for an Oscar. Sobiloff, however, recognized that his verse was less than perfect and paid Conrad Aiken, Anatole Broyard, and later Delmore Schwartz to give him weekly poetry lessons, though he did have to park his limousine around the corner to avoid infuriating Schwartz.

There were then at least half a dozen important American poets, and many minor ones, who were also businessmen. While this is an interest-ing fact in itself, it is also one that requires some qualification lest it be misleading. The exceptional careers these poets pursued while writing stand in such sharp contrast to the more conventionally "literary" careers of their contemporaries that it is easy to overlook the similarities. For both the lives and the works of these businessmen have more in common with the mainstream of American poetry than one might suspect. It is first necessary to recall that none of them chose to make careers in busi-ness. Initially all of them attempted some conventional literary career. The young Stevens began enthusiastically as a journalist in New York. Eliot studied philosophy and then, like Dickey and Ammons, taught briefly. Eberhart studied at several universities and later became private tutor to the son of the King of Siam. Phillips served as a university ad-ministrator and teacher. But soon, because of exhaustion, failure, dissatis-faction, or poverty, all of these poets left their vocations for business jobs. Business was the most convenient alternative that society offered them when their earliest ambitions went sour, and they made what their par-ents and family probably called a sensible choice.

That poetry was a long-standing vocation in the minds of these men has an importance beyond biographical accuracy. It is a necessary element in understanding their development as writers. When one sees how these well-educated men had professed poetry since youth, it becomes obvious that it is both naïve and ill-informed to portray them as primitives emerg-ing from the dark woods of corporate life suddenly able to speak with the tongues of men and angels. Too many critics have expressed a sort of in-nocent amazement that businessmen could actually write poetry, not to mention good and even great poetry. In different ways the public images of Stevens and Dickey have been especially distorted by this type of mythologizing. And it is easy to see why. The businessman-by-day–poet-by-night contrast makes good copy. Everyone enjoys stories of double lives and secret identities. Children have Superman; intellectuals have Wallace Stevens.

Even first-rate critics found it impossible to avoid sensationalizing the paradox of the mild-mannered insurance executive who wrote uncompromisingly Modernist poetry at home. Witness Delmore Schwartz's mischievous glee in beginning his discussion of Stevens's poetry with a description of his office life. But was Stevens's gift to create supreme fictions while working in Hartford more surprising than Ezra Pound's ability to write majestically of life's beauty while living in a Pisan detention camp? The course of Stevens's career, like those of the other businessmen-poets, was hardly unusual. Was it really surprising that a Harvard man, formerly editor of the *Advocate* and a fledgling writer in New York, would eventually become a major American poet? Rather it seems a classical background for an American writer of that generation. What was most odd about Stevens was not his occupation, but rather that he never visited Paris or Rome, since most corporate vice presidents do that.

For some American poets, then, business was just one more way of surviving. While it was not the career that any of them originally wanted, it did support them until that other, more difficult career became reality. Let the naïve think that the support they needed was only financial. Certainly a job in business paid the bills, but it also provided each poet with more than money. At least outwardly, it gave direction to his life, providing him with a sense of place and purpose in his society. It gave him attainable goals—raises, promotions, pensions—in contrast to the seemingly unattainable goals of his artistic life. (Witness Eliot's pride at each of his promotions in the Lloyd's Bank international department during his early London years.) The routines of office life could be anaesthetizing, but this very feature also had its advantages for a poet. The pattern each job imposed on his life helped numb the anxiety he felt between poems, in those long, dry periods when it seemed he would never write again. For a job is more tangible than talent. It can't vanish suddenly the way that inspiration often seems to. In short, business provided these men with the same security and satisfaction that many of their contemporaries found in teaching. Young poets chose between the two careers looking for the same rewards. Which direction they took was ultimately a matter of temperament and values.

4. The First Voice

The first voice is the voice of the poet talking to himself—or to nobody.

—T. S. ELIOT, "The Three Voices of Poetry"

STEVENS, ELIOT, AMMONS, DICKEY, and the other poets I have mentioned form an extremely diverse group. They differ as much in the types of companies they worked for as in the poetry they wrote. They come from different parts of the country and different levels of society. They share no obvious spiritual or literary affinities. Their careers exhibit little similarity, except that they all wrote poetry while working in business. Yet if one studies the lives of the poets about whom some biographical information is available, curious resemblances begin to emerge.

All of these poets were successful in their business careers and soon achieved a comfortable, secure standard of living. Yet once they had achieved any level of fame, they quit their jobs (all except Stevens, that is, for whom real fame came very late in life). And finally and most significantly, although they wrote much of their best work during their years of employment, none of them had anything to say about their experiences at work, at least in their poetry. While their working lives may have had an important influence on the course of their writing, this influence was never directly manifested. They maintained a disinterested silence about their workaday worlds. Confessional poetry may be a dominant mode in American poetry, but while it has unlocked the doors to a poet's study, living room, and bedroom, it has stayed away from his office—unless the office happened to be located in an English department.

Given the strongly personal and often autobiographical character of most American poetry, it seems astonishing that these men did not use the images and situations of their daily occupations as what Marianne Moore called the "raw material" of their poetry (which, as she pointed out earlier in the same poem, should not "discriminate against business documents"). Their aversion to using this part of their lives is an indication of how strongly the prevailing fashions in American poetry have determined what is written even by its most gifted poets. It is also proof of

Northrop Frye's conjecture that what a poet writes more often comes from other poetry than from life experience. And finally their collective taciturnity suggests that in the creative process of businessmen-writers there is a form of voluntary censorship that often determines what and how the poet will write.

The inability of these businessmen-poets to write about their professional worlds is symptomatic of a larger failure in American verse—namely its difficulty in discussing most public concerns. If business is nonexistent as a poetic subject, there is also a surprising paucity of serious verse on political and social themes. Not only has our poetry been unable to create a meaningful public idiom, but it even lacks most of the elements out of which such an idiom might be formed. At present, most American poetry has little in common with the world outside of literature—no reciprocal sense of mission, no mutual set of ideas and concerns, no shared symbolic structure, no overlapping feeling of tradition. Often it seems that the two worlds don't even share a common language. At its best our poetry has been private rather than public, intimate rather than social, ideological rather than political. It has discussed symbolic places rather than real ones, even when it has given the symbols real names. It dwells more easily in timeless places than historical ones. For many reasons—some of them compelling—most of our poets have rejected the vernacular of educated men and tried to develop conspicuously personal and often private languages of their own.

Much was gained in this process of refinement—greater accuracy and intensity in language, intellectual rigor, and surprising originality. Much was also lost, not the least of which was the poet's audience. But long before his audience disappeared, a more important thing had happened: the poet had lost his sense of addressing a public, lost the belief that he and they had anything significant in common. This failure of assurance changed everything he wrote. There still could be occasional public statements or popular successes, but they seemed incidental to the general course of the art. Readers still existed, but no longer did they form a cohesive or important group. Nor did they matter economically. They were too few and too scattered to reward the poet with either wealth or fame. At times they almost seemed to exist in spite of him, and he in spite of them.

Paradoxically, the poet in business has thrived in this neglect. His job, like the academic's, has sheltered him from the economic consequences of writing without an audience. It even tutored him in surviving alienation. Every day at the office reminds him what an outwardly futile spiritual life he leads. If they knew about his writing, his business associates would surely see no more value in such unlucrative endeavors than his fellow poets would see in his drab job. The poet then is doubly dismissed—by his peers in both professions. Meanwhile he is doubly busy with both vocations. If he survives as an artist, he will certainly be able to face the neglect of an invisible public without much additional difficulty. If he perseveres as a poet, he will be writing primarily for himself, but performing for such an appreciative and discerning audience has its advantages (though fame and wealth are not among them). Writing for oneself makes autobiographical exposition unnecessary. The poet can plunge immediately into the particular idea or experience that interests him. The organization can be complex, the ideas difficult, and the symbolism private. It doesn't matter as long as the poet himself can follow them. They belong to the private world that is the poet's mind. His poems are what Stevens described in "The Planet on the Table":

> Ariel was glad he had written his poems.
> They were of a remembered time
> Or of something seen that he liked.
>
> Other makings of the sun
> Were waste and welter
> And the ripe shrub writhed.
>
> His self and the sun were one
> And his poems, although makings of his self,
> Were no less makings of the sun.
>
> It was not important that they survive.
> What mattered was that they should bear
> Some lineament or character,
>
> Some affluence, if only half-perceived,
> In the poverty of their words,
> Of the planet of which they were part.

5. The Uncommon Voice

Then surely the splendour of the language is something in excess of the sense, adding enormously to our pleasure but not assisting (rather obstructing) our understanding.

—DONALD DAVIE, "Essential Gaudiness:
The Poems of Wallace Stevens"

I am a man of fortune greeting heirs.

—WALLACE STEVENS

OFFICE LIFE, investments, interest rates, corporate politics, quarterly profits—these are not subjects that would seem especially congenial to poetry, and one can understand how a poet, even one for whom these topics were matters of daily concern, would ignore them. Certainly Eliot, Stevens, Ammons, and the others managed to ignore them without damaging their art. But must one conclude then that there was no fruitful interchange whatever between these poets' literary and professional lives? Could there not have been a less obvious connection? Knowing that these poets made careers in business, would it not be reasonable to assume that some of them at least might have written poetry more closely related to the language and concerns of the average man than did their academic and bohemian contemporaries? Yet this was not the case.

It is surprising to notice how consistently extreme these poets often were in developing private literary languages. While poets as dissimilar as the academic Yvor Winters and the bohemian hermit Robinson Jeffers kept their diction and syntax scrupulously within the bounds of common speech, the businessmen Stevens and Eliot pushed vocabulary and grammar not only to the limits of comprehensibility but quite often beyond. Stevens in particular sometimes wrote with the wild, inventive abandon of a Shakespearean clown who has suddenly found himself the protagonist of a tragedy. Nonsense can be serious stuff, and from this point of view Stevens is the finest nonsense poet in American literature, an Edward Lear for epistemologists. Unfortunately, this endearing aspect of his talent is too often missed by his sober academic commentators.

Another nonacademic professional, Dr. William Carlos Williams, often remarked that while his daily work as an obstetrician exhausted him, it also exercised a good influence on his poetry. Working with common people filled his ears with the contemporary American speech he would use so distinctively in his poems. Surprisingly, for Stevens, Eliot, Ammons, and the others, the similar experience of working in business had the opposite effect. Rather than pushing their work in the direction of colloquial language, their professional lives seem to have given them a deep dissatisfaction with the general spoken idiom as a medium for poetry. Perhaps after a full working day of no-nonsense talk in the office, these poets received a rebellious pleasure at night from writing extravagantly.

Only after work could Stevens, who wore conservative gray suits and drank coffee at the office, write "Tea at the Palaz of Hoon," which begins:

> Not less because in purple I descended
> The western day through what you called
> The loneliest air, not less was I myself.

Being Wallace Stevens at home meant letting himself go by inventing foreign-sounding words and names, prizing paradoxes, and giving his difficult poems brilliant but mysterious titles.

Returning home from an eight-hour day of tabulating the balance sheets of correspondent foreign banks, Eliot wrote some of the most allusive and elusive poetry in English, poems more difficult than any he had written while a student of philosophy. Few great poems in our language are as difficult as those Eliot wrote while working at Lloyd's. The difficulties of *The Waste Land* are well known, but even Eliot's minor poems of this period often read like purposefully forbidding private jokes. One poem begins:

> Polyphiloprogenitive
> The sapient sutlers of the Lord
> Drift across the window-panes.
> In the beginning was the Word.

The poem continues with neologisms and conspicuously unusual diction (often rhyme words designed to call attention to themselves)— "superfetation," "mensual," "piaculative," "epicene." As in Stevens, one must often pause to determine what is going on beneath the playful verbal surface. In a poem like the one above, "Mr. Eliot's Sunday Morning Service," the social commentary has been transformed into an exercise in private sensibility. Significantly, Eliot also developed his gift for nonsense poetry during this period.

Stevens and Eliot left a valuable heritage of how language could be used aggressively in poems, and the later businessmen-poets have been conspicuous among their heirs. While Robert Creeley, a bohemian academic, was adapting Williams's "American idiom" to distill a poetry of austere diction and syntax, his exact contemporary, A. R. Ammons, a salesman, developed the same idiom into a complex, almost mandarin style. Whatever one thinks of Ammons's long, syncopated sentences, his ostentatious puns, or his sometimes knotty diction, it is impossible to deny that his poetry uses language in a forceful and individual way. Likewise, James Dickey's poems often seem to carry themselves on by the sheer energy of their verbal invention. Whether he is imitating the sermon of a fervent woman evangelist or re-creating the wandering mind of a drunken telephone lineman, Dickey puts his trust (sometimes undeservedly) in the force of the speaking voice and allows it to spill relentlessly from line to line. There is, in short, a degree of verbal aggression in the work of both Dickey and Ammons that one does not often notice in the poetry of their academic contemporaries.

The poetry of William Bronk is uncommon in a somewhat different way, though it too can be seen in relation to the work of Stevens. Like Stevens, Bronk really has one principal subject underlying his poetry—the perception of reality. His characteristic form is the short, imageless poem:

> We aren't even here but in a real here
> Elsewhere—a long way off. Not a place
> To go but where we are: there.
> Here is there. This is not a real world.

Concise, abstract, and earnest, Bronk's poems are as extreme as Ammons's or Eliot's most difficult work in their rejection of the imprecision and ease of common speech. They are poems of solitude and isolation, as austere as a mathematical equation. Every word bears the weight of deliberate reflection. Bronk is not an ingratiating poet. He does not want to be. In order to appreciate him one must accept his work totally on its own terms. Otherwise it seems trivial or pompous. The whiteness of the page is his universe, not ours. Like Stevens, he tries to become a god capable of filling that whiteness with a world of poems.

These examples are not presented to prove that working in business played the primary role in developing these poets' particularly extravagant or abstract styles. That development was the result of their personal background—their taste, education, personality, and ambitions. What matters is that business had no overtly countervailing effect of simplifying their styles or concerns. The paradox is simply that these "men of the world" wrote out of a much more private universe than their supposedly sheltered academic counterparts. Perhaps because they worked in isolation, or because their private calling to poetry had so little to do with their daily work, these men had trouble addressing any audience but themselves.

6. Some Conclusions

> Though Stevens found it tiresome when others pointed to his dual career as businessman-poet, that afternoon he himself called attention to it and the way he handled it. Louis Martz, his campus host that day, recalls ". . . he opened up his briefcase and he said, 'Now you see everything is neatly sorted out here. Over here in this compartment . . . is my insurance business with the farmers, and over here in this compartment is my lecture and some poems that I want to read. I keep them completely separated.' At other times though, Stevens might argue just the opposite, stressing the seamlessness of his career. . . .
>
> —PETER BRAZEAU, "Wallace Stevens on the Podium:
> The Poet as Public Man of Letters"

THE PURPOSE OF this study so far has been to challenge some assumptions normally made about American poets and to raise a few unorthodox questions about the relationship between life and art. The discussion has centered on a curious collection of modern poets who were also businessmen—a group whose very existence no scholar has previously noted. Sticking close to biographical facts and textual examples from these writers, it has pointed out a few unexpected features and demonstrated the difficulty of making easy judgments about the problematic interaction between their two careers. The issues raised in this discussion, however, extend far beyond this small group. Ultimately they concern how any serious artist survives in modern society. Looking at poets who worked in business merely focused the discussion on one of the more extreme and paradoxical examples of the alienated modern artist. In further exploring the broader issues raised by this odd group of individuals, I will try to deal with the more general problem of how American poets, who cannot make a living from their art, still manage to write and develop.

First, it is necessary to recapitulate the key questions raised thus far in this discussion. How did their business careers affect the lives and works of these poets? Why did these men write nothing about their working lives? What personal and artistic changes did they undergo in the years they spent in jobs that were alien if not antagonistic to their vocations as poets? Were these jobs only ways of surviving until fame caught up with them? Is anything even gained by segregating them as a distinct group of writers and comparing them to other poets whose lives seem more typical? These are serious questions that anyone who looks closely at the lives of these poets must ask. And for the most part they are impossible to answer directly. The facts, as they exist, point toward an almost absolute separation between their business careers and imaginative lives. But can this really be all there is to say about the matter? Common sense instinctively demands a more direct relationship between life and art. Parts of the same man's life can't be split apart as easily as Stevens claimed to Louis Martz. While it is certainly true that for many years these poets led strictly divided lives, there must also have been deeper connections between their two careers. Here the critic must become a speculator, using not only scholarship and analysis but also inference and intuition. My conclusions here are admittedly both tentative and subjective, but the investigation nonetheless seems worthwhile. Risks are sometimes necessary to achieve difficult goals. One law of investment remains constant between business and poetry—the higher the risk, the higher the potential reward.

There is no need to dwell on the unfortunate effects of business careers on each of these poets. The personal difficulties these men faced are obvious. Their careers took up the greater part of their time and energy. Coupled with the responsibilities of family life (all of these poets were married), their careers forced their reading and writing into odd hours (late evenings, weekends, brief vacations) and probably prevented them from reading and writing as much as they would have liked. Stevens and Eliot both complained about this deprivation, and it is reasonable to assume that one would hear similar complaints from Dickey, Ammons, Bronk, and others if one had access to their letters and journals. In Eliot's and Stevens's cases at least, the strain of managing two careers also put severe pressure on their marriages. Their business careers also isolated them to a greater or lesser degree from the society of other writers, artists, and intellectuals. Unless like Eliot they had the friendship of a Pound, they lived very much on the margins of the literary world. Working in regular jobs, they did not have the flexibility or leisure to participate fully in either the formal or informal artistic life of their times. There was little freedom to travel, give readings, lecture, edit magazines or anthologies, accept residencies at universities, or even much time for mixing at the parties, festivals, and conferences where writers so often meet. Business turned these poets into outsiders in the literary world.

These are considerable disadvantages. Time to think, time to read, time for idle but intelligent conversation—all of these are essential for most young writers' development, and it is foolish to think that without them a poet's performance wouldn't suffer in some way. It is hard, discouraging work to write in isolation during one's few spare hours after working a full day in an office (or a classroom). How inconceivably private the act of writing must have been for Stevens drafting out poems night after night in the dull solitude of suburban Hartford.

From another perspective, however, these unsupportive conditions might well seem like advantages. For example, while working in business might have cut these poets off from the literary world, it also sheltered them from it. Working obviously helped them economically. It gave them an income independent from writing, freeing them from most literary hackwork. They did not have to review uninteresting books, write matter-of-fact lectures, teach unwanted classes, or quickly sell every poem and essay. They could afford to choose what to write and where to publish.

An outsider has another advantage. While he may feel intense pressure to prove himself as a writer to the people he rightly or wrongly perceives as "insiders" (editors, reviewers, academics, self-supporting writers), he has the advantage of setting his own pace. Paradoxically, this doubly busy man enjoys a leisure that professional poets both inside and outside the academy do not. The outsider can wait however long it takes to mature as a writer, whereas the professional poet must try to speed up the process. Hence Stevens could wait until he was forty-three before publishing *Harmonium,* perhaps the most remarkable first book in American poetry, and then could afford another thirteen years of silence before bringing out a second collection. Ammons managed a decade of quiet growth between the publication of his first, privately printed volume and his second, widely acclaimed book. And Eliot, in another way, could carefully conserve his energy, waiting months or years between perfectly achieved poems. By contrast, for the creative-writing teacher the pressures of "publish or perish" may be fatal. The same university job that frees a young poet from many financial worries can also add the irresistible pressure to write too much too soon, and the writing may become slick, automatic, and superfluous. Of course, poets inside the academy can survive these pressures, but it is not easy, given the demands of tenure, promotion, and professional prestige.

There may even be advantages in missing the society of other writers. One may lose the fun of talking with professional wordsmiths or miss the confidence of knowing the people whose names one sees on bylines and editorial mastheads, but one also doesn't waste ideas in conversation. Talking is easier than writing and much more immediately gratifying. More than one poet has poured his genius into conversation at the expense of his poetry. A person working in business is also not constantly besieged by the latest artistic and political fads. A poet's sense of his own direction might sharpen best if he is not forced to defend or discuss it every day in a classroom or café. Witness how steadfastly Stevens followed his independent imaginative course during the frenetically political thirties. Would he have been able to maintain his quirky integrity had he not been working in a Hartford insurance office? Eliot, Ammons, Bronk, and Dickey show the same stubborn independence in following their own sensibilities. Whatever their faults, they are clearly strongly individual writers.

Eliot saw an additional advantage in being constantly busy with another career. It kept one from writing unnecessary poems. Eliot frowned on poets who wrote when they had nothing new to say. Nor was it necessary, he felt, to make oneself write, since the really important poems would force themselves out. When George Seferis, the modern Greek poet, visited Eliot in London, he complained that his duties as a diplomat left him no time for writing. Eliot chided him, saying that this was actually a blessing and his poems would be better for the wait. The unconscious, he told Seferis, is working all the time.

As usual, Eliot had a point. For some poets at least, long silences are an essential stage in their creative growth. The classic examples are Rilke and Valéry, for whom many years of poetic silence became the necessary preparation for writing their greatest work. Their cases are extreme, but silences of more modest duration have often proved necessary for many authors, especially at turning points in their careers. A few poets like Hardy or Lawrence apparently manage to write continuously throughout their lives, but for most poets, even great ones, writing is an exhausting, intermittent process. A competent poet can usually turn out some lines of verse for any occasion, but a serious poet at some crucial point in his artistic development may hesitate to write at all. His old style may no longer seem authentic or appropriate, and a new form of expression that answers his particular needs may still seem impossible to find.

How poets overcome these imaginative challenges in life is an interesting study. Stevens, whose confidence was shattered after the uneventful debut of *Harmonium,* stopped writing for years and devoted himself to office work and private reading. Eliot, on the other hand, abandoned poetry at the height of his career after the triumphant reception of *Four Quartets,* turning his creative attention entirely to writing for the theater. Many poets, however, undergo less dramatic transitions, which nonetheless demonstrate the courage to endure months or even years of self-doubt while they wait between poems. Like Rilke, they will not write when there is nothing to say. They let the work mature slowly in the back of their minds or shape itself through innumerable drafts and revisions. It is essential for these poets not to force themselves to write too much or too quickly.

Business is a helpful shelter for this careful and introspective kind of writer because his job keeps him sufficiently occupied to take away some of the guilt and self-questioning of not being able to write. For other poets, teaching or translation fills a similar need, but these undertakings may be too closely related to writing to offer comfort for everyone. To businessman-poets like Stevens and Eliot, the steady rhythm of office life provided a sense of security and relief. While such regulation would have been unbearable to extroverted poets like Pound or Auden, for some of their more private contemporaries it obviously worked, and the proof is in their poetry.

Outside careers also sheltered these men from other dangers. In some way hard to pin down, their jobs protected them from the occupational hazards of writing poetry. For whatever reasons, the profession of poetry is a dangerous one in America, perhaps because it is so damnably difficult to succeed at in any meaningful way. Some poets have literally killed themselves for fame, destroying themselves slowly in public before distastefully appreciative audiences. Suicide, alcoholism, drug addiction, poverty, and madness are all too often fellow-travelers of poetry in this country, as the biographies of our poets tragically demonstrate. This essay is not the place to speculate on why this should be so, but the lives of writers like Vachel Lindsay, Hart Crane, H. D., Delmore Schwartz, John Berryman, Weldon Kees, Robert Lowell, Winfield Townley Scott, Sylvia Plath, and Anne Sexton show it to be the case. Nor is this self-destructiveness new. Baudelaire noticed this distinctively American curse in the life of Poe, and it creeps less overtly even into the lives of writers like Robert Frost, Conrad Aiken, Randall Jarrell, Elizabeth Bishop, and Theodore Roethke.

Somehow, working in business gave the poets I have discussed a saner perspective on their careers as writers. It gave them other accomplishments that helped soften the recurrent sense of frustration and failure any poet at times experiences. It also tutored them in the difficult virtue of patience. But most important, working in nonliterary careers taught them a lesson too few American writers learn—that poetry is only one part of life, that there are some things more important than writing poetry. This is an obvious statement to anyone but a writer, yet it is one that few American poets have ever learned because it addresses life and not art. It has nothing to do with writing poetry, and knowing it will never help a writer gain fame or perfect his craft. But learning it may help him or her survive.

F. Scott Fitzgerald's dictum that "there are no second acts in American lives" is too often true about our poets. But it need not be so. The young Eliot survived a disastrous marriage, the agonizing physical and mental decline of his wife, and his own mental breakdown. The middle-aged Stevens weathered the public failure of *Harmonium* and the more bitter private failure of his family life. Yet both kept their sense of artistic purpose intact, and both went on to write their most ambitious and influential work because they possessed a hard-earned realism about their lives. They did not define themselves as men by poetry alone but recognized other ambitions and responsibilities—even when the resulting actions were painfully at odds with their literary dreams. They knowingly sacrificed time and energy away from their writing. Paradoxically those compromises saved them as artists. By refusing to simplify themselves into the conventional image of a poet, they affirmed their own spiritual individuality, and the daily friction of their jobs toughened their resolve. Ultimately the decisions they made forced them to choose between abandoning poetry and practicing it without illusions. Anyone who studies the lives and works of the men who combined careers in business and poetry finds this hard-won sense of maturity and realism at the center. Their lives may not always provide other poets with overtly inspiring examples, but their careers offer pragmatic and important lessons in spiritual survival. In a society that destroys or distracts most artists, they found a paradoxical means to prosper—both as men and writers. In American literature that is not a small accomplishment.

The Sense of the Sleight-of-Hand Man

—

WALLACE STEVENS has long been the most enigmatic of major twentieth-century American poets. Neither his life nor his work fits any familiar pattern, and sometimes they both seem cunningly calculated to defy any comfortable definition. The more one sought Stevens the whole man the more assuredly one found either of his two fragmentary personae—the stolid burgher or the playful aesthete. Few poets ever wrote so much and betrayed so little about their personal lives. And, strangely, the same sensibility that created a brilliantly idiosyncratic and unmistakably individual style was also drawn exclusively to abstract and universal themes.

One wonders if it wasn't a conscious decision on Stevens's part to exclude his active life from his imaginative one, as if he feared risking his daily world by putting it too explicitly into his poetry. Only in a few late poems does one sense him trying to assimilate both parts of his life. In contrast, one could read all of the early *Harmonium* and have no idea about the man behind the poetry—where he lived, whether he was young or old, single or married, settled or peripatetic, how he made his living, what he was like in daily life. Not that such matters determine the quality of the poetry, but one cannot help noticing their conspicuous absence. Readers are not angels, and they wonder about the human figures who create the books they read.

Nor did the little that was publicly known about Stevens's life help clarify the mystery. To learn that the author of the most flamboyant book of American poetry was a middle-aged insurance man in Hartford only added to the confusion. Here one knows Stevens deliberately created an unassailably proper image both to protect himself professionally within the Hartford insurance world and to deflect the pressures of a literary reputation. By the time he achieved literary fame in his sixties, it no longer really mattered to him. It was an occasional luxury to be enjoyed sparingly. Moreover, by then he realized the importance privacy played in his inner life and knew that his solitude must be maintained at all costs. He avoided all publicity about his personal life, turning down offers for self-promotion many of his contemporaries would have killed for. He provided the public with a tantalizingly vague general image—the vice president in the steel gray suit—and carefully withheld any other details. This situation proved too tempting for some of his readers, who, like Delmore Schwartz, made up anecdotes about the man behind the poems. But despite creative writing from an occasional critic, Stevens's strategy worked magnificently. The literary establishment was very willing to treat him as a myth rather than a man, and even thirty years after his death when (at least in the academy) he was considered as the most significant American poet of the century and his books were elevated to the status of sacred texts for the learned to elucidate, almost nothing substantial was known about the life he led while writing those works. Like the accomplished sleight-of-hand man in one of his titles, he had masterfully made himself disappear.

But no one disappears without a trace, at least no one as amazing as Wallace Stevens, and now through the remarkable research of Peter Brazeau the first credible portrait of this elusive poet has been written. In 1975, twenty years after Stevens's death, Brazeau began searching out and interviewing everyone who had known him—poets, insurance men, lawyers, professors, neighbors, relatives, editors. Brazeau found Stevens's office valet, his maid, the manager of his club, his secretary, even his confessor—people, in short, who saw Stevens in every aspect of his life, sometimes on a daily basis for years. (It is curious how these mundane acquaintances despite the frequent awkwardness and banality of their language, usually provide more vivid and convincing portraits than the poet's more illustrious literary friends, who often reminisce more tellingly about themselves than about Stevens.) Brazeau has arranged this material thematically in *Parts of a World: Wallace Stevens Remembered,* an oral biography, in which the exact words of his sources are quoted. What emerges from this mosaic is one of the most carefully detailed portraits of a poet ever assembled.

Brazeau's book, however, does not qualify as a true biography. That book is yet to be written. While Brazeau presents an unexpected wealth of material, he does not arrange it in a consistently sequential manner (though his thematic arrangement does have a subtle dramatic quality).

Nor does the book survey all of Stevens's life. It literally begins *nel mezzo del cammin* in the poet's thirty-sixth year as he made the difficult decision to leave New York for Hartford. Stevens's youth has been largely lost. Brazeau could find no one living who knew Stevens before his move to Connecticut, and so perforce *Parts of a World* became a chronicle of the poet's Hartford years. Within these limits, however, Brazeau succeeds admirably in providing a rich portrait of Stevens and his daily world. There is nothing like it in all the voluminous literature written on Stevens.

Parts of a World is not a perfect book by any means. Like any oral biography, it is frustrating to read at long stretches. One longs for the author to have shaped the material into an extended, balanced narrative rather than the asymmetrical crazy quilt of separate interviews. Brazeau is a careful editor, but even he cannot eliminate all the repetition and circumlocution of his sources. Sometimes too his zeal for reportorial accuracy leaves in the false starts, vague focus, and non sequiturs of the actual interviews. While this method heightens the documentary air of the book, I for one would not have minded a more liberal editorial hand from time to time.

But these small reservations do not diminish this book's status as a remarkable act of creative scholarship. While many critics have been turning out marginal studies of Stevens's poetry, Brazeau has assembled one of the few permanently indispensable books on the poet. *Parts of a World* fills an enormous gap in our understanding of Stevens, and it provides the first real foundation for all subsequent biographies. *Parts of a World* also stands as an important act of conservation. Had not Brazeau spent nine years gathering this information, who would have? Most of it would have been irretrievably lost. I noted in reading the appendix that several of the people interviewed have already died. One wishes that more academics showed Brazeau's imagination and resourcefulness in attempting significant projects off the beaten track of literary scholarship.

Brazeau's book also illuminates what in addition to the dual career in business and poetry will probably become the central issues in Stevens's biography, i.e., his unhappy marriage, his move from New York to Hartford, and his deathbed conversion to Catholicism. The strain in Stevens's marriage has long been known. Indeed, it is one of the few biographical facts that could be surmised from the poetry. That so prolific and effusive a poet could have written so much and so rigorously excluded his wife's presence speaks "of the woe that is in marriage." How strange to come upon the lines prefacing "Notes Toward a Supreme Fiction" and realize they were written not to Stevens's wife but to the aesthete Henry Church:

> And for what, except for you, do I feel love?
> Do I press the extremest book of the wisest man
> Close to me, hidden in me day and night?

Brazeau's book gives the first full outline of Stevens's courtship and marriage, but even here the essential mystery behind its unhappiness remains. In June 1904, having just completed the New York Bar exams, the twenty-five-year-old Stevens returned to Reading, Pennsylvania, to spend the summer with his parents before beginning his law practice. Here he met Elsie Kachel, an eighteen-year-old salesgirl with a grammar-school education who was reportedly "the prettiest girl in Reading." The reaction of Stevens's respectable father to this girl "from the wrong side of town" was not hard to predict, and long before Stevens's marriage to Elsie five years later, the poet had cut off relations with his father and most of the family.

Whatever their differences, Mr. and Mrs. Stevens shared a great discretion, and one will never know just how or when their romantic infatuation turned into the joyless stalemate of later years when the couple lived in separate sections of the house. Most likely there was no sudden collapse of affection but just the gradual revelation of how incompatible the domineering, intellectual, and expansive Stevens was with the shy, nervous, and unliterary Elsie. Whereas Stevens emerges from Brazeau's pages a fully fleshed, credible individual, Mrs. Stevens remains a shadowy figure. The reader gets many glimpses of her often eccentric behavior, but no real sense of her interior life.

A generic danger of oral biographies is that they can easily degenerate into gossip, but in the case of Mrs. Stevens, Brazeau's book has almost no choice. There is little trustworthy information about her, since Stevens allowed virtually no one into his house, and he always attended literary and business social events by himself. Therefore, much of what is reported about Mrs. Stevens in Brazeau's book is only surmise. She was widely considered by her neighbors to be a little crazy, and the state of the Stevenses' marriage was the butt of many jokes at the office. Local kids referred to her as "the witch." And yet the few people who met the retiring, dowdy Mrs. Stevens disagree. To some she seemed quiet but gracious, to others eccentric to the point of insanity. Perhaps the most convincing portrait comes from a former maid, who depicts her as a serious, demanding, and inflexible woman: "She was just not a happy person, and she didn't try to make other people happy either."

Brazeau also provides the first real account of Stevens's early legal career and the professional crises of 1916 that forced him to leave his beloved, cosmopolitan New York for provincial Hartford. Between finishing law school in 1903 and being fired from the bankrupt New England Equitable Insurance Company in 1916, Stevens had drifted through five law firms and four insurance companies (if one counts mergers). This is hardly the career path of a successful lawyer. One has the sense that the distractions of Manhattan may have undermined Stevens's concentration. Even his choice of surety bonds as his specialization, one of the dullest corners in all jurisprudence, did not provide him with job security. Now jobless at thirty-six, the eminently practical Stevens must have realized that he had to concentrate on his career as never before. Obtaining a job through an ex-colleague at the newly formed Hartford Accident and Indemnity Company, Stevens reluctantly left New York for Hartford, a move of great personal and artistic significance for the poet.

Hartford fed the reclusive, meditative side of Stevens's personality just as New York had developed his *bon vivant,* aesthetic side. While he would frequently return to Manhattan for short sprees of jovial socializing in galleries and restaurants, speakeasies and literary salons, it was in Hartford that he made his living. In vast anonymous New York he could temporarily play the dandy, but in smaller Hartford he was a key vice president in one of the town's largest companies. He never trusted Hartford to accept him as both a poet and a businessman. Though, contrary to legend, Stevens did not hide his literary career from his office associates, he actively discouraged an interest in it. He answered their references to his poetry with rude stares, enigmatic comments, or modest dismissals. Likewise, he refused to read his poetry locally, would not deliver lectures in Hartford he had given in other cities, and remained aloof from the town's not inconsiderable artistic life. In Hartford he wanted to be known only as an insurance executive. Biographical interpretations of literature are still out of favor—and rightfully so for real criticism. But book reviewers are allowed to speculate in undisciplined ways. Consequently, one wonders if Stevens's demi-exile to Hartford was not one of the major factors shaping his development as a poet. Would his poetry have taken the same course of development, from the brilliant sensuousness of his early pieces in *Harmonium* to the austere intellectuality of "The Rock," had he remained in the convivial artistic circles of New York?

The most startling new information published in Brazeau's book is the account of Stevens's deathbed conversion to Catholicism. (News of his baptism had previously been suppressed by the local archbishop, who feared that it would harm the reputation of Catholic hospitals among non-Catholics.) Whether this act was a denial or vindication of Stevens's artistic credo will surely be one of the major issues in any comprehensive criticism of his oeuvre. His request for baptism was not an act that can be easily dismissed. On one subject all of Brazeau's ninety informants agree—i.e., Stevens was not a man to make commitments lightly. Nor were his final months marked by emotional or intellectual weakness. As Manning Heard, later president of Hartford Accident and Indemnity, said, "Of all the individuals I've seen go through this, he was the most capable in knowing how to die." In his final bout with stomach cancer Stevens maintained a stoic calm and intellectual lucidity worthy of his old philosopher in Rome as "The human end in the spirit's greatest reach. / The extreme of the known in the presence of the extreme / Of the unknown."

Nor was his conversion unprefigured in his life and work. Like his hero Santayana, Stevens had used Christian concepts throughout his work, however agnostic his articulated philosophy seemed. Likewise, unknown to all but a few of his closest friends, for years Stevens had often spent part of his seemingly sybaritic visits to New York meditating in churches, usually St. Patrick's Cathedral.

The fun of reading *Parts of a World* comes from the hundreds of anecdotes and observations throughout the book: old-school Stevens wearing a crimson feather in his cap at the Harvard–Yale game; philistine Stevens attending wrestling matches with the "boys" from the office; drunken Stevens dancing a polka with a colleague from work; imperious Stevens commanding a junior executive to drive him down to the New York World's Fair for lunch; sophomoric Stevens roaring with laughter over silly jokes. One could go on listing anecdotes for pages, as indeed most of Brazeau's reviewers already have, but there is at least one deeper observation that has eluded them, the strength of Stevens's character. Unexpectedly, the Stevens that emerges from these pages is not unlike the protagonist of one of his own later poems—a strong philosophic man of taste and imagination, a person who lives in his time and place without being of it. To see Stevens's cantankerous reclusivity and aloofness merely as eccentricities misses the point. They were also expressions of his values. In lonely, unliterary Hartford, Stevens learned that the private act of writing was important, not the public life of the writer. He cared for literary politics no more than office politics, and just as he deliberately passed up promotions that could have led him to the presidency of Hartford Accident and Indemnity, he continually turned down other opportunities that would have made him a literary celebrity. Immune to vanity, he would not let either *Life* or the *New Yorker* do profiles on him (honors his friend William Carlos Williams actively courted). Instead he lived in Hartford like "a veritable monk," as Dr. Williams complained. And though Williams did not intend that epithet as a compliment, one sees many of the ancient monastic virtues in Stevens—the love of solitude and meditation, the steadfast dedication to one's quest for enlightenment, and paradoxically for so successful a businessman, a distance from the City of Man. American poetry could do much worse in selecting a patron saint.

The Emperor
of Hartford

———

WHEN ASKED to name the greatest French poet of the nineteenth century, André Gide replied, "Victor Hugo—hélas!" Some American readers, if asked to choose their foremost modern poet, might echo Gide's perplexity by answering, "Wallace Stevens, alas." For though Stevens ranks high among the most deserving candidates, he hardly offers Americans the sort of national poet they might like. Affluent, aloof, and undemocratic, Stevens so deeply contradicted the available stereotypes of the American poet that for years bewildered critics inaccurately classified him as *sui generis,* an inexplicable hybrid of two seemingly irreconcilable sides of the American experience—business and poetry. That the two sides of Stevens's life never overlapped, that no trace of his office life ever appeared in his poetry and that his literary career was never discussed with his fellow workers, only heightened the mystery of how this insurance lawyer with the body of a football player wrote some of the great Modernist poetry in English.

Milton J. Bates's comprehensive biographical study, *Wallace Stevens: A Mythology of Self,* documents how the poet's life ran a soberly determined course worthy of his most stolid Pennsylvania-Dutch ancestor. The young Stevens accepted his father's stern advice that his primary concern should be, "Starting with nothing, how shall I sustain myself and perhaps a wife and family—and send my boys to College and live comfortably in my old age?" Although his estranged father considered him "as Romantic as Cinderella," for years Stevens suppressed the exuberant side of his nature to pursue this bourgeois ideal. After leaving Harvard University in 1900 he spent only nine months as a journalist in New York before switching to law. He chose a dull but lucrative legal specialty, postponed his marriage to "the prettiest girl in Reading" for years out of an exaggerated financial prudence, delayed having his first child for another fifteen years, and eventually left his beloved New York for Hartford to recoup a faltering career. Not until he was in his mid-thirties, when his personal and professional life seemed secure, did he seriously return to his undergraduate dream of poetry.

By the time Stevens achieved literary fame late in life, it no longer mattered to him. Successful in business, reconciled to Hartford and inured to an unhappy but stable marriage, he had already created a sustaining cycle of office routine and domestic privacy. He enjoyed his business associates but allowed no intimate friendships. Virtually no one was admitted into his home. He also largely ignored the literary world, usually turning down the readings, lectures, recordings, and interviews for which his contemporaries furiously competed. He wanted only to continue thinking and writing in private, as he had done for decades.

Criticism in the thirty years since the poet's death has made the stature of his work unassailable, but until recently it contributed little to explain the man. Until the publication in 1977 of the collection *Souvenirs and Prophecies: The Young Wallace Stevens,* edited by his daughter, Holly, and Peter Brazeau's 1983 oral biography, *Parts of a World: Wallace Stevens Remembered,* the intensely private man behind the poems seemed a mystery. Even now he remains an enigma.

Most troubling to the average reader is not the intellectual challenge of Stevens's poetry, which is considerable, but the relentlessly abstract and impersonal focus. Directly or indirectly, almost all of his poems are about poetry. Few poets have written so obsessively about a single subject, and probably no lyric poet has written so well so often and revealed so little about his personal life. Consciously or unconsciously, Stevens excluded "the grey particulars of man's life." Even during his twenties, he considered his professional life unreconcilable with his imagination. "There is no everyday Wallace," he wrote his fiancée, "apart from the one at work—and that one is tedious." While his youthful poems strike the conventional personal notes, by the time he returned to poetry in early middle age he had sublimated any confessional need in writing. "I am a lawyer and live in Hartford," he wrote the managing editor of the *Dial* when asked for a biographical note. "But such facts are neither gay nor instructive."

Bates maintains that, if not gay, the facts of this poet's life are instructive. Using material from the Holly Stevens and Brazeau books as well as from considerable original research in the family papers, he parallels the

facts of Stevens's life with the development of his poetry. While what
emerges is hardly satisfactory as biography, it is a convincing account of
Stevens's growth as a poet. Bates's study rests on the simple proposition
that no matter how hard a writer tries to separate his life and work (and
Stevens consciously tried), the two inform each other. In the nineteenth
century critics usually linked specific events in a writer's life with episodes
in the work. Bates attempts nothing so literal or old-fashioned with the
uneventful facts of Stevens's life. Instead, he argues persuasively that the
ways Stevens thought and spoke about himself in letters, journals, and reported conversations were very literally transposed into his poetry.

The central link Mr. Bates establishes between Stevens's life and work
is the "mythology of self" in his title. This theory of dynamic multiple
identities is actually a commonsense proposition; to borrow the un-
scholarly definition Jaques gives in *As You Like It,* "one man in his time
plays many parts." While the average citizen makes do with the traditional
seven in strict chronological sequence, Stevens demanded a broader
repertory. The role of the successful Hartford insurance lawyer was only
one of his more convincing and enduring performances. Bates illuminates the "variety of selves conversing behind the burgherly façade" and
shows how Stevens restlessly adopted numerous poses in his quest for
self-definition and growth.

Most of the information about Stevens's life comes from his letters,
and not the least interesting aspect of Bates's book is his virtual construc-
tion of a miniature biography from these frequently reticent documents.
Bates judiciously examines them and compares their rhetoric, preoccupations, and ideas to poems written around the same time. These comparisons reveal some surprising things, especially in poems and letters from
the thirties, when Stevens confronted Marxism. Challenged by a harsh
review in the Marxist journal *New Masses,* the politically conservative
Stevens tried to reconcile the differing demands of the imagination and
communism in a series of surprisingly sympathetic poems. Bates sees
these poems, published by a private press in a small volume, *Owl's Clover,*
but excluded from Stevens's *Collected Poems,* as crucial in the poet's ultimate affirmation of pure poetry. Bates handles these comparisons deftly,
although in his chapter on Stevens's courtship and marriage he occasionally links Mrs. Stevens too literally with figures in the poetry, especially
the "Interior Paramour" of the final poems. One wonders if this uncharacteristic pushiness comes from his wish to humanize the unromantic,

impersonal Stevens, whose ample mature oeuvre conspicuously lacks love poems to his wife.

Many of Bates's critical observations are not original. Stevens's use of personae, for example, has been much discussed elsewhere. Bates's innovation comes from integrating previous literary scholarship into an extended biographical examination of the poetry. In doing so he demonstrates how frequently the manner and concerns of Stevens's poetry emerged from the pressures of his life. Stevens, for example, devastated by the deaths of his siblings, became obsessed with recapturing the past through genealogy. Meanwhile, his highly philosophical poetry became increasingly grounded in the images of rural Pennsylvania and concerned with themes of familial identity. Bates's intelligence and discretion in applying evidence from Stevens's life to his poetry makes this study a model for the new biographical literary criticism currently enjoying a revival in the universities.

Intending his book to be useful to the novice, Bates, who teaches English at Marquette University, has also digested much contemporary Stevens scholarship. Occasionally his approach creates some unnecessary detours for the seasoned reader, but his commitment to clarity also yields some excellent short analyses of certain poems. Avoiding jargon, he talks perceptively about individual poems in a way that balances the differing needs of the scholarly and general audiences.

There is, however, one central criticism to be made of this ambitious study, which does not diminish its quality, but unavoidably suggests its limitations. Relatively little is known about the first half of Stevens's life, beyond his own accounts in letters and journals (parts of which were mutilated and destroyed by his wife). Even his later years are poorly documented by modern standards. For example, Stevens's deathbed conversion to Roman Catholicism, still disputed by his daughter, remained hidden for nearly thirty years by the Archbishop of Hartford. If such a crucial episode almost escaped record, what else was lost? A guarded, private man with an old-fashioned sense of propriety, Stevens was at the very least a selective chronicler of his own life. Undoubtedly many important events were never committed to paper. His letters and surviving journals are models of discretion. (This situation is not without its advantages. No one will have to read about the poet's domestic squabbles or sex life, and a little less information is precisely what contemporary biography needs.) How complete a view of Stevens's life emerges from these documents is therefore debatable. Although he works well within these limitations, Bates largely underplays this central issue.

Ultimately, the portrait in Bates's book seems convincingly human, however incomplete. At last one feels the intimate connections between the businessman who led a life of exemplary caution and the angel who wrote poems of splendid extravagance. Stevens once commented that "poetry seeks out the relation of men to facts." Focusing on a particularly difficult relation to discern, Bates has shown how well criticism can make those same discoveries.

Bourgeois
in Bohemia

—

IN JUNE 1915, Thomas Stearns Eliot, a twenty-six-year-old American graduate student on a traveling fellowship to Oxford, committed the one rash act of his life. He married Vivien Haigh-Wood, a vivacious young Englishwoman he had met only a few months before. Handsome, self-conscious, and exaggeratedly decorous, Eliot entered marriage with little romantic and no sexual experience in his sheltered past. Since early childhood his life had been spent in one or another school, all of them elite—the Milton Academy, Harvard University, the Sorbonne, Oxford's Merton College. He had never had a job.

Neither set of parents knew of the marriage beforehand, and Eliot correctly guessed that his family would disapprove. His parents hoped he would begin a brilliant academic career the next fall at Harvard, a plan this hasty alliance could only upset. His father, Henry Ware Eliot, was a St. Louis brick manufacturer from a distinguished Massachusetts family and had patiently supported Tom's training to become a professor of philosophy. His mother, Charlotte Champe Eliot, was passionately attached to her youngest and brightest child. Haunted by her own frustrated literary ambitions, she desperately desired Tom to achieve the fame she "strove for and failed." Without warning their son had married an unknown foreigner, lost his fellowship, resigned from his Harvard assistantship, made plans to remain in wartime London, and announced his scheme to support his wife and himself with unspecified literary work.

No wonder Eliot hesitated writing his father directly to discuss his plans. Instead, two days after the wedding he enlisted his new friend and fellow expatriate Ezra Pound to defend his decision to stay in England and pursue a literary career. Pound was delighted to oblige. From the moment Pound had read the manuscript of the unpublished "Love Song of

J. Alfred Prufrock" he had recognized Eliot's genius. It was, he wrote the editor of *Poetry,* "the best poem I have yet had or seen by an American." Yet the reserved Eliot had always kept him at a distance. Now, worried and confused, Eliot asked Pound for help in his intimate affairs.

Pound's long letter to the senior Eliot, a brilliant and quirky defense of expatriate literary life, remains an important document of international Modernism, but it was not the epistle to soothe a worried father's nerves. Even on his best behavior, Pound could not talk about one expatriate poet for long without returning to himself. "As to T. S. E.'s work," he confided, "I think it is the most interesting stuff that has appeared since my own first book, five years ago." But after lecturing Eliot's father on assorted developments in modern American poetry—mostly initiated by Ezra Pound—he came down to practical terms. Mr. Eliot needed to support Tom for two years while his son built a literary reputation capable of sustaining a family.

Henry Ware Eliot was not convinced. Letters and cables crisscrossed the Atlantic. Finally, in late July, the dutiful son returned to face his family alone. (The nervous Vivien had refused to sail with him partly from fear of German U-boats.) This short visit proved uncomfortable for everyone. His mother was overcome with anxiety. His father questioned his son's judgment. Eliot wavered between resuming his Harvard studies and remaining in London. In either case he promised his parents he would finish his dissertation. Satisfied that Tom would not throw away his academic career, his father generously offered to continue his allowance. Suddenly news came from England that Vivien was ill, and Eliot hurried back. Leaving his family's summerhouse in East Gloucester, Massachusetts, the poet had no idea how decisive his return voyage would prove. He would never see his father again, never resettle in America, never become a university professor, and, by his own reckoning, not for the next forty years be genuinely happy.

Back in England Eliot's romantic and literary dreams quickly faded before the difficulty of his situation. Each time Vivien recovered from one illness, she soon collapsed into another. A family visit could leave her prostrate for days with nervous anxiety. Desperate to become the good provider his own father had always been, Eliot took a series of temporary teaching jobs, but they proved inadequate to support even his frugal household, especially as living costs rose with the war. "I must do everything I can to earn more money," he wrote his former teacher Bertrand

Russell. He began reviewing both to supplement his income and to gain notoriety for the permanent literary job he hoped to acquire. But gradually this responsible and realistic young poet recognized the ugly truth. His bride was a chronic invalid utterly dependent on him. Literary work was ill-paying and irregular. His teaching and domestic duties left him too exhausted to write poetry. While a small circle of literary acquaintances now acknowledged his poetic talent, his growing reputation did little to alleviate the burdensome problems of his daily life.

Bohemia offered the once securely middle-class young poet no escape from this "most awful nightmare of anxiety the mind of man could conceive." Money worries continued. Poetry ceased to come. Vivien's illnesses proliferated until Eliot's letters home sounded like catalogues of pathology. Each time her name is mentioned, one learns to expect some gruesome new malady—colitis, neuritis, catarrh, gastric influenza, neuralgia, hemicranial migraines, rheumatism, defective secretion of the glands. What he did not confide in his letters was her increasingly destructive addiction to the sedatives and painkillers her doctors so liberally prescribed. The long, futile nights of nursing Vivien in their squalid apartment taught Eliot the completeness of his failure as a husband. For all his love and idealism he could bring her neither health nor security. He became obsessed with fears of his own death and her destitution. Finally, in March 1917, the twenty-eight-year-old Eliot astounded his wife, family, and friends by taking a full-time job in the Colonial and Foreign Department of Lloyd's Bank. "You will be surprised to hear of me in this capacity," he wrote his mother, "but I enjoy it."

This absorbing personal drama forms the human setting of the long-awaited first volume of *The Letters of T. S. Eliot.* Although this hefty and thoroughly annotated collection officially spans twenty-five years of Eliot's life (from ages nine through thirty-four), its actual focus is much narrower. Nearly 600 pages of the 639-page tome chronicle a crucial eight-year period of Eliot's personal and public development. This period begins in August 1914, when the young poet unexpectedly arrived in London (fleeing from the University of Marburg at the outbreak of World War I), and runs through the end of 1922, when Eliot achieved sudden fame with the simultaneous publication of *The Waste Land* in both England and America and the commencement of his influential critical quarterly, the *Criterion.* The record this volume provides is impressive in both quantity and quality. It gives weekly and sometimes daily accounts of the personal, literary, and business affairs of this complex and secretive writer.

No profession enjoys malicious gossip more than that of literary academics, and some early reviewers of this volume have already expressed much high-minded exasperation that the Eliot letters do not contain more graphic confessions of the poet's private life. One senses that the guardians of literary culture are disappointed to read a book this long that does not contain lurid revelations of Eliot's sexual activities. The shit-stained knickers and florid hard-ons that make James Joyce's correspondence a monument of *Weltliteratur* are conspicuously absent here. Instead, one finds only the apparently boring spectacle of a brilliant and introspective young man candidly discussing the major problems of his life.

"Letters should be indiscretions—otherwise they are simply official bulletins," Eliot wrote fellow poet Conrad Aiken. While this volume contains a few too many official bulletins—letters of mainly documentary interest, which chronicle social engagements, lectures, trips, etc.—the overwhelming bulk of them are frank and personal accounts of his often troubled existence. If he is sometimes reticent about the details, he usually speaks directly about the problems he faced, and he always writes intelligently and well. The volume's real surprise is that Eliot's letters are so consistently personal. The laconic public man of later years is not yet in evidence. While he frequently discusses literature and ideas, his primary topic is his own difficult domestic and professional life.

If there is a problem with this volume, it is one of editorial permissiveness. During his lifetime Eliot did his best to suppress biographical information. An intensely private and rigidly proper man, he was deeply ashamed of his failed first marriage and Vivien's eventual confinement in an insane asylum. He expressly forbade that any biography be written of him. He also destroyed many family and personal letters. His secrecy, of course, only fueled speculation about what he was trying to hide. Pseudoscholarly guesswork has gone to absurd lengths, especially lately, for instance, when one critic maintained without any documentary evidence that Eliot had a youthful homosexual affair with Jean Verdenal, a French medical student later killed in World War I, whom the poet met while studying in Paris.

Confronting such assertions, Eliot's second wife and widow, Valerie, obviously edited the volume to set the record straight—at least as she sees it. Consequently, in addition to the poet's own letters, she intermittently includes various correspondence from family, friends, teachers, and associates. These secondary contributors include Eliot's father, mother, and first wife, as well as Ezra Pound, Betrand Russell, André Gide, Richard Aldington, and, inevitably, Jean Verdenal (who emerges as a bright, conventional, and heterosexual bourgeois who always addressed Eliot with the formal "Vous"). The letters from Vivien prove invaluable. Her nervous, intelligent, but disjointed correspondence provides a vivid portrait of the woman who, sick or well, dominated the poet's existence for nearly twenty years. Her letters also frequently amplify personal and social circumstances Eliot only partially describes. Letters like those of Verdenal, however, belong in a scholarly journal. Their inclusion sometimes brings the volume too close to a documentary history full of interesting but inconsequential information.

But Eliot's own letters transcend their documentary surroundings. Read together, his early correspondence constitutes a powerful and unified narrative that reveals the unknown Eliot, a vulnerable and obscure young poet that the dignified and internationally famous elder writer wished forgotten. On a human level the story the letters tell may seem almost prosaic, but being genuine it soon proves emotionally compelling. It is the commonplace tale of a sensitive youth unprepared for the bitter difficulties of adulthood. As the story progresses, however, Eliot proves no ordinary protagonist. Disastrously married, accidentally expatriated, emotionally dependent on his distant family, habitually short of cash, and hopelessly drunk on the unprofitable art of poetry, Eliot consciously trades freedom for survival, then happiness for success. These hard-driven bargains were not so much Faustian as commercial. Like the prudent banker he became, Eliot gradually learned the necessity of repressing the open, emotional side of his nature in favor of the rational and deliberate. The extraordinary drama of these letters comes from watching Eliot transform himself into a consummate realist and politic public man of letters while somehow still protecting the poet inside. The metamorphosis cost him a nervous breakdown and much of his humanity. It also made him into the most influential English-language poet and critic of the century.

The public Eliot who emerges at the end of these letters is a survivor—wise but disillusioned, socially astute but cold, stiffly middle-aged at thirty-four. He saw literary life as petty and sordid. "Poetry is a mug's game," he once remarked in the British English he gradually adopted (a

mug being a dupe). By 1922 Eliot had resolved to be a mug no longer.
He negotiated lucrative deals for his books and plays. He grew modestly
wealthy by giving readings and lectures. And he advised every youth who
would listen to avoid poetry as a career. He knew too well its emotional
cost. The Greek Nobel Prize laureate George Seferis recounted that when
Eliot heard about a young man who wanted to dedicate himself to
poetry, he remarked with unenviable authority, "He's getting ready for a
sad life."

If Eliot had a sad life, he was unwittingly much to blame. Like all of
the major first-generation Modernist American poets, Eliot was the product of the educated upper-middle class. In a town only a few decades
removed from the frontier, his father was unusual not only for his prosperity but also his college education. Much of the difficulty Eliot faced in
early adulthood came from his inability to distance himself from his parents' bourgeois Republican values. Although Eliot wanted to become a
poet, he never expected to give up his comfortable standard of living.
While Pound contentedly accepted an existence at subsistence level,
hardly worrying about next month's rent or this week's groceries, Eliot
could not bear even the possibility of economic uncertainty. What Pound
saw as *la vie bohème,* Eliot viewed as squalid poverty. In his twenties he
already worried over life insurance and retirement savings. He frequently
asked his family for money—not just to cover current expenses but also
to put into a savings account for possible emergencies. More than once
he complained to his mother that his funds were so low he might have to
let Vivien's charwoman go. No wonder Mrs. Eliot fretted so much when
her pampered youngest son decided to become a freelance writer in
London. "Tom has always had every reasonable desire gratified," she told
Bertrand Russell, "without any thought of ways and means, up to the
present time." His stay in literary bohemia lasted only eighteen nerve-
racking months before he escaped to Lloyd's. Starting over in banking
actually reduced Eliot's income, but the job offered promotions and security. Pound objected. Eliot's wife shed tears. But the poet knew what he
needed. He no longer had to depend on writing for money. He had regained his middle-class self-respect. "It is a relief to be no longer on the
hunt and a nuisance to everyone I know," he wrote on starting the job.

Yet if Eliot's middle-class expectations contributed to his problems,
that same set of values also helped him succeed. While his career may not

prove Edison's maxim that "genius is one per cent inspiration and ninety-nine per cent perspiration," his example certainly does not contradict it. Once he joined Lloyd's Bank, Eliot settled down to a bone-crushing schedule of fourteen- or fifteen-hour days from which he never relaxed until forced to in old age by emphysema. He rose early in the morning to write for two hours before going to the office. He then worked at the bank from 9:15 A.M. to 5:30 P.M., six days a week, translating correspondence and analyzing the balance sheets of foreign banks. Returning home, he spent the evening on writing and editorial projects in addition to nursing his wife. He was driven as much by shame as ambition. Having faltered once as a literary freelancer, knowing his family thought his marriage a fiasco, bearing the disapproval of his literary friends for entering business, Eliot was determined never to fail again. He would succeed at both careers, and to everyone's surprise he did. He was quickly promoted at the bank, then promoted twice again, and he kept on writing—at an incredible rate.

"There are only two ways in which a writer can become important," the banker Eliot confided to an old Harvard professor. "To write a great deal, and have his writing appear everywhere, or to write very little. . . . I write very little." The numerical facts, however, dispute Eliot's modest self-assessment. During the nine years he spent at Lloyd's (1917 through 1925) Eliot changed the course of modern poetry and criticism. He published more than 130 essays, articles, and reviews, including "Tradition and the Individual Talent," "The Metaphysical Poets," and "The Function of Criticism." He began his influential reassessment of the Elizabethan and Jacobean dramatists. He wrote about a third of his mature poetry, most notably *The Waste Land*, "Geronition," "The Hollow Men," and most of *Sweeney Agonistes*. He composed or collected eight books and pamphlets. He taught evening courses in literature. He became assistant editor of the *Egoist*, the London correspondent for the *Dial*, and in 1922 started the *Criterion*, of which he was the sole editor.

The pressure of this work load strained his health and eventually led him to a nervous breakdown in late 1921 (the exact medical nature of which the *Letters* does little to clarify), but even his recuperation in a Lausanne sanatorium proved a working vacation. The convalescent Eliot used the time to finish *The Waste Land*. His daily schedule both compensated for his painful marriage and made it worse. His personal life gradually shrank to a laborious routine. But his effort made him the most famous Modernist poet in English. He realized the nature of the exchange he had made but never regretted it. Raised in the professional class, he knew that success always comes at a price.

Studying Eliot's life, one ponders that price carefully. Except for his brief breakdown and Vivien's slow decline, Eliot's biography lacks the tangible tragedy of the archetypal doomed poet. He did not pay for his genius with madness like H. D. or suicide like Crane or treason like Pound. Instead, in private, he made the quiet everyday sacrifices of personal freedom, sexual love, and domestic happiness. He protected the tender side of his humanity by learning to repress it so that the pain was invisible to the outside. That rarely successful creature, a bourgeois artist, Eliot refused to put his craft above his values. He rejected the idealistic egotism that George Bernard Shaw once characterized by saying, "The true artist will let his wife starve, his children go barefoot, his mother drudge for his living at seventy, sooner than work at anything but his art." Eliot—like his Harvard contemporary Wallace Stevens—was determined to lead a responsible life. Neither would abandon his middle-class morality for art. But the Muse demanded sacrifice, and they offered their youth, their marriages, their friendships, even, all evidence suggests, their sexuality. No Americans ever wrote greater poems. Was it a fair exchange? The question can't be answered, but it remains worth asking.

The Successful Career of Robert Bly

—

ROBERT BLY is one of the most famous and influential poets now writing in America. The author, editor, and translator of over eighty books and pamphlets, Bly has been a constant and outspoken presence in American poetry for the past three decades. Now, at sixty, he is one of the few contemporary poets who, like a rock star or sports celebrity, seems bigger than life. Indeed, in parts of the academy Bly has already achieved canonic stature. His poetry has entered the curriculum and inspired a sizable secondary literature of books, dissertations, and articles. He has demonstrated that it is still possible for a contemporary poet to become a public figure.

Bly's fame did not come by accident. He has poured immense energy not only into the solitary act of writing but also into developing his public personality as a writer. No contemporary poet (except Allen Ginsberg) has better understood the value of publicity or used it more aggressively to his own advantage. Bly realized early in his career how important it was for a poet to create an attractive public image independent of his work. There was little fame in the poetry world and many contenders. To become well known, one had to court a broader public—and not by poetry but personality. Bly knew that the mass media would always have room for a few poets, provided that they were sufficiently colorful.

Bly created a series of timely public images, each suited to a particular decade. The sixties saw Bly as a fiery antiwar activist, the seventies as a mysterious shaman explaining the myths of contemporary culture, the eighties as a gentle spiritual counselor healing the psychic wounds of modern life. In the meantime, he gave more interviews than a Hollywood starlet, campaigned more miles than a presidential hopeful. He appeared on television, spoke on radio, made recordings, even engineered mass-market mailings to announce his books and seminars. Though he professes a preference for the contemplative life, Bly is not shy about sharing his talents. Traveling for months each year to give readings, performances, lectures, and workshops, he has probably reached a broader public than any American poet since Robert Frost.

Although Bly has achieved considerable literary fame, his position in contemporary letters remains curiously ambiguous. His importance to recent literary history seems incontestable, but his achievements as a poet are open to question. No comprehensive account of American poetry since 1950 can ignore Bly's manifold contributions as a poet, translator, editor, critic, performer, and personality. One might even claim him as the most influential poet of the sixties and seventies. He helped introduce surrealism into American poetry, popularize Latin American verse, renew interest in literary translation, strengthen the identity of regional poetry from the Midwest, and lead the movement of political poetry during the Vietnam War. He also played a critical role in discrediting the American tradition of formal poetry, offering as an alternative his own vision of poems that would be, as Charles Molesworth has summarized, "more open in form, associative in structure, and ecstatic in intention."

This much Bly has certainly done. The debate begins when one stops chronicling and begins evaluating his achievements. Bly's advocates esteem him as a contemporary Ezra Pound, a multitalented pioneer who has used poetry, translation, and criticism innovatively to create an authentic and genuinely new style. His detractors see him as an industrious opportunist, a writer of immense but overwhelmingly pernicious influence and shallow achievement. Such controversy is not unexpected for so prolific and mercurial a writer. While criticism usually clarifies a writer's achievement, in Bly's case critics have been hard-pressed merely to keep up with his latest transformation. But now with the publication of his *Selected Poems* and the appearance of several critical books about his work, the time for an informed and frank appraisal has arrived.

Bly's work profits by being seen in the context of his life and background because he is one of the few twentieth-century American poets who have remained deeply rooted in their native landscapes. Born in Madison, Minnesota, in 1926, the poet grew up on a farm in the tightly knit Norwegian-Lutheran society of the Great Plains. Although Bly left Minnesota to join the Navy in World War II and then spent more than a decade elsewhere, he returned to rural Minnesota in 1958 and has kept it as his base during his entire public literary life.

For all his later eccentricity, Bly began his literary career in the most conventional way for an ambitious young poet of his generation. In 1947 after a year at St. Olaf, a stolid Lutheran college in Minnesota, Bly fled his native pastures for Harvard Yard. In those postwar years, Cambridge was the right place for an aspiring poet. John Ciardi and Archibald MacLeish were on the faculty. Richard Wilbur was a university fellow. Bly's fellow undergraduates included John Ashbery, Donald Hall, Kenneth Koch, Frank O'Hara, and L. E. Sissman, with Adrienne Rich at Radcliffe. Like everyone else literary, Bly competed for the staff of the *Harvard Advocate* and, as always, competition suited him. Eventually, the *Advocate* not only made him a senior editor but published his lively essays and awkward, metrical poems. In 1950 he left Harvard with a *magna cum laude* in English, and, not surprisingly, moved to New York City to write. This relocation proved unsuccessful, and he wrote very little. Several frustrating years later, Bly took the next conventional step and left for the University of Iowa to earn an M.A. in Creative Writing. His time at Iowa remains murky because he has maintained an uncharacteristic silence about this period, consistently skipping over it in his many autobiographical interviews and essays. Perhaps the most telling testimony of his years in the famed Writers' Workshop comes from his current advice to aspiring authors. When asked how to become a poet, Bly now replies that one should go off alone for two years and talk to no one. In 1956, however, having himself spent two years talking to his teachers and fellow graduate students, Bly left with his bride for Norway on a Fulbright. At the age of thirty, Bly seemed headed for a comfortable academic career.

Europe was the turning point in Bly's creative life. His subsidized scholarly project was to translate Norwegian poetry (although he knew no Norwegian at the time, Bly has never lacked self-confidence). Instead, in Oslo he discovered modern European and Latin American poetry, especially the work of Georg Trakl and Pablo Neruda. Returning to the United States in 1958, he was filled with a religious mission to reform American poetry. His aim was to push aside the now decrepit "Puritan, American isolationist tradition" of Pound, Eliot, and Williams and replace it with a vital new international style. The old tradition, he claimed, strived for clarity and reason, which created "a spare, bare poetry" with few images. The new movement would create *"poetry heavy with images from the unconscious"* (Bly's italics).

Bly saw himself at odds with the literary establishment—both in the academy and in New York—against which he waged a wily generational and geographical war. If rural Minnesota was remote from the center of American literary life, he would then bring it closer to the mainstream of world poetry. If he was a young man with no critical authority, he would discredit the older generation of literary arbiters. Not employed on any faculty, Bly could ignore the restraints of standard scholarly and critical writing and leap instead into polemic, satire, and speculation to accomplish his ends. He would overstep the narrow boundaries of academic departments and explore not only literatures in foreign languages but also ideas from sociology, psychology, and anthropology. He would fight on his own terms to transform the poetic standards of the coming decade.

To accomplish this transformation, Bly began what would become the most influential small poetry magazine of the next decade, *The Fifties* (later updated to *The Sixties,* to *The Seventies,* and eventually to *The Eighties*). Though it published the work of other writers, *The Fifties* was largely a one-man show with Bly supplying poems, translations, reviews, editorials, and fillers from cover to cover. For an average issue Bly wrote about two thirds of the material, mostly under his own name but often under pseudonyms (including that of the arch-critic, Crunk). It was an exciting performance and one that quickly revealed Bly's strengths and weaknesses. His clarity of purpose gave vitality and direction to every page. His intellectual curiosity rejected the conventional limits for literary discourse set by the New Critics. He was not interested in careful, textual analysis but in ambitious cultural criticism. Bly responded to poetry with the whole of his intelligence, frequently making illuminating political, psychological, and sociological observations. One sensed a bold, original mind with a true talent for making unexpected associations. Bly also understood how a living literature needed innovation to avoid stagnation. In *The Fifties* he brought news to American poetry—news of foreign poets, critical alternatives, and revolutionary aesthetics.

The Fifties was an overtly didactic magazine, a paperbound church with the Reverend Bly permanently at the pulpit. There might be a little poetic music to work up the crowd, but the sermon was the main attraction. There were souls to be saved. Bly's articles were not carefully crafted essays. Indeed, the scholarship he proudly flaunts on all occasions often proves embarrassing under scrutiny, as when he analyzes Lucretius's image of "the tears of things," not realizing he is quoting one of Virgil's most famous phrases. The didactic impulse rarely leads to perfectionism, and too often the excitement of Bly's best prose coincides with an enthusiastic hastiness.

Not only Bly's prose was spoiled by his didacticism. Nowhere are its damaging effects more evident than in his copious translations. In *The Fifties* Bly translated the work of foreign writers, especially those involved in the surrealist and expressionist movements (which had not yet entered the mainstream of American literature) to illustrate how contemporary poems might be written. For all his fascination with contemplative figures like Meister Eckhart, Bly has always chosen action and involvement. As a propagandist for a new poetics, he quickly discovered that translation was more important than his own poetry for demonstrating his theories in convincing, concrete terms. But as a translator, Bly reveals the aesthetic simplification inherent in his "deep image" school of poetry.

Bly's versions usually conveyed the surface sense and images of the original, but the careful shapes of sound which embody them and the nuances of meaning which enliven them were largely ignored. The main problem a translator of poetry faces is not in bringing across the surface sense. That task, at least in modern languages, is relatively easy. The difficulty comes in re-creating the complex design of sound and connotation that charges the original with energy. Bly usually solved this problem by ignoring its existence. He merely provided prose translations, often curiously awkward ones, lineated as verse. His versions were usually good enough to make a particular critical point. Unfortunately, they were rarely strong enough to bring the poetry itself across with the theory. In the pages of *The Fifties,* poetry truly became what got lost in translation.

Is this judgment an exaggeration? Here are the opening stanzas of two famous poems in the original French and German. (I offer two languages to increase the chances that the reader will be able to compare at least one of Bly's versions with the original text.) First the opening quatrain of Mallarmé's "Sonnet":

> *Sur les bois oubliés quand passe l'hiver sombre*
> *Tu te plains, ô captif solitaire du seuil,*
> *Que ce sépulcre à deux qui fera notre orgueil*
> *Hélas! du manque seul des lourds bouqets s'encombre . . .*

And now the beginning of Rilke's famous "Der Panther," describing a caged panther in the Jardin des Plantes in Paris:

> *Sein Blick ist vom Vorübergehn der Stäbe*
> *so müd geworden, dass es nichts mehr hält.*
> *Ihm ist, als ob es tausend Stäbe gäbe*
> *und hinter tausend Stäben keine Welt.*

Here are Bly's versions. First the Mallarmé:

While the dark winter is passing over the woods now forgotten
Lonesome man imprisoned by the sill, you are complaining
That the mausoleum for two which will be our pride
Is unfortunately burdened down with the absence of masses of flowers . . .

Now the Rilke:

> From seeing and seeing the seeing has become so exhausted
> It no longer sees anything anymore.
> The world is made of bars, a hundred thousand
> bars, and behind the bars, nothing.

As an impromptu translation in a French II oral exam, the Mallarmé might eke out a passing grade, but as poetry in English is fails the most rudimentary test. Not only does it not seem like the verse of an accomplished poet, it doesn't even sound like the language of a native speaker. Nor does the Rilke exhibit the virtues of a smooth literal translation. It transforms the tight, musical German into loose, pretentious doggerel. In the first line, Bly gratuitously introduces awkward, unidiomatic repetitions as equivalents to Rilke's clean phrasing, and substitutes a long limp line for the original's appropriately controlled iambic pentameter. ("The Panther" is a poem about the repetition of confinement.) In the second line Bly indulges in more vague, clumsy wordplay ("anything anymore") and meaninglessly varies the rhythm of the line from his opening, once again discarding Rilke's tight stanza design for no apparent benefit. In the third and fourth lines, Bly yet again shifts the sense of rhythm and lineation with a jerky enjambment falling in the middle of a phrase ("a hundred thousand/bars") before tightening up his syntax suddenly.

If this language is indeed verse, it is verse of the most amateurish variety. Not only are Rilke's subtle repetitions vulgarized in Bly's heavy-handed language, but the intense spiritual identification between the poet and the caged animal is clumsily undercut in Bly's English. In the German Rilke implicitly presents the panther as masculine. It is "his" glance on the bars. The image of a thousand bars occurs "to him." Of course, this sexual identification comes from the masculine gender of the German word for "panther." But, like other great poets, Rilke uses the deep structure of the language to heighten the meaning of his images. Focusing such subtle connotations gives poetry its intensity. Bly, who has repeatedly cited this particular poem as a source for his theory of "twofold consciousness," misses the nuance entirely. While understanding the central idea of the poem, Bly is strangely deaf to the subtler side of its language, and he mechanically neuters this imprisoned masculine panther into an "it," although English grammar can neatly duplicate German in this case, and common American speech characteristically uses gender to personalize animals. What can one say about translations so insensitive to both the sound and nuance of the originals?

By propagating this minimal kind of translation Bly has done immense damage to American poetry. Translating quickly and superficially, he not only misrepresented the work of many great poets, he also distorted some of the basic standards of poetic excellence. His slapdash method ignored both the obvious formal qualities of the originals (like rhyme and meter) and, more crucially, those subtler organizing principles such as diction, tone, rhythm, and texture that frequently gave the poems their intensity. Concentrating almost entirely on syntax and imagery, Bly reduced the complex originals into abstract visual blueprints. In his hands, dramatically different poets like Lorca and Rilke, Montale and Machado, not only all sounded alike, they all sounded like Robert Bly, and even then not like Bly at his best. But as if that weren't bad enough, Bly consistently held up these diminished versions as models of poetic excellence worthy of emulation. In promoting his new poetics (based on his specially chosen foreign models), he set standards so low that he helped create a school of mediocrities largely ignorant of the premodern poetry in English and familiar with foreign poetry only through oversimplified translations.

Bly's weaknesses as a translator underscore his central failings as a poet. He is simplistic, monotonous, insensitive to sound, enslaved by literary diction, and pompously sentimental. Moreover, these are not accidental faults. They are the consequences of his poetic method and they are exacerbated by his didactic impulse. Curiously, Bly's prose rarely exhibits these problems. Whatever its intellectual failings, it is usually fresh, vigorous, and diverse. Much of the poetry, however, suffers from being written according to a method.

As *Selected Poems* makes clear, Bly's earliest work was awful. A few lines written when the young Bly lived in New York City will suffice to show his wisdom in waiting till thirty-five to publish a book:

> There is a joyful night in which we lose
> Everything, and drift
> Like a radish
> Rising and falling, and the ocean
> At last throws us into the ocean . . .

By the time his premier volume, *Silence in the Snowy Fields,* appeared in 1962, Bly had developed a quiet, personal style capable of creating fine short poems within a limited range. The most noticeable qualities of this style were simplicity, coolness, and compression. Even eighty volumes later this strangely unified book remains the central Bly collection, the one most often praised by critics and cherished by readers. Now in its thirteenth printing, it appears on many university course lists. Its contents are frequently anthologized (not infrequently by Bly himself), and in his *Selected Poems,* Bly preserves more poems from it than any other collection. Here Bly created a type of poem that would not only become his trademark but also influence two generations of poets. Here, too, one sees the beginning of the problems that would weaken most of Bly's later work.

"Old Boards" from *Silence in the Snowy Fields* demonstrates the usual Bly manner:

> *I*
>
> I love to see boards lying on the ground in early spring:
> The ground beneath them is wet and muddy—
> Perhaps covered with chicken tracks—
> And they are dry and eternal.

II

This is the wood one sees on the decks of ocean ships,
Wood that carries us far from land,
With a dryness of something used for simple tasks,
Like a horse's tail.

III

This wood is like a man who has a simple life,
Living through the spring and winter on the ship of his own desire.
He sits on dry wood surrounded by half-melted snow
As the rooster walks away springily over the dampened hay.

"Old Boards," like all the "country poems" from *Silence in the Snowy Fields,* is short and undeceptively simple. The rhythm is calm and deliberate. All of the lines are end-stopped with the line lengths matching the units of sense. The vocabulary is ordinary and traditional. One cannot find a single word or image that is specifically modern. The diction is flat and old-fashioned or, to use Bly's more ambitious formulation, "dry and eternal." The tone, like the rhythm, never departs from a cheery peacefulness. Roman numerals have been placed before each stanza to slow the reader down and put each section in isolation. The first stanza presents an ordinary farm scene. Old boards have been laid over the muddy ground to make a walkway in spring. The second stanza equates this commonplace sight with something unexpected, the wood used to build the decks of ships that take men on voyages. The final stanza combines these notions to show how a farmer's seemingly ordinary life also encompasses a spiritual voyage. "Old Boards" is a simple, honest poem. While not particularly exciting or memorable, it has the modest virtues of brevity, directness, and precision.

The problem with Bly's work is that he has rewritten "Old Boards" several hundred times, usually less well. Not only is every poem in *Silence in the Snowy Fields* similar both technically and thematically, but so is most of Bly's subsequent verse. The style that this early book achieved through compression and discipline quickly relaxed into an uninteresting set of mannerisms. Worse yet, as the style grew more slack, the intellectual demands Bly placed on it became more onerous. Bly's "country" style works best for simple, static scenes. It operates in isolated flashes that generate no complex narrative or intellectual energy. Despite their gestures of spiritual profundity, the poems operate too superficially to recreate any but the most elementary spiritual insights, and even these they usually assert rather than dramatize—and, as Bly develops, assert with increasing crudity. Bly's initial clarity and simplicity soon became pious pretension like this section from "Six Winter Privacy Poems," which opened *Sleepers Joining Hands* (1973):

> There is a solitude like black mud!
> Sitting in this darkness singing,
> I can't tell if this joy
> is from the body, or the soul, or a third place!

This short poem deserves scrutiny because it is a microcosm of Bly's faults. It begins with the supposedly bold but ultimately corny "deep image" of solitude as "black mud." Anyone schooled in Bly's poetics will know that mud is a positive, profound symbol. It is earthy and elemental, especially when modified by black, the favorite "deep image" color after white. Although Bly's opening line is flat and abstract, he announces his metaphor in great excitement. (One can always tell when Bly is excited. He adds an exclamation point.) He then switches to an image that attests to his spiritual discipline. After all, how many of us desire spiritual growth strongly enough to spend time sitting alone singing in the dark? After one line of such grueling discipline, Bly is properly rewarded by a transfiguring joy that so confuses him that he is unable to determine whether it comes from his body, his soul, or, in his inimitable phrase, "a third place" (second exclamation point). At this abrupt climax the reader may want to go back to the beginning to see what he or she has missed. A second look will probably not help much. One may even begin to wonder what "black mud" is doing in the poem besides sitting around seeming profound. This indescribable quality is apparently what makes it a "deep image." Reaching the end a second time, the reader should simply appreciate the last line for what it is, a small masterpiece of bathos, a Hallmark Cards version of mysticism.

This poem also demonstrates the pompous sentimentality that pervades much of Bly's work. In poetry sentimentality represents the failure of language to carry the emotional weight an author intends. There is an excess of some lofty emotion that the reader understands but cannot participate in. Instead the reader remains outside the emotional action of the poem, a little embarrassed by it all, like a person sharing a train compartment with a couple whispering romantically in baby talk.

This edifying sentimentality is one of the keys to Bly's popularity. Most people like sentimental art, as long as its emotions are stylish. The last century sentimentalized tender emotions like love and pity. This Old Sentimentality is now passé. The New Sentimentality prefers other ennobling qualities like alienation, loneliness, and especially sincerity. But traditional or contemporary, the sentimentalist always asks the reader to experience more emotion than the poem generates. Poets know that many readers will collaborate in the deception. A few bells will suffice to set off emotions readers want to experience anyway.

Reading Bly, one continually comes across purple passages of the New Sentimentality:

> There is a restless gloom in my mind.
> I walk grieving. The leaves are down.
> I come at dusk
> where, sheltered by poplars, a low pond lies.
> The sun abandons the sky, speaking through cold leaves.

Is it possible for a stanza of poetry to be both unadorned and overwritten? Here every phrase contains at least one heavy-handed hint to the author's mood. (Excerpting these clues, one could easily compose a telegram version of the poem: "Restless gloom grieving leaves down dusk low abandons cold.") But despite its crude overstatement, the language remains weirdly inert for a lyric poem. Characteristically, Bly simply asserts his emotions. His utilitarian language does little to re-create them in the reader. Instead, in the manner of the New Sentimentality, he tries to bully the reader into an instant epiphany of alienation and self-pity.

If Bly writes this sentimentally about the weather, watch out when he talks about love, as in *Loving a Woman in Two Worlds* (1985). Here the Old and the New Sentimentality meet with truly gooey results. The gap between the intense emotions Bly intends and the tepid language he employs is broad enough for parody, but unfortunately, the poems are not intended to be funny. Sincerity alone cannot save a poem like "Letter to Her," which opens with this stanza:

> What I did I did.
> I knew that I loved you
> and told you that.
> Then I lied to you
> often so you would love me,
> hid the truth,
> shammed, lied.

Is Bly only a sentimental poet with mystical pretensions? From much of his *Selected Poems* it would appear so, but then in the middle of all the early work one suddenly comes across sharp, startling poems like "Counting Small-Boned Bodies":

> Let's count the bodies over again.
>
> If we could only make the bodies smaller,
> the size of skulls,
> we could make a whole plain white with skulls in the moonlight.
>
> If we could only make the bodies smaller,
> maybe we could fit
> a whole year's kill in front of us on a desk.
>
> If we could only make the bodies smaller,
> we could fit
> a body into a finger ring, for a keepsake forever.

This remarkable short poem appeared in Bly's second full-length collection, *The Light Around the Body,* published in 1967 just as the movement against the Vietnam War hit full stride. This moment in American history became crucially important to Bly. His leadership in organizing poets to protest U.S. military involvement in Southeast Asia gave him national notoriety. His decision to write political poems incorporating the lessons he had learned from translating Neruda, Lorca, Vallejo, Trakl, and others produced his finest poems. And his cross-country trips to give readings against the Vietnam War created in him the hunger for celebrity and attention that characterized his later career. This historical episode was therefore doubly ironic for Bly. The political events that cheapened the poetry of so many of his contemporaries invigorated his work, while the occasion for his national fame eventually created the conditions for his literary decline. The politician produced a poet of rare quality just as the shaman degenerated into a showman.

One sees this transformation in the poems from *The Light Around the Body* and the pamphlet *The Teeth Mother Naked at Last* (1970). Several things happen there that rarely occur in his other work. First, the language breaks out of the monotonously literary diction of his "country" poems. Fresh, unexpected words and images appear. Second, the languid mood and syntax of the earlier poems give way to an urgency and excitement. Third, a powerful, illuminating anger disperses the fuzzy sentimentalism that weakens so much of his other work. Finally, Bly's view now broadens from his narrow private concerns to confront the rest of humanity. The poems no longer confine themselves to the easy juxtaposition of the poet alone with nature. They face the difficult world of human history. Bly seemed to be developing from the minor mode of his early work into a major new identity. In the process he wrote a few of the most stunning political poems in American literature—strange, frightening pieces like "Romans Angry About the Inner World," "Johnson's Cabinet Watched by Ants," and especially "The Teeth Mother Naked at Last" (which, like many of the *Selected Poems,* has now been significantly revised by the author). Here Bly truly created a new type of American poem, driven by stunning images and startling associational connections for which nothing earlier in the national literature fully prepared one:

> Massive engines lift beautifully from the deck.
> Wings appear over the trees, wings with eight hundred rivets.
>
> Engines burning a thousand gallons of gasoline a minute sweep
>   over the huts with dirt floors.
> Chickens feel the fear deep in the pits of their beaks.
> Buddha and Padma Sambhava.

Meanwhile out on the China Sea
immense gray bodies are floating,
born in Roanoke,
the ocean to both sides expanding, "buoyed on the dense marine."

Helicopters flutter overhead. The death-
bee is coming. Super Sabres
like knots of neurotic energy sweep
around and return.
This is Hamilton's triumph.
This is the triumph of a centralized bank.
B-52s come from Guam. Teachers
die in flames. The hopes of Tolstoy fall asleep in the ant heap.
Do not ask for mercy.

Unfortunately, this exciting phase lasted only a few years. By the time "The Teeth Mother Naked at Last" appeared in the volume *Sleepers Joining Hands* (1973), Bly's political poetry had already dulled into a method as monotonous as his "country" poems. Bly's immense facility had again proven his undoing. The once-frightening juxtaposition of myth and politics had become another easy routine. The new style and content were roughly similar to the best poems from *The Light Around the Body,* but the intensity and surprise had vanished. From now on Bly's writing becomes depressing to survey. When he risks large new themes, as in the long poem "Sleepers Joining Hands," the work fails (as even he now senses, having broken this "too expansive and excitable" long poem into a number of shorter pieces in the *Selected Poems*). More often Bly remains content to revisit familiar themes with increasingly less compression and precision. A book like *This Tree Will Be Here For a Thousand Years* (1979) repeats self-consciously the mode of *Silence in the Snowy Fields.* Nor was this sentimental journey enough. As one of Bly's notes in *Selected Poems* makes clear, a third volume of "country poems" is on its way. This retrenchment would be less disappointing if Bly could still handle this mode as well as he did earlier in his career. Instead, one sees a decline in quality, as well as a failure of real imaginative growth.

Bly's failure to build on the achievement of his best poems and his subsequent decline into self-parody make *Selected Poems* a major disappointment. Whatever my reservations about Bly, I like the sensibility behind the work. I admire most of his basic values. I delight in his energy and irreverence. I want him to bring his poems to life—to dazzle, frighten, and move me. Instead I read page after page of predictable, edifying poetic exercises. The experience would not be quite so bad if I did not hear the author so energetically applauding his own performances. Bly insists on being judged as a major poet, but his verse cannot bear the weight of that demand.

There is nothing subtle in Bly's bid for major stature. He has unabashedly organized his *Selected Poems* to demonstrate his own importance. He argues for this position overtly by chronicling each and every change in his poetry and equating them with growth. (One of the most interesting critical assumptions currently prevalent seems to be that the more a poet changes his work the more he grows in stature.) For Bly there is no subject so thoroughly engrossing as himself, and in recent years even his literary criticism, once so exciting and iconoclastic, has veered into pious autobiography. In *Selected Poems* this compulsion to annotate his own work proceeds unchecked by the Harper & Row editorial department. In only 204 pages of text the author has provided no fewer than eleven substantial prose commentaries. There is an introduction for each of the nine sections of the book, plus two "afterthoughts" at the end, short essays that link the poet's technique with that of Smart, Blake, Whitman, Baudelaire, Ponge, and Jiménez. Of course, a *Selected Poems* should advertise a poet's achievement. Usually a volume accomplishes this by presenting an author's best poems and letting the reader evaluate them. From the organization of this book, however, it would seem that Bly distrusts either his readers or his own work.

What use is poetry that cannot speak to its contemporary audience without the support of intermediary prose? Perhaps these insistent commentaries are only the miscalculations of an overly eager author. But in Bly's case even a sympathetic reader may begin to wonder about what is really going on. Reading the commentary in this volume is like watching a ball game from the stands while listening to someone describe it on the radio. The announcer, however, seems to be describing an altogether different game, one much more exciting than the humdrum contest down on the field. One should not be too surprised, though. It is just that gift for self-marketing that has built Bly's successful career. Some readers enjoy the sales pitch enough to accept the poetry on faith. I advise a more critical reading of these *Selected Poems.* There are a few breathtaking moments here, as well as many quiet revelations. If only one did not have to push through all the dullness and pretension to find them or shut out the author's eager guided tours along the way. Bly's best poems make this volume worth the effort, but, unfortunately, it is an effort.

Short Views

—

"... trust in God
And take short views."

—W. H. AUDEN

IF YOU WANT TO WRITE about new poetry for magazines and news-papers, you will usually be obliged to undertake "omnibus" reviews. The format requires you to discuss between three and a dozen individual volumes together under a common heading like "Christmas Poetry Picks" or "Eleven New Voices." The more humane journals like the *Hudson Review* allow you to pick most of the books for discussion. The journal sends forty or fifty freshly printed collections, and you sift through them to find the most interesting offerings.

I have done more omnibus reviews than I care to remember. They require an immense amount of time. They pay miserably. And they usually attract little attention. They are, in short, the very model of poetry criticism. Omnibus reviews, however, do offer one genuine advantage to the critic. They broaden his or her sense of what is actually being written—the good, the bad, and the unendurably awful. One always finishes these overviews with a new appreciation for one's ignorance of the full diversity of contemporary poetry, and that awareness is healthy for any critic.

I offer a few selections from the many group reviews I have done. Since there seemed no point in reprinting my more conventional opinions, I have deliberately chosen books about which my judgment differed from the critical consensus.

1. John Ashbery

SHADOW TRAIN will change no one's mind about John Ashbery's merits as a poet. His admirers will praise the newfound discipline and concentration in this collection of sixteen-line, "sonnet-like" poems. His detractors will grumble about the emperor's new briefs. And the rest will continue to play Pontius Pilate, washing their hands of the whole matter. Yet *Shadow Train* is an interesting book that can give a careful reader a new understanding of Ashbery's strengths and weaknesses as a poet.

Part of the pleasure of reading Ashbery comes from the variety of words, images, moods, and styles he can fit so seamlessly into his work. He continually surprises one with things not usually found in a poem. *Shadow Train* encompasses everything from Warren G. Harding to the Keystone Kops, from the idea of God to the "Image of the Little Match Girl." He can move convincingly from pathos to low humor in the same stanza or turn a piece of slang into a remarkable metaphor. Yet sometimes this diversity works against him. He often indulges in gross sentimentality, and though he tries to distance it with an ironic title, as in "Some Old Tires," the burden of his clichés sometimes sinks the entire poem:

> This was mine, and I let it slip through my fingers.
> Nevertheless, I do not want, in this airy and pleasant city,
> To be held back by valors that were mine
> Only for the space of a dream instant . . .

It takes more than irony to save this sort of writing, but these obvious lapses are rare. Ashbery's pervasive sentimentality is usually better balanced by flashes of wit or at least the pleasant chiaroscuro of deliberate ambiguity. Even in "Some Old Tires" he later partially redeems himself with lines like ". . . To have always / Had the wind for a friend is no recommendation." Elsewhere he cleverly describes "angels elbowing each other on the head of a pin." His usual style is nostalgic but in a suave and worldly way—the tone of a man who has seen it all stoically looking back on life.

> Another season, proposing a name and a distant resolution.
> And, like the wind, all attention. Those thirsting ears,

Climbers on what rickety heights, have swept you
All alone into their confession, for it is as alone

Each of us stands and surveys this empty cell of time . . .

("The Ivory Tower")

As *Shadow Train* demonstrates, Ashbery still has a good ear for spoken language. While there is not much traditional music in his recent poetry, it bristles with striking lines and phrases. This gift is felicitous, natural phrasing is the key to Ashbery's unique sound. Whereas most poets use the stressed word or the metrical foot for their rhythmic unit, Ashbery uses the larger unit of the phrase. This choice gives his verse its speed and distinctively supple rhythms. This practice also has its dangers. In his longer poems it can allow Ashbery's complex syntax to run away with him. The self-imposed limits of *Shadow Train* (fifty short poems of identical length) keep him from spinning the elegant camouflage that typifies his longer work. Here one can see how Ashbery's imagination works. Since the poems are short enough to be seen as a whole, their underlying structure, usually so elusive, becomes clearer than before. The abrupt transitions from scene to scene, image to image, are now easier to follow. They may still seem arbitrary, but at least now one can hold both unrelated parts in mind for comparison.

Shadow Train therefore shows the same Ashbery as *Self-Portrait in a Convex Mirror* or *Houseboat Days* but in a form that is easier to grasp. He is still not a poet one would recommend without reservations, but at least this volume provides a manageable introduction to his prolific and difficult work. If one is prepared to approach him uncritically, he is very entertaining, but his work must not be read so much as overheard—like an attractive voice talking at another table. Under scrutiny, however, his elegant poems often seem arbitrary and overlong. Their unity is mainly stylistic. Their meaning is in their method.

Ashbery is a discursive poet without a subject. Although he deals indirectly with several recurrent themes, themes that have become increasingly dark and personal as he has grown older, the poems are mainly the surface play of words and images. One never remembers ideas from an Ashbery poem, one recalls the tones and textures. If ideas are dealt with at all, they are present only as faint echoes heard remotely in some turn of phrase. Ideas in Ashbery are like the melodies in some jazz improvisation where the musicians have left out the original tune to avoid paying royalties. They are wild variations on a missing theme with only the original chord changes as a clue. This sort of music can be fun as long as someone doesn't try to analyze it like a Beethoven symphony. A skillful and sympathetic critic like Helen Vendler can trace major themes in Ashbery, but somehow in reading him, even repeatedly, one does not see the deeper side of his work emerge so satisfactorily. Despite the awards and attention, he lacks the weight of the major poet his defenders claim he has become. Paradoxically, his work becomes more pleasurable and interesting the fewer claims one makes for it. He is a marvelous minor poet, but an uncomfortable major one.

2. Margaret Atwood

MARGARET ATWOOD'S *Two-Headed Poems* are full of interesting ideas, memorable images, and intelligent observations. She has a deep understanding of human motivation, and her poetry deals naturally with the intricate sort of psychology most poets ignore. Her poems are often painfully accurate when dealing with the relationships between men and women or mothers and daughters. She also has the experienced novelist's skill of putting complex situations into clear and satisfying shapes. And yet with all these strengths, Atwood is rarely an effective poet. She writes poetry with ideas and images, not with words. Her language, through flawless by prose standards, lies dead on the page. Her poems have a conceptual and structural integrity, but the words never build the heightened sense of awareness one looks for in poetry. The problem centers on her rhythms, not only the movement of words and syllables within the line, but also the larger rhythms of the poem, the movements from line to line and stanza to stanza. While the sequence of her ideas works beautifully, her language never gains force.

One notices the curious neutrality of Atwood's language most clearly in her sequence of prose poems, "Marrying the Hangman," which obliquely tells the story of Françoise Laurent, a woman sentenced to death for stealing who legally avoids punishment by convincing the man in the next cell to become a hangman and then marrying him. (Atwood uses a real historic incident here, but the plot still seems like something out of a forgotten Mascagni opera.) The language in these prose poems is not different from the language of her verse, except that it has no line breaks. It most resembles a passage of elevated prose, like an excerpt from Joan Didon's histrionic *Book of Common Prayer.* Returning to the poems, one finds the same windy quality. Images are used in a profligate, casual way. The line breaks add little force to the rhythms.

The few times in *Two-Headed Poems* that Atwood's language condenses into genuinely arresting cadences, the results are fresh and convincing, as in "Foretelling the Future," which begins:

> It doesn't matter how it's done,
> these hints, these whispers:
>
> Whether it is some god
> blowing through your head
> as through a round bone
> flute, or bright
> stones fallen on the sand . . .

But such moments come too rarely. Imaginative in conception, these *Two-Headed Poems* are mostly flat and perfunctory in execution. If images and ideas alone could make poetry, Atwood would be a major poet.

3. Jared Carter

TOO OFTEN in reading a new book of poetry, one wonders why the author has bothered to include many of the poems. Most books are full of superfluous material—pieces of botched intention, false direction, or middling intensity, pieces that read more like exercises than poems. How many books would be twice as good at half the length, especially those by authors who insist on collecting nearly every scrap they write and force their readers to become their editors? Is it any wonder that readers become fiercely loyal to the writers who never waste their time, to poets like Philip Larkin or Elizabeth Bishop, who never collect a superfluous poem?

Yet even in a period of loose standards, some poets refuse to make easy compromises; they wait years for a book to find its inevitable shape. There are no superfluous poems in Jared Carter's *Work, for the Night Is*

Coming, which The Academy of American Poets chose for its 1980 Walt Whitman Award. Publishing this first book at the age of forty-two, Carter has made a memorable debut. From beginning to end, this volume has the quiet passion of conviction, the voice of a poet who knows exactly what he wants to say and how to say it.

Work, for the Night Is Coming is unusually unified, especially for a collection that spans many years of an author's development. Behind the range of styles and approaches, one recognizes a single honest and contemporary voice. The book is also unified by the people and places it describes; all of the poems with specific locations are set in Indiana, where Carter was born and still lives. Working in the tradition of *Winesburg, Ohio* and the *Spoon River Anthology,* he has created Mississinewa County, an imaginary landscape of small towns and family farms that seems more real than most actual places.

Carter's characteristic tone is elegiac. Aware of how much the Midwest has changed during his lifetime, he writes out of a deeply felt desire to preserve the landscape and people of this world. His subject matter is the culture of small-town Indiana, although "culture" is not the word one would normally use in describing places that seem so average. Talking about local customs, legends, buildings, and people, he creates a richly populated world in the process of passing away. A typical poem is "Monument City," in which the poet visits a favorite aunt whose house is being destroyed to make room for a reservoir. Describing the last evening spent waiting there for the rain to clear, so that a family friend (the local undertaker) can take a photograph of the house, Carter preserves all that is about to vanish in this woman's life. It is a quiet but extraordinary moment, made even stronger by another poem nearby that describes how the same undertaker must supervise the moving of a graveyard that will also be flooded by the reservoir.

Even when he is writing about supposedly neutral objects, Carter imbues them with personal importance, usually the human necessity to believe that something one does will resist Time. In "Geodes," for example, the crystallized stones he collects gradually become his own poems as well. It begins:

> They are useless, there is nothing
> To be done with them, no reason, only

The finding: letting myself down holding
To ironwood and the dry bristle of roots

Into the creekbed, into clear water . . .

And ends:

. . . It is all waiting there in the darkness.

I want to know only that things gather themselves
With great patience, that they do this forever.

Reading Carter, one notices how elegiac the poetry of small Midwestern towns has been from the beginning. Starting with the *Spoon River Anthology,* this poetry has shown how vulnerable these human communities are in comparison to the great natural spaces around them. It was as if even the earliest settlers knew that their children wouldn't stay on, but would soon go running off to Chicago or California. Today the landscape cries out for a poet to explain what has happened, to reconcile the empty storefronts, abandoned farmhouses, and miles of lonely highways to those who have stayed on.

There are so many good poems in *Work, for the Night Is Coming* that it makes no sense to list them all, but it is interesting to note the kind of successes Carter achieves. He never manages a really dazzling triumph in any one poem, but rather brings off one modest success after another. A poet who waited forty-two years to publish his first book must often have wondered if it was worthwhile to bide his time and perfect his craft. The answer in Carter's case is an unqualified yes.

4. James Dickey

JAMES DICKEY is understandably one of the most widely read poets in America. He has probably done as much as any living writer to broaden the subject matter of our poetry. His contributions have come not from searching out exotic areas of the American experience, but from bringing over the mythology of the Southern redneck into poetry—complete with all its lurid trimmings of drunkenness, brutality, sex, and ignorance. Dickey created a new literary landscape that, however un-attractive, still seemed both credible and relevant to contemporary read-ers. His was a poetry about Americans who didn't go abroad, unless they were drafted—a poetry that found stranger things in backwoods Georgia than in remotest Asia. He wrote about people one had met in real life but had never before encountered in verse—telephone linemen, foot-ball players, airline stewardesses, Baptist preachers—and in pieces like "Lifeguard," "The Sheep Child," "The Scarred Girl," and "Cherrylog Road," he created a powerful, original, and utterly American kind of poetry.

Another rarely acknowledged source of Dickey's popularity is his be-lief that heroism is still possible in the normal course of American life. While most American poets have created characters who seem like varia-tions on E. A. Robinson's hard-drinking fatalist, Miniver Cheevey, Dickey filled his work with extroverted, active men—hunters, soldiers, athletes, truck drivers—who managed to assert their individuality in a hostile world, sometimes by risking their lives in elemental acts of courage, sometimes merely by doing their difficult, thankless jobs. While certain critics have found the particular form of Dickey's heroics too *macho* to endorse, his values have certainly struck a responsive chord in many read-ers from Hollywood to the White House.

From such an author one has high expectations, but what is one to make of Dickey's much-heralded new volume of eighteen interconnected love poems, *Puella*? Although it has been widely praised, and sections of it have already won the prestigious Levinson Prize from *Poetry,* the new book is an unqualified disaster.

The dedication of *Puella* reads "To Deborah—/*her girlhood, male imag-ined,*" and the book is a series of poems in which Dickey muses on the life his young wife led before they met. Each section begins with a vague, at-mospheric title (e.g., "Deborah, Moon, Mirror, Right Hand Rising") and immediately plunges into a wild imagistic reverie:

> Rising behind me
> And coming into my right hand
>
> Is the wide-open collisionless color of the whole night
> Ringed-in, pure surface.   All pores cold with cream,

> I have reached the bright reception of my palm, the full
> Steady of the oval,
>
> Afterglowing in the hang-time of my image . . .

It takes a certain genius to write this badly. Unfortunately, this passage is typical of the entire book. The language is lyric, impassioned, and consummately imprecise. The image Dickey conjures up here could have been very beautiful—a young woman preparing for bed catches the reflection of the moon rising behind her face in a hand mirror. But his language obscures the image with a profusion of tired verbal tricks—arbitrarily compounded words ("Afterglowing in the hang-time"), hopelessly vague description ("the wide-open collisionless color"), and clumsy wordplay ("All pores cold with cream"). These strained, self-conscious local effects dominate the language of *Puella* so completely that it is frequently impossible to make out the general sense of a passage—the whole is so hidden by its parts. Dickey seems so enraptured by his subject that he has lost all perspective. He sees each emotionally charged scene too clearly to imagine that his readers might have trouble understanding what is happening. Ironically, Dickey, once the most extroverted poet in America, has become a solipsist.

The poems in *Puella* are private and provisional—a random parade of images that the reader can dimly observe but never quite construe. Nor do repeated readings help. The more one scrutinizes the language of *Puella,* the more it seems improvised and approximate, nothing but pure, old-fashioned Southern sound and fury. Dickey demands that the reader surrender to the flow of the lines, but unfortunately they lack the purely lyric beauty necessary to seduce the reader's reason away from their puzzling sense. In fact, the organizing principle of Dickey's language often seems more visual than auditory, with the idiosyncratic placement of words and phrases on the page frequently crippling the underlying rhythms.

Sometimes even grammar itself collapses under the weight of so much lyricism. Consider the beginning of "Veer-Voices: Two Sisters Under Crows" (often even the titles don't make much sense). The poem's opening sentence reads like a word-for-word translation from an inflected dead language.

> Sometimes are living those who have been seen
>   Together   those farthest leaning
>   With some dark birds and fielded
> Below them   countercrying and hawing in savage openness
>   For every reason.

When a poet as talented as Dickey writes a book as muddled as
Puella, one must wonder what went wrong. Here, I think, Dickey mis-
judged his talents by choosing an extended lyric form (what the ancients
would have called a dithyramb) when his poetic gifts are primarily narrative and dramatic. His gift for language *per se* has always been limited.
His best poems have usually been based on arresting characters or situations, and their power has come primarily from the psychological particulars of the human scene they describe. By contrast, the girl in *Puella*
remains a misty, unrealized presence, an *Ewig-Weibliche* already assumed
into heaven rather than one of the flesh-and-blood, earthbound people
of Dickey's strongest poetry. *Puella* also lacks any underlying dramatic
sense that would have placed the details of the poems in perspective.
Dickey tries to place the poems with specific titles and subtitles, but such
framing devices are not enough to hold the verse together. They help
only because without them the reader usually would have no idea whatsoever what the poems are about. *Puella* is a sad book, saddest of all for
Dickey's admirers.

5. Tom Disch

THERE HAS BEEN a great deal of talk lately about a rebirth of formal
poetry. Over the past two years the literary press has singled out several
young poets with particular praise for their command of traditional technique. Meanwhile, several older poets like John Frederick Nims and
George Starbuck—formerly *poetae non grati*—have reissued their out-of-
print work to generally favorable reviews. Rhymed poems have begun to
reappear in all the wrong magazines, and (as always happens during the
revolution) the recent past is being subtly rewritten by the new conspira-
tors, with the reputations of once neglected formal poets like Edward
Thomas, Louise Bogan, and even Roy Campbell being revived.

The most unusual of the younger formal poets is probably Tom Disch,
whose third and best collection, *Burn This,* has just appeared in London.

Although Disch is well known in this country as a science-fiction writer, only one volume of his poetry has been published here (and that one by an Iowa fine press in a limited edition). Disch's lack of acceptance in the poetry world is not altogether surprising, however. Genre writers with serious ambitions are viewed with extreme suspicion and condescension by the literary establishment.

As if his literary credentials weren't dubious enough already, Disch's poetry is as unusual as his background. One could virtually use *Burn This* to define the current mainstream of contemporary poetry dialectically through its opposites, so consistently antithetical is its approach from contemporary practice. Disch is concerned primarily with ideas not emotions (the free play of ideas, that is, not any particular ideology). His subjects are rarely personal, except insofar as Disch represents himself as what Auden once called the "average thinking man." He therefore cultivates a general rather than a private voice. His tone is cosmopolitan and public rather than intimate and sincere. The structure of his poems more often depends on the logical progression of his ideas than on the associational links of his images. His natural manner is witty and discursive, not serious and lyrical. Most of his poems fall into traditional forms and genres, not the preferred nonce forms of contemporary poetics (when he does adopt the forms of contemporary poetry, it is almost always for parody). And, most amazingly, one gathers in reading him that Disch is more interested in writing verse than poetry (though there is certainly no surer way to good poetry than to begin by producing good verse). In short, Disch is every bit at one with his age as John Dryden would be in a surrealist café.

Like most good verse, the poems in *Burn This* have the virtues of clarity, grace, wit, and intelligence. Poetry may prosper in an atmosphere of dark and subjective innocence, but verse needs the informed perspective of maturity. Reading through this book, one experiences a type of pleasure that is unusual for a book of poems. One enjoys what is being said as much as how it is being said. There is real paraphrasable substance in these poems, and the flow of ideas is never predictable. Disch has not only a first-class mind but also a highly original one. One sees this originality most clearly when he discusses literature—and indeed fully half the poems in this volume directly concern literature and the imagination. Poetry about literature, especially poems about writing poems, can be excruciatingly dull (witness the work of some of our most decorated contemporaries). But Disch's quick mind, his lively sense of humor, and his unique perspective on serious literature (being as he is an illegal immigrant from across the literary Rio Grande that separates serious from popular writing) turn these poems into compelling reading.

The overall structure of the volume is no less lucid than the style of its individual poems. *Burn This* is divided into five discrete sections, each of which exploits different poetic forms and genres. Part 1, entitled "Homages," contains poems written in borrowed styles including parodies of A. R. Ammons, Joyce Kilmer, Walt Whitman, Robert Bly, and Robert Creeley. Part 2, "The Life of Poetry, and Lives of the Poets," is made up of intellectual light verse that speculates on the sources of poetry. Part 3 is all sonnets. Part 4 exploits a common form of contemporary poetry, the pseudo-instructional poem, which purports to explain some activity—usually elemental—to the uninitiated listener. Disch handles this form brilliantly, creating a series of "instructions" on poetics, including two poems that seem to me as good as didactic verse can possibly be: "Ars Poetica," a discussion of the practice and aesthetics of haiku written in a haiku stanza, and "The Thirty-nine Articles," a remarkable sestina about the challenge of writing a sestina. Finally, the book concludes with "Theories," a set of long discursive poems on literature, the best of which are "On Science Fiction," and "Literature as a Career," which ends with a defense of self-supporting writers like himself:

> So sell it, and don't feel ashamed.
> If the world, in the form
> Of critic or poet, asks who we are
> And why our wages are higher than his
> (If they are), answer his question politely
> And say we are tailors who fit out the minds
> Of paying multitudes eager to wear
> Whatever our beloved emperor appeared in
> Yesterday. Or say, if such hyperbole won't do,
> That we are failures who would give
> A pound of bloodless intellect to live
> Among the Imagination's upper-middle classes
> On the franchised slopes of Mount Parnassus.
> Say what you will, however absurd,
> But see that they pay you a penny a word.

With all the mediocre volumes of poetry issued in this country each year, it is shocking that a book this strong and original had to go to England for a publisher.

6. Maxine Kumin

OUR GROUND TIME HERE WILL BE BRIEF provides a comprehensive selection from Maxine Kumin's six previous books of verse, including her Pulitzer Prize–winning volume, *Up Country,* in addition to twenty-nine new poems. Kumin is understandably a popular poet. She is an intelligent and sensitive person who writes on the enduring themes of life and death, place and family. Essentially a domestic poet, she takes as her material the world of her everyday life in rural New Hampshire—her home, children, neighbors, land, and animals, especially horses, which she has loved since girlhood. She is a strong woman whose independence is natural, not ideological, and the usual modesty of her tone does not hide her underlying self-assurance. She writes confidently about what she knows—the death of friends, the departures of her children, the landscape around her—and she does so honestly and directly without striking fashionable postures.

Even when she tries a trick in a poem, as in this passage from "The Retrieval System," it seems candid and unimpeachable:

> I remember the funeral. *The Lord is my shepherd,*
> we said. I don't want to brood. Fact: it is people who fade,
> it is animals that retrieve them. A boy
> I loved once keeps coming back as my yearling colt,
> cocksure at the gallop, racing his shadow
> for the hell of it. He runs merely to be.
> A boy who was lost in the war thirty years ago
> and buried at sea.

There is much to enjoy in Kumin's volume, especially among the new poems. Her readers will be glad to see further reports on her engaging neighbor, Henry Manley, the eighty-two-year-old Yankee bachelor, whose presence has enlivened Kumin's poetry since his first appearance in *The Nightmare Factory.* There is also a very moving group of poems about her brother and his brave struggle against the crippling nervous disease that killed him, and there is an affecting elegy for her friend, Anne Sexton, written "on being interviewed by her biographer." The people in Kumin's poetry come alive. She captures their personalities and makes her affection for them contagious.

Yet with all these strengths, there is a curious thinness to Kumin's verse. She uses language in a skillful but utilitarian way. It is a medium to communicate the facts of her poetry, and even in her formal poems one finds little evidence of joy in language for its own sake. The rhymes seem forced and incidental, the metrical pattern filled out rather than exploited. Even Kumin's most lyrical outbursts sound flat and perfunctory, as in the climax to "Sunbathing on a Rooftop in Berkeley":

> O summers without end, the exact truth is
> we are expanding sideways as haplessly
> as in the mirrors of the Fun House.
> We bulge toward the separate fates that await us
> sometimes touching, as sleeves will, whether
> or not a hug was intended.

Perhaps it is this dependence on "the exact truth" that sets the limits on Kumin's achievement. When her poems succeed, they do so mainly on the strength of the characters they introduce, the scenes they describe, the stories they tell. While her language presents the subject matter clearly enough, it rarely heightens it sufficiently to make the exact words definitive. Her poems are moving without being memorable. Ultimately Kumin is a writer who has applied her diligence more to exploring her own life than to the possibilities of her medium. The truth is an honorable limit for a poet to set on her work; nonetheless, it does at times remain a limit.

7. Radcliffe Squires

MANY NEW BOOKS of poetry are interesting. Some are entertaining. A handful are really memorable. But how rarely a new book comes along that is so exciting that it leaves one slightly dizzy. Nothing in Radcliffe Squires's first five books of poetry will have prepared readers for *Gardens of the World*. Somehow at the age of sixty-three, long after the point when most writers settle into comfortable repetition, this little-known poet has focused all of his talent into one stunning and original collection. Not that *Gardens of the World* is a perfect book. It contains some poems that seem stiff and mannered. But the good poems are so strong that one forgets the momentary lapses, and the best four or five poems rank, in my opinion, with any new American poems of the last ten years.

The first poem in the book, "One Day in Salamanca," lets the reader know this will be no ordinary collection. The poem describes a strange incident in a Salamanca café where a young beggar threatens to crush a captured sparrow unless an American tourist buys its freedom. Squires turns this anecdote into an amazing parable. The scene, the characters, the action are all brilliantly described. Most collections could not survive an opening this powerful. Everything else would seem anticlimactic. In *Gardens of the World* it sets a high standard that is matched many times. It also establishes the strange tone that dominates the book, which unexpectedly shifts between gentleness and cruelty.

The poems that follow are set mostly in the dry, empty landscapes of the West. Born in Utah, Squires sees the plains and deserts with the unromantic eye of a native. He can masterfully re-create the exact look and feel of a place, but he is not content merely to describe. A landscape exists only insofar as someone sees it, and Squires's Western poems explore the relationship between the human viewer and the inhuman terrain. He understands how people cannot watch a place without somehow transforming it, however subtly, into subjective human terms. Squires's landscape poems are his most openly personal ones. By defining his relation to the natural world, he defines himself. In "Chasms" the landscape becomes a symbol for human imperfection and mortality:

> I wonder why we come again and again
> To these places where footpaths suddenly end,
> And beneath us lies a chasm. Sometimes it is
> A sea like a vast grapevine.
> We watch, its veined, overlapping leaves
> Shifting out of phase until they break at the horizon.
> Sometimes we come to these great holes
> In the desert where nothing shifts at all,
> And, it seems, will never shift again and yet
> Remains all unfinished.

In passages like this, one hears Squires's unmistakable voice. It is calm, insistent, and authoritative. The rhythms are strong but conversational, and no matter how complex the syntax, one never loses track of the sense. Though there is often a subtle metrical system at work (the passage above is based on a four-stress line), one rarely notices it since the rhythms follow natural speech patterns so closely. Metaphors are used sparingly, but when introduced, they are carefully placed and elaborated. One always has the sense of a single, insinuatingly familiar, and worldly voice behind the lines—the voice of an old man without illusions but still sensual and alert.

The last section of Squires's book is a series of nine interrelated poems each re-creating a visit to a mythological garden. On the basis of these pieces alone I feel that Squires deserves consideration as one of the finest American poets writing today. They are overwhelming. Packed with so many arresting scenes, images, characters, and ideas, they are impossible to take in all at once. Reading them, one experiences a sense of excitement mixed with awe that one rarely gets with contemporary poetry. No, they are not quite a masterpiece. They have occasional flaws and miscalculations, and after a dozen readings, I am still not convinced that they form an integrated sequence. But at their best, as in "The Garden of Medusa" and "The Garden of Hecate," they are among the finest and most original new poems I have read in years.

Each of the Garden poems presents the end of a journey—a journey inward climaxing in a mysterious confrontation. The form of the poems is quasi-dramatic. Written in the present tense, they project the reader into the scene and force him through the action of the poem. While each garden is similar in that it becomes the scene of the action, each has an appearance and atmosphere different from the others. The Garden of Hecate, for example, is a quiet, untended spot haunted by an undefinably sinister force:

> The gate is heavy and the hinge stubborn, but
> It is not locked. Lean on it with all
> Your being. It will give just enough
> For you to enter and pass under the white poplar tree
> From which albino worms descend on glittering threads.

Each garden is not just a landscape but a troubling symbol for memory and imagination. If it can be visited, the arrival is not without risk.

Squires explores the fine line between self-discovery and self-destruction. What one sees in the mirror may be more than one expects. The vision of one's destiny may be of death. And yet even death may become an alluring temptation, as in "The Garden of Medusa" where the dead champions, who have looked on the Gorgon's face, acquire a terrifying beauty:

> . . . where those who were turned
> To stone still stand. How beautifully they
> Have weathered. The grasp has run from the hands.
> Frail honeycomb of limestone shows in the hollowed
> Cheek. And the eyes, hardly eyes now,
> More nearly birds' eggs nested in stone, are all
> Turned calmly in the same direction. It is as if
> Sunlight had broken through the roof of the
> Underworld, and all the dead had forgotten
> Their living sins as wind and rain moved on them.
> You may, after all, choose to forget the mirror and
> See what the face really looks like.

These lush, mythical gardens stand in contrast to the dry, open landscapes of Squires's Western poems, and in some ways they represent the two sides of his imagination—the visionary and the realistic, the Western American and the classicist. There is ultimately no dichotomy, however. Each type of poem makes the same journey in a different direction. The desert poems, which begin so realistically, typically end in a quiet visionary moment, just as the gardens for all their intricate fantasy often turn out to be inhabited by worldly individuals. As different as they seem on the surface, both types of poem confront the same question—how does man, who is created by history, escape from it? Squires has written critical studies of two American poets who have little in common except their position as dark, philosophic loners—Robert Frost and Robinson Jeffers—and he, too, shares their determined individuality. He is a philosophic poet who has no need for easy answers. And like Frost or Jeffers, he is complex without being difficult, serious without being pointlessly depressing. It has taken him a lifetime of experience and forty years of writing to translate his vision as successfully as in *Gardens of the World*. This is not a book to ignore.

8. Theodore Weiss

VIEWS AND SPECTACLES is an extremely severe selection of Theodore Weiss's shorter works. From his seven published volumes, Weiss has chosen only thirty-five poems to outline in his career, adding a few new pieces to bring the volume up to date. He has omitted many well-known poems and excluded his longer work entirely, except for a few excerpts treated as independent poems. While this approach may have some disadvantages, it does provide the new reader with a manageable entrée into Weiss's often intimidating work, as well as give the familiar reader fresh perspective on his unique achievement.

Almost every commentator on Weiss's work has made the same observation: he is not easy to read. Although at first sight there are no overwhelming difficulties in his work, no long untranslated passages in Greek or cryptic typographical arrangements on the page, there are some essential qualities that make it strenuous reading. Each poem tries to do something different, explores a new subject or finds an unexpected way of expressing itself. Intellectual, allusive, and complex, he is a learned man who does not hesitate to show erudition in his work.

The restless quality of Weiss's imagination demonstrates itself in the complex, dynamic syntax that is the most important and original feature of his style. For Weiss, syntax has become a way of thinking. It not only drives the rhythm of the poem but also controls the movement of images and ideas. Sentences stretch themselves across lines, building phrase upon phrase, image upon image, holding fragments of perception together in uneasy equilibrium, via colons, commas, and dashes. Weiss pushes syntax to its extreme until the reader sees ideas and images in a new relationship, hears words and phrases in a new way. The effect is one of extreme, indeed dangerous, compression. So much verbal and intellectual energy is contained that the poems sometimes seem about to explode into sharp, fiery fragments.

Poetry committed to compression and innovation risks many failures, and even in a carefully selected volume like *Views and Spectacles* Weiss does not always succeed in controlling his dynamic experiments. But, when he does succeed, he achieves poems of excitement and originality. Weiss is one of the few American poets of his generation who has created new verse rhythms. Many poets started out, as he did, from Pound and Williams, but most of them never achieved such a personal sound.

One notices what makes Weiss's work so individual more easily in his complex poems, but even at his most accessible, in poems like the justly celebrated "The Fire of Alexandria," one sees all the characteristic qualities—its strong conception, learning, wit, and rhythmic originality (an originality all the more remarkable for coming through in a poem written, uncharacteristically, in iambic pentameter):

> Imagine it, a Sophocles complete,
> the lost epic of Homer, including no doubt
> his notes, his journals, and his observations
> on blindness. But what occupies me most,
> with the greatest hurt of grandeur, are those
> magnificent authors, kept in scholarly rows,
> whose names we have no passing record of:
> scrolls unrolling Aphrodite like Cleopatra
> bundled in a rug, the spoils of love.

Perhaps this sort of poetry—thick with allusion, spiced with scholarship—is difficult for some readers. I find it exciting. How good to see intelligence combined with passion, and imagination provoked by scholarship. However much we pretend otherwise, poetry is a bookish art, and learning for most poets is as essential an experience as travel or romance. *Views and Spectacles* demonstrates how intimately related love and learning can become in poetry.

The Difficult Case
of Howard Moss

—

FOR NEARLY FORTY YEARS Howard Moss was one of the most famous figures in contemporary American poetry. He published twelve collections of verse, three volumes of criticism, and two plays, as well as several anthologies. He won the National Book Award and the *Nation*'s Lenore Marshall Prize in Poetry. His work appears in most anthologies of contemporary verse. His poems were also frequently set to music by distinguished American composers. Moss, however, was best known as the poetry editor of the *New Yorker,* a position he held for thirty-eight years. The magazine's preeminence and Moss's long tenure on its staff made him the only poetry editor most American writers knew by name. But fame, as the proverb warns, can be a double-edged sword, and for Moss the notoriety he achieved as one of the most perceptive judges of other people's verse served not only to obscure his own accomplishments as a poet but also frequently to distort them through irrelevant literary politics.

The *New Yorker* casts a long shadow over its contributors, and the epithet "*New Yorker* author" followed even E. B. White and John Cheever to their graves, as if they had never done more than master some common house style. Moss's own obituary in the *New York Times* spent more time discussing *New Yorker* editorial policy than examining his career as a writer. Moss's long association with the *New Yorker* posed even more problems. Not only did he select virtually all of its verse since mid-century, he also published much of his own work there, a situation his detractors never ceased to criticize.

A poetry editor has a difficult time on any magazine. The writers he or she publishes often feel they have only been given their due, while those rejected think that aesthetic blindness or bad taste prevented their work from being chosen. Nowhere is this problem more exaggerated than at the *New Yorker,* which receives over a thousand poems per week and publishes about two. Imagine the cumulative frustration of over 50,000 rejections a year multiplied across nearly four decades, and one understands the difficulty of Moss's position among his fellow poets. Was it any wonder that disinterested views of his own poetry were hard to find?

Moss's real achievements as an editor were rarely understood. His detractors often implied that there had been some golden age of poetry at the *New Yorker* before his arrival. Few realized that when Moss became poetry editor in 1950, the *New Yorker* did not occupy an especially important place for poets, but was best known for its light-verse writers like Ogden Nash, E. B. White, Morris Bishop, and Phyllis McGinley. Before him there had never even been a full-time poetry editor. Moss was responsible for shifting the magazine's focus toward serious, indeed often demanding verse (a shift for which advocates of light verse never forgave him). If the *New Yorker* is now one of the most prestigious showcases for new poetry in America, Moss largely made it so. He not only set high standards but also, more important, made poetry seem central to the magazine's identity, whereas other large journals usually treated verse as filler. As a result, Moss probably did more to shape the mainstream of contemporary American poetry—for both the better and the worse—than any other editor in the past half century. He also helped create the large supportive audience for poetry the *New Yorker* now enjoys.

The list of poets Moss helped bring to prominence is too long to give here, but it includes Elizabeth Bishop, Theodore Roethke, L. E. Sissman, Anne Sexton, Sylvia Plath, Richard Wilbur, Galway Kinnell, James Dickey, John Updike, James Merrill, Mark Strand, Donald Justice, Adrienne Rich, Charles Wright, Amy Clampitt, John Ashbery, W. S. Merwin, and James Wright. Moss's taste was not universal. It did not encompass the extremes of J. V. Cunningham's compressed formality or William Everson's rhapsodic expansion, but his sympathies were impressively broad. Moss could publish Sexton and Wilbur, Sissman and Strand, Rich and Updike side by side. He was also open to new voices. When Kinnell's work was first accepted by the *New Yorker,* he had only two published poems to his name. More recently Moss printed more than a dozen poems by the then unknown Amy Clampitt before her collection, *The Kingfisher,* appeared. He gave many young poets their first broad public exposure.

If he had been only an editor, Moss would have earned a place in the history of American poetry. But he made a more enduring if less cele-brated contribution in his own poetry. That his creative achievement was not well understood does not diminish its importance, though this situa-tion does make his verse difficult to discuss without what may sound to some like special pleading. His professional position placed him in the midst of every debate about the *New Yorker's* oversize influence on poetic reputations, and those controversies colored discussions of his work. They not only left some readers skeptical about both the positive and negative reviews of his poetry, they also made disinterested criticism al-most impossible to write. As a result, Moss's poetry attracted much pub-licity but little serious or sustained criticism. Ironically, only with his death in 1987 did his personal identity as a writer separate from his profes-sional identity as an editor, and the substantial legacy of his poetry begin to be evaluated properly.

How sad to begin a review of Moss's *New Selected Poems,* which sur-veys a poet's lifework, with a digression on the politics of literary reputa-tion, but in this case it seems impossible to discuss the book objectively without confronting the issues that surround it for reader and reviewer alike. The need now, however, is to push those issues aside and concen-trate solely on the poetry. The relevant issues are entirely literary, namely the questions one asks when reading any comprehensive selection of a serious poet's oeuvre. How good is the poetry? What are its particular strengths and weaknesses? Did the author develop over time, and if so, what was the outcome of that change? And, finally, how does this work compare to the best poetry of its time?

New Selected Poems preserves very little from Moss's precocious first collection, *The Wound and the Weather* (1946), which was published when the author was only twenty-four. Moss the veteran editor rightly recognized this book as Moss the poet's weakest volume. The missing poems are well crafted but generally dull. All of Moss's best early work is formal, but here he merely fills in forms rather than reinventing them in his own image. The formal language frequently seems so stiff and second-hand that the occasional echoes of Auden and Stevens sometimes provide the volume's livelier moments:

> I gnarled me where the spinster tree
> Unwound its green hosanna

> And built its sorrow, leaf by knee,
> A lachrymal cabana . . .

But these prosodic high jinks are rare, and the three surviving poems give ample demonstration of Moss's suave but brittle youthful work.

In his second book, *The Toy Fair* (1954), Moss already discovered the pure, intensely lyric style he would develop over the next decade. This style is formal, compressed, and almost preternaturally lucid. Rhyme and meter provide a well-defined basic architecture over which an elaborate sequential syntax is often superimposed. There is also a strong sense of the line, which almost always coincides with some basic unit of syntax, so that while the lines are rarely end-stopped, they move together naturally with the surface meaning of the poem. Usually a limited number of sounds and images is introduced like a set of musical themes that are then developed in focused variations.

Although Moss's early style bears a resemblance to the mainstream fifties formalism of Wilbur, Hecht, or Nemerov, it uses poetic language differently in some crucial respects. Moss's language is less intellectual and ironic, his diction more colloquial and less flamboyant, though equally controlled. If Wilbur had a genius for the unusual word, Moss excelled at using the commonplace one with unexpected clarity. Moss's craftsmanship is no less accomplished than Wilbur's, but he lacks Wilbur's extravagant formal inventiveness. Unlike reading an early Wilbur lyric, one rarely finishes an early Moss poem with the sense of amazement that the poet made some ingenious form work without tripping. Moss mastered quiet rather than virtuoso forms. Finally, he wrote more directly than most of his contemporaries, who often seemed to specialize in approaching personal subjects sideways. The peculiar power of his early poetry comes from the energy needed to balance its intense emotion with the cool precision of the language.

One example of Moss's early *poésie pure* is "Burning Love Letters," which begins:

> I.
> Fire that cancels all that is
> Devours paper and pen,
> And makes of the heart's histories

A cold hearth warm again.
It could as well consume a branch,
Blank paper or black coal
That now, in ashy avalanche,
Scatters the heart whole.

2.
What words led to the end of words?
Coldly, all separate sighs
Shiver in flame, flying upwards,
Merged into burnt lies.
In somersaults of light, words burn
To nothingness, then roll
In dead scrolls, delicate as fern,
Or hiss like a waterfall.

Not only their emotional intensity but also their directness of statement separates these stanzas from contemporary poems by Wilbur (or Hecht or Nemerov). Moss's language is eloquently musical without being lush or exotic. His diction comes from conversational American English but has been purified of both its highest and lowest registers. One finds neither any slang nor erudite vocabulary. Nor are there any allusions beyond the immediate reach of the average reader. The metaphors come from everyday experience. The poem uses universal images organized in immediately apprehensible musical language to create its emotional effect. Technically, this is poetry in the plain style of Jonson or Herrick but used in an uncharacteristically romantic way that few of its other contemporary masters (like Yvor Winters or J. V. Cunningham) would have found comfortable. Compare the dramatic end of Moss's poem with Cunningham's dispassionate epigram on essentially the same theme:

Love's ashes lie and will not rise
As fire dies to a black sun
And makes of the heart's histories
A warm hearth cold again.
Cremation's scattered dust confronts

Dead vision, and in these
Ashes I write your name once,
Bending on cold knees.

                                                    (Moss)

The once hooked ever after lives in lack,
And the once said never finds its way back.

                                                    (Cunningham)

Both poets use language similarly. They write with clarity and precision in a purified colloquial English. They also seem to share a common human experience behind the poem. Cunningham's speaker removes himself from this highly charged emotional experience to universalize it in perfectly phrased abstractions, whereas Moss's persona speaks directly out of the experience to dramatize it in emotional terms. Obviously, neither approach is intrinsically superior. They are, however, essentially different, despite the similarity of the language that embodies them.

In his early work, therefore, Moss created a powerfully individual lyric style that used the formal elements of mainstream fifties verse to different ends. Unlike the work of his most distinguished contemporaries, his poetry dramatized its subjects in simple musical language, and it spoke in an emotionally direct and accessible way alien to the ironic, intellectual, and frequently elitist style of much of the period's best verse.

Moss developed this style in *A Swimmer in the Air* (1957) and *A Winter Come, A Summer Gone* (1960), his first new and selected volume. By the end of the decade he had written at least five of the most memorable American lyric poems of the fifties: "Burning Love Letters," "Elegy for My Father," "If You Can," "A Summer Gone," and "A Winter Come" (as well as one of the decade's funniest poems, "Tourists"). Critics have taken little note of this work, even in the better surveys of the period, possibly because simplicity, emotion, and musical perfection are not qualities that produce compelling literary scholarship. But these poems have aged well without the assistance of a scholarly facelift.

Thirty years is a surprisingly long time, and few poems survive even this short span of years. Yet Moss's best early work still glitters with its tense brilliance, as in this stanza from "A Summer Gone" describing the autumn migration of local birds:

> There is a time when feeling knows two things:
> The dead bird lying, and the whir of wings.
> Those travelers who beat the upper air
> Have clarities in mind—a south somewhere,
> Where clouds are higher and the sea more blue.
> Diviners of the tropics have to go
> Where summer is still spoken. Autumn wings
> Time the distances between two things.

These early poems also confront the themes that would haunt Moss across his subsequent career—the difficulty of love, the decay of the body, the passing of time, and the inevitability of death, all counterpointed against the inexhaustible beauty of the natural world. These are obviously not original subjects. They are the classical themes of lyric poetry. In a period when most poets approached them indirectly or ironically, Moss risked the emotional investment of addressing them simply and directly. This early work also conveys the gentle elegiac tone that would carry through his later work:

> A child lay down in his imagined grave
> To see the form he'd make engraved in snow,
> But even that feigned hollow filled with snow,
> And, rising on a landscape blurred a bit
> By shadows of an adumbrated blue,
> He came upon two worlds he had not known:
> One was his being, one his mind let go
> Until the light would take the blue from snow.

Among the new work in *A Winter Come, A Summer Gone* there was a sequence of ten dramatic poems called *King Midas*. This sequence (which, though overwritten in parts, contains two of Moss's most simple and beautiful lyrics, "The Princess' Speech" and "The Princess' Song") marks a pivotal point in the poet's development. These poems, each spoken by one or more of seven characters, tell the story of Midas through a series of songs and speeches. Moss had always preferred a dramatic stance in his poems. Now he began to develop the possibilities of this stance by creating characters more distinct from himself.

So much literary criticism concentrates on the question of influences that, surrounded by these exhaustive poetic genealogies, one can easily lose sight of the seldom-stated truth that for most real poets above the age of thirty-five the strongest influence comes from their own previous work. The burden of a writer's past can exert its influence in different ways. One writer tries to escape from his earlier limitations, while another struggles, perhaps vainly, to recapture his lost vitality. Young poets quite properly are concerned with technique—how to bring off what they want to say memorably in words. But once the techniques are mastered and the early poems successfully written, new problems arise. The mature poet realizes how small a fraction of his own experience, of the world's experience, he has re-created in his work. The very techniques he mastered to capture one part of experience often excluded another. Slowly he realizes that the only way he can continue to be true to himself is to change himself.

One of the great clichés of contemporary criticism is that change automatically equals growth, but how seldom this really happens. Most poets who change styles or subjects in mid-career write no better or deeper than before. They simply write differently. Frequently a writer ends up worse, having abandoned the sources of his own early strength. Artistic growth involves more than mastering new techniques, though that mastery remains essential. It demands a spiritual commitment for which a writer's earlier habits may have left him unprepared. Only the writer whose stylistic transformations reflect real personal development truly grows. Other writers just change.

With his first retrospective volume behind him, Moss began transforming his poetry in some fundamental ways. Rather than trying to capture universal moods as he had in his early lyric work, he now focused more on creating characters in his verse. Sometimes he portrayed these characters in third-person sketches; more frequently he presented them indirectly in undefined but alien first-person voices. For poets new themes almost inevitably demand new forms. As he crated new personae, Moss began developing a new kind of highly compressed dramatic monologue. These poems seldom run more than two or three pages, for although Moss was exploring dramatic subjects, he still gave his work the concentration of lyric poetry. These speaking voices also bring a more diverse diction into his poetry as the pure, universal vocabulary of the early lyrics broadens to include the range of contemporary speech. Finally, Moss now begins to use free verse for the first time, but he uses it with a distinctive concision and musicality. Sometimes it even rhymes.

From this point on it becomes especially dangerous to identify the speaker or protagonist of any Moss poem with its author. Increasingly Moss creates alternate versions of himself, including a variety of madmen and neurasthenics, even in poems that seem to overlap at points with his own life. He also summons up more obviously foreign speakers, including nonhuman voices like the ocean or a tree to explore alien forms of experience. If his early work analyzed normal experience, especially the psychology of love, this new poetry focused most often on abnormal or extreme states of mind. Sometimes these poems even take the form of case studies, as in the group of four portraits ("Lu," "Eva," "Miriam," and "Jane") originally published under the collective title of "Lifelines."

Few reviewers fully understood this shift. While they recognized what Moss was attempting in his third-person portraits, many of them continued to make the automatic identification of the poet with his first-person narrators, especially if the poem had anything to do with New York (after all, Moss was an editor of the *New Yorker*). Needless to say, this critical methodology resulted in some far-fetched interpretations. But then reviewers sometimes help by providing interpretations so absurd that they force the reader to set his own mind working straight.

These shifts begin in *Finding Them Lost* (1965) and continue in *Second Nature* (1968). Moss is now writing a more fluent and complex kind of poem. One feels the same delicate sensibility, alive to every nuance of a particular scene, but now it takes unexpected turns. The best poems in these volumes ("Going to Sleep in the Country," "Painting a Wave," "Arsenic," "A Dead Leaf," or "The Pruned Tree") are remarkable not only for their diversity of style and theme but also for their insistence on surprising the reader. "A Dead Leaf," for example, begins with a witty conversational voice speaking in a stately four-stress line and then suddenly switches into compressed, imagistic free verse only to switch again a few lines later. Moss is no longer writing perfectly tuned lyrics, all of a piece, that carefully build on one set theme. Instead, his poems now restlessly explore the diverse, even discordant, possibilities of a particular situation. He also risks sudden breaks between scenes, leaving the reader to fill in the missing connections between stanzas. When this technique does not work, as in "Front Street," the reader is left with an unsatisfying ambiguity that the distinction of language cannot redeem. But when the central inspiration is strong enough to create the unspoken connections between the glittering fragments, as in "A Dead Leaf" or "Arsenic," Moss achieves a remarkably original poetry that has the richness of a dramatic monologue but the intensity of a lyric.

Even the simpler poems of this period often create an exquisite and original kind of beauty. In "The Pruned Tree," Moss projects himself into the alien consciousness of a plant that—and this is the hauntingly unexpected turn in the poem—rejoices in its own mutilation, since that dismemberment is the price of its destiny. The poem speaks gently in the imagined voice of the tree:

> As a torn paper might seal up its side,
> Or a streak of water stitch itself to silk
> And disappear, my wound has been my healing,
> And I am made more beautiful by losses.
> See the flat water in the distance nodding
> Approval, the light that fell in love with statues,
> Seeing me alive, turn its motion toward me.
> Shorn, I rejoice in what was taken from me.
>
> What can the moonlight do with my new shape
> But trace and retrace its miracle of order? . . .

Resounding with a quiet, almost mystic joy, "The Pruned Tree" works on at least three levels. First, on its literal level, the poem projects the human imagination into the semi-animate mind of a plant and rejects human sentimentality by celebrating the naturalistic irony that a tree can be made stronger and more fruitful by most of its branches being cut away. Second, "The Pruned Tree" constitutes an objective correlative for the subjective emotional states found in Moss's early love poetry. One only has to read the opening stanza without reference to the poem's title to see how clearly, despite the central metaphor, it also expresses the author's earlier theme of the heart's growth through pain and loss. Finally, the poem subtly represents Moss's indirect *ars poetica,* not only claiming but also demonstrating how expression can be more powerful through restraint and order, virtues that are not achieved except through loss and pain.

In 1971 Moss published his *Selected Poems,* a carefully chosen collection that earned him his first major literary prize, the National Book Award in Poetry. Although this volume amply demonstrated the unique achievement of Moss's earlier work, of the seven new poems included, only the autobiographical "Long Island Springs" bore comparison with his best previous verse. The other poems were frequently witty and always impeccably written, but their elegant lines lacked the sharp cutting edge of "The Pruned Tree" or "A Dead Leaf." At mid-career the poet seemed to be reaching an impasse raised by his own facility.

In *Buried City* (1975) Moss broke the impasse by writing the two most complex and ambitious poems of his career, "Chekhov" and "Buried City." Neither poem allows an easy summary. Both are extended lyric monologues that discuss serious human issues—love and responsibility, property and freedom, art and illusion—in highly charged, figurative language. Moss, however, develops these moral themes like musical ideas. Rather than weakening the intellectual impact of the poem, this development strangely intensifies it as images, emotions, and ideas all play together in the reader's imagination.

In "Chekhov," the finer of these two exceptional poems, Moss freely rearranges images, ideas, settings, and characters from Chekhov's work to superimpose two interrelated themes. First, he dramatizes the irreconcilable conflict of what property and place mean in a traditional society ruled by familial and feudal responsibility, as compared to a modern capitalist economy in which money depersonalizes and dislocates everything. Meanwhile, Moss interweaves this grim ideological conflict with the mystery of art transforming illusion into reality. The unexpected combination of these themes expressed in images drawn or seemingly drawn from Chekhov creates a rich and original lyric texture:

> If the temporary brilliancies gather once more
> In the middle distance, and the modal lark
> Persuades the summer evening to reveal
> One private little splendor not for sale,
> Still, a gunshot, onstage or off,
> Tells us what no one is prepared to know:
> Love is a tourniquet tightening its bands

> Around the slowly dying wrist of freedom,
> Futility's a spinster bending over
> A book of household accounts forever.

There are other strong poems in *Buried City*—"Cold Water Flats," "Shore Lines," "Bay Days"—but they work in simpler terms, more reminiscent of Moss's earlier pieces. Indeed, the poet seems to have retrenched from the scope of "Chekhov" and "Buried City" soon after writing them. His next book, *A Swim off the Rocks* (1976), lies outside the discussion at hand, since it gathered Moss's light verse, much of it written years earlier; but the next collection of poems, *Notes from the Castle* (1979), marked a notable falling off. The few memorable poems in this volume, which ranks as Moss's least distinguished mature collection, are compressed and obsessive expressions of a single mood, like "The Long Island Night." The entire poem runs:

> Nothing as miserable has happened before.
> The Long Island night has refused its moon.
> *La belle dame sans merci*'s next door.
> The Prince of Darkness is on the phone.
>
> Certain famous phrases of our time
> Have taken on the glitter of poems,
> Like "Catch me before I kill again,"
> And "Why are you sitting in the dark alone?"

The longer works in *Notes from the Castle* generally read like superior occasional poems, for example the moving "Elegy for My Sister" or "Stars," a witty verse epistle to James Merrill. These poems are accomplished but so diffuse that their best parts excel the whole. Too often Moss's wit hardens into mannerism, and his verbal dexterity grows out of proportion to its subject, as in the beginning of "The Night Express":

> That moment we neared the reservoir
> Dry wit dried up aware that water
> Was no longer there for the taking. Hazel
> And birch, those secret, solitary drinkers,

Were suddenly duplicated everywhere,
Even the ground consuming its potion.
The word on every lip was "parched."
Could the desert be a stone's throw away. . . ?

If Moss's poetic range appeared to be narrowing, that fear was dismissed by his last single collection, *Rules of Sleep* (1984). Here, he once again reaffirms his mastery of familiar themes in short lyrics like "Morning Glory" or "Venice: A Still Life," while also performing the unexpected in a bizarrely delicate monologue like "Einstein's Bathrobe." The range of voices Moss displays in this volume is noteworthy even for a poet of his stylistic dexterity—from the laconic delivery of "Making a Bed" to the lush description of the Italian poems to the urbane narration of "The Restaurant Window." He entered his sixties with all his skill intact and capable of new development, as in "The Miles Between," where direct syntax and indirect language combine with emotional intensity to create a rhetorically extraordinary love poem. All a single sentence, the poem piles metaphor on metaphor to evoke but never depict a lost love:

Ambassador of rain to the night snow,
Custodian of all the miles between,
Who brought the morning tray of light and shadow,
Emissary sun, editing each form,
Illusion's minister who prints the leaf,
Goldsmith of autumn, and you, greenhorn
Conjuror of shoreline and sea storm,

The past's long unforgotten amateur,
Tearstruck highbrow, touchy and extreme,
Reaching for the heights to climb but one,
Soulmate looking for a place to lie,
By the talented flow of Iceland's lava,
By darkness coming down on Hungary,
I swear that you and I will meet again.

This new poetry matches depth of emotion with skillful extravagance of language. Memorable, original, and intense, it shows how Moss once again has transformed the style and substance of his earliest work while remaining constant to its spirit.

His accomplishments, however, were not unmixed. While the *New Selected Poems* show how rarely Moss wrote a bad poem, they also reveal how often he composed accomplished but uncompelling ones. The quiet tone, which give his finest lyrics their unforced sincerity, sometimes conspires to subdue the emotional focus of the poem just as the very qualities that distinguish his best work—the precision, delicacy, and polish—usually create a texture so pellucid that the slightest flaw becomes apparent. Likewise Moss had a genius for description that too often operated independently of any equally forceful inspiration. Such writing becomes a kind of superior verse in which the whole sometimes amounts to less than the sum of its brilliant parts. At these times Moss fell prisoner to his own too perfectly refined sensibility.

If a poet must have faults, a superabundance of taste, a weakness for description, and a tendency to overpolish seem rather agreeable ones. But to some critics these misdemeanors rank as capital offenses, and like the cheerless judges of a revolutionary tribunal they have sentenced Moss for the heinous crime of having a bourgeois and urbane sensibility—as if all true art were produced by only one class, one region, one kind of imagination. They bristle at the gentility of Moss's work as if poise and refinement automatically resulted in diffuseness and insincerity. Some of these critics also equate poetic form with narrow-minded literary reactionism, and they peremptorily dismiss any contemporary poem written in meter as irrelevant. Some of Moss's contemporaries have suffered from this critical "Know Nothingism," most conspicuously Richard Wilbur, but no poet met with it so consistently as Moss, and the reason must almost certainly be his long association with the *New Yorker* and his presumed membership in the New York literary establishment.

Ultimately, however, literary squabbles fade away, and what remains is the work—or at least that part of it, large or small, that continues to fascinate future readers. A poet will be judged by his best poems because posterity will forget the others. Their power, range, freshness, and—there is no way of avoiding it—their word-for-word perfection will determine the author's reputation. In the long run, therefore, critics who carp about the failings of Moss's weaker poems may be accurate but irrelevant. At his best Moss was a superb lyric poet. One may quibble about his rank among his contemporaries, but one need only read "A Summer Gone," "A Pruned Tree," or "Chekhov" to know that he wrote poems of permanent value. Of how many other Americans of his generation could one say the same?

Tradition and an Individual Talent

—

ANYONE WHO READS Donald Justice's poetry at length will eventually note how often his poems seem to originate out of other literary texts. While most poems conduct a conversation with the past—if only by employing a form or genre their audience will recognize—authors, especially Americans, often exert immense effort and ingenuity to disguise their literary antecedents. If poetry grows out of the dialectic between innovation and emulation, our literature has always prized originality over continuity. Originality is, after all, America's one strict tradition.

Donald Justice, however, appears unconcerned about revealing the extent to which his poems rely on the literary tradition. *Departures, Selected Poems, The Sunset Maker,* and *A Donald Justice Reader* all end with "Notes" in which the author identifies the sources of particular poems, including some borrowings that even a sophisticated reader would not have detected. Other poems begin with clearly labeled epigraphs that contain images or phrases used later in the text. Even Justice's titles openly advertise their genealogy: "Sestina on Six Words by Weldon Kees," "Last Days of Prospero," "After a Phrase Abandoned by Wallace Stevens," "Variations on a Text by Vallejo," "Henry James by the Pacific." Whereas most writers diligently hide their literary debts, Justice practices what accountants call "full disclosure." In this respect he writes as a historian would, carefully crediting all of his predecessors to acknowledge that scholarship—like literature itself—is a collective enterprise. Justice's meticulous notation not only attests to his integrity as a writer, but it also suggests that his borrowings are a conscious and central aspect of his poetics.

Until going through all of Justice's published poetry, however, even a careful reader may not realize the full extent and diversity of the author's appropriations. Moreover, such an examination also reveals the surprising fact that Justice's conscious employment of other texts for his own imaginative purposes is not part of an early imitative stage but has increased with each collection. Whereas his first volume, *The Summer Anniversaries* (1960), contains only five poems (out of thirty-two total) that have overt literary sources, Justice's second collection, *Night Light* (1967), includes no less than eleven (out of forty). In *Departures* (1973), the ratio increases with ten out of twenty-nine poems openly drawing material from other literary works. In *Selected Poems* (1979), four of the sixteen previously uncollected poems employ borrowed literary models. (This count does not include the Tremayne poems, which show an oblique debt to Kees's Robinson and Berryman's Henry poems.) Finally, in *The Sunset Maker* (1987), not only do nine of the twenty-five poems owe debts to other literary works (three are translations), but the last half of the book constitutes two internally referential sequences of poems, stories, and memoir that borrow and develop material from one another.

I do not claim this census is scientific. Another critic might arrive at a slightly different total or make a convincing argument why a particular poem does or does not belong on the list. But by any count, it appears that at least one quarter of Justice's published poems utilize openly borrowed material—even if it is only something as small as a memorable phrase. His appropriations vary from entire poems (like Attila József's 1927 "O Europe," which Justice rewrote about the American landscape as "1971") to borrowed situations and characters ("Last Days of Prospero"). He may steal an opening line (as he did from the beginning of John Peale Bishop's "Ode," which now also starts Justice's "The Grandfathers"). He may adopt elements of a poet's style (as in his Guillevic homages) or a particular typographical arrangement (like Hart Crane's use of marginal commentary in *The Bridge,* which found its way into one version of Justice's "Childhood" before being revised away). He also has reshaped prose passages into verse while keeping much of the original phrasing, as in "Young Girls Growing Up (1911)," which recasts an incident from Kafka's diaries. And sometimes he simply quotes an author in a passing allusion. The sheer diversity of his textual appropriations is not only impressive but unusual, as is his habit of underscoring each debt with a conspicuous epigraph or end-note that heightens the reader's awareness of the transaction. One often reads an allusive author unconscious of his borrowings. Justice, a lifelong teacher, intends his allusions to be recognized—whether the reader is prepared for them or not.

When critics discuss the debt one poem owes to another, they usually analyze the relationship in terms of influence. In understanding the nature of Justice's textual appropriations, however, traditional concepts of influence are not especially helpful. Except for a few early poems influenced by Auden (one of which, "Sonnet," is equal to anything in its model, Auden's "In Time of War"), Justice has always had an identifiable tone and manner. His obsession with formal experimentation and his impatience with writing the same kind of poem for very long have given his work an extraordinary stylistic variety out of proportion with its relatively small size. But his poetic signature remains constant—clarity of expression, relentless economy of means, self-conscious formal design, unpretentious intelligence, and quiet but memorable musicality. Reading his work, one always senses an integrating and independent imagination.

Discussing literary influences, one also looks for the critical relationships between an author and one or two dominant predecessors. Reading Blake, one recognizes the crucial importance of Milton as a model. Studying Baudelaire, one considers his obsessive relationship with Poe. A contemporary writer like William Everson, for example, cannot be understood without constant reference to his lifelong master, Robinson Jeffers. Harold Bloom insists that such dominant influences must be seen in Freudian terms as decisive psychic struggles. In order to become strong and mature, a younger poet must assimilate and then overpower his elder authority figures. Such theories, however, do little to clarify Justice's case. Not only does one not sense any psychic wrestling with his three dominant early masters—Stevens, Baudelaire, and Auden—one also doesn't find much evidence of them in his poems outside of a few deliberate homages. Likewise, the broad range of Justice's borrowings— from T. S. Eliot's prose and Hart Crane's marginalia to Duke Ellington's lyrics and Mother Goose's syntax—makes it impossible to discuss dominant single influences. If Justice is, to use Bloom's term, a "strong poet," one aspect of his strength is the ability to draw from the breadth of world literature.

The one critic who provides a helpful model for Justice's appropriations is T. S. Eliot. In his 1920 essay on the Elizabethan dramatist Philip Massinger, Eliot wrote that one could learn a great deal about a poet by understanding the way in which he borrows:

> Immature poets imitate; mature poets steal; bad poets deface what
> they take, and good poets make it into something better, or at least

something different. The good poet welds his theft into a whole of feeling which is unique, utterly different from that from which it was torn; the bad poet throws it into something which has no cohesion. A good poet will usually borrow from authors remote in time, or alien in language, or diverse in interest.

Except in his conscious homages, Justice does not imitate the styles or employ the thematics of the texts from which he draws material. Instead, like Eliot's mature poet, he steals an image or idea, or phrase or pattern to use in a new imaginative context. In "Counting the Mad," for example, Justice borrowed the meter and syntax of the Mother Goose toe-and-finger counting rhyme, "This little pig went to market." But Justice's poem imitates neither the style nor effect of its source:

> This one was put in a jacket,
> This one was sent home,
> This one was given bread and meat
> But would eat none,
> And this one cried No No No No
> All day long.
>
> This one looked at the window
> As though it were a wall,
> This one saw things that were not there,
> This one things that were,
> And this one cried No No No No
> All day long.
>
> This one thought himself a bird,
> This one a dog,
> And this one thought himself a man,
> An ordinary man,
> And cried and cried No No No No
> All day long.

The original nursery rhyme (or at least the most common modern variant, which Justice uses as his model) is playful and intimate — as befitting a verbal and tactile game a mother shares with a small child. By keeping the syntactic pattern of the original more or less intact but substituting shocking new subject matter, Justice achieves the double effect of familiarity and dislocation. The harmless market-day adventures of five childlike pigs become a nightmarish tour of an insane asylum. Significantly, Justice formalizes the idiosyncratic rhythms of the original nursery rhyme into a fixed stanza. Repeating this pattern three times, always ending with the staccato cries of the inmate who "thought himself a man, / An ordinary man," Justice creates a formal feeling of confinement analogous to the mad's physical incarceration. Imaginative literature about insanity often tries to re-create the disjunctive mental processes of the mad. This method tends to create complex imitations of the mad's interior monologue. In "Counting the Mad," however, Justice views the insane from a largely exterior perspective. He reproduces what a visitor would see or hear, and in doing so also reproduces the horror a visitor would feel. The only projection into the interior life of the mad is in the final stanza, where he states the central figure's self-image of normality. Although Justice's subject is potentially complex and unknowable, by using the Mother Goose paradigm he makes the finished poem simple, lucid, and accessible.

"Counting the Mad" also illustrates Eliot's point that good poets improve or transform what they take because Justice's poem is both more ambitious than and different from its model. This sort of appropriation is typical of Justice. He takes something from one context and uses it in another. Reading in a newspaper about "a hatbox of old letters" to be sold at auction, he transformed the item into the elegiac poem "To the Unknown Lady Who Wrote the Letters Found in the Hatbox." Finding a striking description in a John D. MacDonald detective novel ("One of those men who can be a car salesman or a tourist from Syracuse or a hired assassin"), Justice—who was then living in Syracuse—expands the passage into a menacing, metaphysical poem, mysterious in ways quite alien to MacDonald. Justice's poem "The Tourist from Syracuse" ends:

> Shall I confess who I am?
> My name is all names and none.
> I am the used-car salesman,
> The tourist from Syracuse,

The hired assassin, waiting.
I will stand here forever
Like one who has missed his bus—
Familiar, anonymous—

On my usual corner,
The corner at which you turn
To approach that place where now
You must not hope to arrive.

The way Justice elaborates MacDonald's brief description into an independent poem is characteristic of his creative method. "The Tourist from Syracuse," however, illustrates this intertextual procedure at its simplest. Although Justice's poem achieves a degree of linguistic and intellectual complexity beyond MacDonald's original, it nonetheless bears a paraphrasable resemblance to its prose parent. Justice rarely develops borrowed material in so linear a fashion. Usually his appropriations only provide a point of departure toward an imaginative end unforeshadowed in the original.

More typical of Justice's creative method is his "After a Phrase Abandoned by Wallace Stevens," which bears as its epigraph an eight-word fragment from Stevens's notebook ("The alp at the end of the street"). Justice has revised the poem significantly since its first appearance as a three-part sequence. Its most current version reads in full:

The alp at the end of the street
Occurs in the dreams of the town.
Over burgher and shopkeeper,
Massive, he broods,
A snowy-headed father
Upon whose knees his children
No longer climb;
Or is reflected
In the cool, unruffled lakes of
Their minds, at evening,
After their day in the shops,
As shadow only, shapeless
As a wind that has stopped blowing.

Grandeur, it seems,
Comes down to this in the end —
A street of shops
With white shutters
Open for business . . .

This poem does bear a family resemblance to Stevens's work. Justice not only borrows the opening line from his Hartford master. He also employs Steven's characteristic dialectic between the sublime and quotidian suggested by the borrowed phrase. Moreover, Justice uses some Stevensian stock characters, the burgher and the shopkeeper. But no sooner has Justice established this Stevensian scene in the three opening lines than he liberates the town from the elder poet's metaphysics. The new poem uses the contrast between the cold, primal presence of the mountain and the increasingly self-contained, man-made reality of the village to make points quite alien to Stevens. Justice observes the psychological situation of the townspeople, who have banished the paternal image of nature to the boundaries of their consciousness. He postulates no Stevensian struggle with abstractions of reality. Rather than transforming his observations into the premises of a supreme fiction, Justice accepts the loss of mythic consciousness as a condition of modern life. Justice even celebrates — despite the touch of irony in the last stanza — the functional beauty of the burghers' workaday world. Without mocking Stevens's fixation on the loss of religious faith, Justice quietly moves beyond this late romantic concern to create a poem of contemporary consciousness.

Justice's poem acknowledges Stevens as its precursor. It even initiates a subtle ontological discussion between the younger and the elder poet. But there is no Bloomian struggle for displacement. Rather than the anxiety of influence, Justice displays a characteristic confidence and respectful tolerance. "True poetic history," Bloom has asserted, "is the story of how poets as poets have suffered from other poets, just as any true biography is the story of how anyone suffered his own family — of his own displacement of family into lovers and friends." Justice's example demonstrates the sheer inadequacy of such Freudian theories of poetic influence. As a means of apprehending how Justice works his intertextual appropriations, Bloomian displacement offers no more insight than does the simple theory of imitation. It is more helpful here to expand Eliot's notion of the "mature poet." No anguished rebel, Justice is a thoroughly mature writer—stylistically, intellectually, psychologically. His authorial identity meets its precursors with the self-assurance, independence, and discriminating affection found in a fully developed and healthy psyche.

"After a Phrase Abandoned by Wallace Stevens" also demonstrates the unusual manner in which Justice uses borrowed material to generate new poems. There were several distinctive ways in which quotations from other texts were commonly incorporated into Modernist poems. They were, for example, used as decorative devices, arresting local effects to add interest to the surface of the poem. Although Modernist poetics minimized the notion of decorative language, properly proportioned decoration remained one of its fundamental poetic techniques. Marianne Moore frequently employed striking quotations in this manner, as in, for example, the second stanza of "England." Quotation was also used as an emphatic device to add force or authority to a passage. Ezra Pound habitually inserted classical quotations into his poems to achieve this effect. Emphatic quotation became a central technique for his "Hugh Selwyn Mauberley." Quotation was also used as a contrapuntal device to provide an ironic contrast to other elements in a poem. Eliot borrowed lines of poems, songs, prayers, and nursery rhymes to use contrapuntally in *The Waste Land* and "The Hollow Men." Sometimes an author even used borrowed language architecturally, as Nabokov did in several of his novels, using, for instance, Poe's "Annabel Lee" as a recurring emotional scaffold in *Lolita*.

Although one finds examples of decorative, emphatic, and contrapuntal quotation in Justice's work ("After a Phrase Abandoned by Wallace Stevens," for instance, borrows a decorative phrase from Auden's song "Fish in the unruffled lakes"), Justice's characteristic method is to use quotation as a generative device. He coaxes a new poem out of the unrealized possibilities suggested by a borrowed phrase or image. His Stevens poem proceeds directly from the images and ideas of the fragment. "The Tourist from Syracuse" likewise uncovers levels of meaning in MacDonald's phrase beyond the normal depth of the detective genre.

In the work of Pound or Eliot, borrowed quotations usually maintain their original identity despite their new context. Even when they are used ironically, one hears them as foreign words imported into the new text. Their quotation marks, as it were, remain intact. The final text often has the texture of a collage in which borrowed and original materials combine to create a novel effect. But in Justice's work, quoted material usually seems totally assimilated into the new poem. Not only does it no longer seem foreign to the text, the new poem appears to have grown organically and seamlessly out of it. One occasionally sees this generative technique in the early Modernists, as in the opening section of Eliot's "Ash-Wednesday," which incorporates a line translated from Cavalcanti ("Because I do not hope to turn again"). But even in "Ash-Wednesday," Eliot ends the passage by returning to emphatic quotation. Having stolen a line to begin his poem, Eliot makes public penance by quoting the end of the "Hail Mary" as a self-standing coda.

Although Justice has appropriated other texts with the imaginative rapacity of an Eliot or a Pound, he has never been much drawn to the techniques of collage. The surfaces of his poems reflect such high polish, his syntax unfolds with such architectural assurance, that one suspects he found the disjunctive energy of High-Modernist collage unappealing. Even when he began poems out of chance fragments (as in the aleatory poems in *Departures*), he left them with a seamless finish. Generative quotation has been a technique more compatible with his tastes, and no American poet has used it more effectively. When Justice titled his third collection *Departures,* he slyly but self-consciously confessed to this obsession. Stylistically the volume was a departure from his earlier formal work, but the book was also built around a series of poems that began as imaginative departures from other texts, some drawn from literary tradition, others from chance methods. Justice's title signals the author's unabashed reliance on the intertextual play between tradition and innovation. Tradition, to tweak Prof. Bloom one last time, is not a threatening father intimidating creation, but a generative matrix for new poems.

The reason why theories of influence as Romantic rebellion have so little applicability to Justice is that he is essentially a Postmodern classicist, a contemporary artist who understands the sustaining power of tradition without seeking to stifle innovation and experiment. "Classicist" and "tradition" have often become code words for aesthetic and political reactionism, but Justice is no traditionalist in the narrow sense. As a poet, critic, and translator, he has assimilated the achievements of international Modernism, but he has from the beginning also recognized that his historical position comes after that aesthetic revolution ended. Justice's

response to the predicament of the Postmodern artist is part of his originality. He fostered no illusions of perpetuating the superannuated avant-
garde aesthetic (a temptation that ruined many artists of his generation,
especially the composers). Instead, he confronted the burden of the past
by exploring and consolidating the enduring techniques of Modernism to
create a style that reconciled the experiments of the previous two generations with the demands of the present.

A central means of achieving this synthesis was to borrow material and
techniques from the major Modernists and determine—in practical poetic
terms rather than the abstract critical concepts—what remained viable for
the contemporary artist. Eliot, Pound, Stevens, James, Williams, Rilke,
Crane, Vallejo, Lorca, Kafka, Rimbaud, Baudelaire, József, Alberti, and
others provided the material for experiment. The imaginative mission of
consolidating the heritage of Modernism also explains why, despite his
voracious appropriations, Justice so rarely borrows from earlier writers.
With only a handful of exceptions, his appropriations begin chronologi-
cally with Baudelaire and Rimbaud, at the start of modern poetry. (And
even his use of earlier sources like Dante in "Hell" often have an Eliotic
or Poundian flavor). Contrasting the chronological range of Justice's allusions and quotations with those of a Pound or Eliot, Kees or Lowell
demonstrates how closely focused Justice has been on Modernism.

In someone less talented or self-critical, Justice's allusive method
might have proved dangerous. To borrow the words of great writers for
inclusion in a new poem forces the reader to compare the new text with
the original. Poetry so openly intertextual also risks seeming remote or
pedantic, something drawn bloodlessly from books rather than learned
firsthand from life. The common complaint of "academic formalism"
leveled at members of Justice's generation is inadequate to address either
the early work or ultimate accomplishments of poets like Richard
Wilbur, Louis Simpson, James Merrill, Donald Hall, William Jay Smith,
or Adrienne Rich. Nonetheless there does remain—as often is the case
with unfair but enduring criticism—an uncomfortable kernel of truth in
that generational stereotype. Some of Justice's contemporaries have produced dully learned and pointlessly self-conscious work. Poets are often
scholarly creatures, and much intelligence and learning goes into every
genuine poem. But intelligence cannot endow a poem with life in the ab-

sence of emotion or imagination. Perhaps a poet can never know too much, but a poem can.

Despite the literary models behind many of his poems, Justice rarely seems bookish. Although subtle in language and sophisticated in technique, his work—except for the overtly experimental pieces in *Departures*—is exemplary in its clarity and accessibility. One always senses the emotional impulse driving the poem (which is frequently a painful sense of loss or, more recently, bittersweet nostalgia), and that intuition clarifies all of the other elements, even when they are complex or deliberately ambiguous. But if Justice's language is often tentative, his poems never display the densely allusive or obscure manner of his teachers, Robert Lowell and John Berryman. His learning is assimilated into the total experience of the poem. One need not know the source of his allusions to understand what they mean in their new context. Even writing about literary subjects such as Henry James or the forgotten poet Robert Boardman Vaughn, Justice remains accessible. In this respect, his work reminds one of the poems of Jorge Luis Borges. Despite their formidable learning, Borges's poems are not difficult, because their intellectual content is always integrated into their imaginative and emotional fabric. Borges might have been speaking for Justice when he said, "I am also living when I dream, when I sleep, when I write, when I read." Reading is a natural part of Justice's poetic process because it is an integral part of his life.

Justice has fulfilled Eliot's challenge in "Tradition and the Individual Talent." He has demonstrated what Eliot called a poet's indispensable "historical sense," the ability to perceive the literary past in order to develop his own contemporary identity. Tradition, Eliot maintained, "cannot be inherited, and if you want it you must obtain it by great labor." Not every poet is willing to make the effort. Most are content to work within a received (and therefore entropic) idea of tradition. Aside from the sheer excellence of his poetry, Justice's importance comes from his determination to explore and redefine the traditions available to contemporary poets. The Modernists accomplished the task for their generation largely in their prose. Justice, however, has conducted his inquiries almost entirely in verse.

Prefacing *Platonic Scripts,* his only prose collection (which includes more pages of interviews than essays), Justice regrets having written so little criticism. "I see now, " he remarks, "that criticism can be of enormous value in helping to define and refine one's own thinking." But even while sharing Justice's regret, one must point out that his poems have performed an important critical function in evaluating the heritage of Modernism. Without ever becoming didactic or dully programmatic, they have clarified the possibilities of contemporary poetry. They are intellectually challenging without losing their emotional force. Although his poems pursue an investigative mission, they never forget that their primary purpose is to be good poetry. They are experimental in the happiest sense—experiments that succeed. His achievement has been to synthesize the diverse strands of Modernism into a powerful, new classical style.

Justice's poetry combines the concentration and energy of Modernism with the clarity and accessibility that typify classical styles. Although the tradition out of which he writes is the Modern movement, his sensibility exhibits the chief features of classicism—unity of design and aim, simplicity of means, clarity of expression, and a governing sense of form, all grounded in an informing tradition. There is also a notable element of restraint, but not in the stereotypical sense of excluding violence and emotion, which classical styles do not do (Beethoven, after all, was the apogee of classicism). Instead, classical styles control and balance emotional energy within a total design. Classicism has never had much good press in America. Our nation prefers the technicolor claims of Romanticism. But classicism is not a single style; rather, it is a sensibility that must in each age reinvent its own means of expression. At its best—which in contemporary art is very rare—classicism can achieve a unique balance of accessibility and profundity, of energy and concentration.

To demonstrate how effectively Justice's style achieves classicism's double aims of simplicity and profundity, we will end by examining "The Grandfathers." In this short, early poem Justice had already created a style with an accessible surface and complex subtext. Characteristically, he did this by appropriating another poet's words to create a subtle intertextual argument. "The Grandfathers" begins with the opening line of "Ode" by John Peale Bishop (a largely forgotten figure who wrote half a dozen of the best American poems of the twenties and thirties). Here is Justice's poem:

The Grandfathers

> *Why will they never sleep?*
> John Peale Bishop

Why will they never sleep,
The old ones, the grandfathers?
Always you find them sitting
On ruined porches, deep
In the back country, at dusk,
Hawking and spitting.
They might have sat there forever,
Tapping their sticks,
Peevish, discredited gods.
Ask the lost traveler how,
At road-end, they will fix
You maybe with the cold
Eye of a snake or a bird
And answer not a word,
Only these blank, oracular
Headshakes or headnods.

On a narrative level "The Grandfathers" is a descriptive poem about taciturn country elders, the sort of old men one might observe while traveling backwoods roads. Read as a realistic lyric examining archetypical figures of American folklore, "The Grandfathers"—with its quirky irregular rhyme scheme and sharp images—is a haunting poem. Aside from compliments, it does not appear to need much commentary. But if one goes back to its source, Bishop's "Ode," one finds an unexpected poem, which begins:

Why will they never sleep
Those great women who sit
Peering at me with parrot eyes?
They sit with grave knees; they keep
Perpetual stare; and their hands move
As though hands could be aware—

Forward and back, to begin again—
As though on tumultuous shuttles of wind they wove
Shrouds out of air.

Bishop's poem describes a frightening vision of the three Fates, who become symbols for a tragic pagan worldview. The three sisters serve as horrific reminders of man's mortality and the transience of human accomplishment. Bishop has no protection from them because his Christian faith, with its promise of salvation and resurrection, is dead. "Ode" ends:

There was One who might have saved
Me from the grave dissolute stones
And parrot eyes. But He is dead,
Christ is dead. And in a grave
Dark as a sightless skull He lies
And of His bones are charnels made.

Returning to "The Grandfathers" after studying Bishop's poem of existential dread, one sees a different text. What seemed like a macabre but naturalistic lyric now also reads as a densely metaphorical examination of how religious anxiety persists even after the religion itself has died. One now notices, for instance, the ambiguity of reference for "they" in the opening line. Does it refer to "the grandfathers," as one might initially have assumed, or to "The old ones," or to something else left unstated (such as the "they" in Bishop's original, quoted in the epigraph)? One also notes that the grandfathers themselves may not be as entirely literal as they at first appeared. These ancient figures consistently operate on both a realistic and metaphorical level. Continuing through the poem, the reader now finds that many of the seemingly realistic details also have sinister, religious meanings. If they are indeed divinities, Justice's "old ones," those "Peevish, discredited gods," may indeed "have sat there forever." Two carefully elaborated levels of meaning coexist in the poem, each becoming a metaphor for the other. On a realistic level, "The Grandfathers" is a study of malign but impotent backcountry elders; on the intertextual and metaphorical level, it describes the silent but troubling gods who still haunt the modern psyche. Characteristically, Justice designs the poem so it can be read satisfyingly on the first level alone, but he also creates a mythic subtext that can be understood only by reference to the poem's source. Justice's headnote from Bishop, therefore, isn't only an acknowledgment of the poet's borrowing; it is also a necessary clue to the poem's tradition, which includes not only Bishop's "Ode" but other Modernist poems about the death of religion.

Poems like "The Grandfathers" demonstrate the centrality of textual appropriation to Justice's aesthetic. Without understanding the inter-textual complexity of his work, one cannot fully read his poems. Placing Justice in his own self-defined Modernist tradition and appreciating the hidden complexity of his sometimes deceptively simple classical style, however, reveals a profound and challenging poet. He has shown that Modernism remains a living tradition for artists strong enough to approach it with imagination and independence.

The Example of Elizabeth Bishop

—

FOR AT LEAST A FEW POETS in my generation Elizabeth Bishop exerted an unusual kind of influence. Her poetry did not directly affect the style in which we wrote. (Even had we tried, a manner as fluent and understated as hers would have proved difficult to imitate.) Nor did she particularly influence our subject matter. Her own interests were too broad and various to provide a fixed point of reference. Likewise, she offered no easily paraphrasable philosophy of life or art for us to espouse. Nor did she, thank God, ever loom above us as a matriarchal predecessor with whom we made anxious Oedipal battle. We found no anxiety in her influence. She was not a dominating parent who inspired rebellion but rather an agreeable and too seldom visited aunt. Indeed, to judge by the conventional measures of literary influence, her presence might have seemed invisible to an outside observer. Nonetheless, by her example she proved a crucial figure in our development as poets.

Not all literary influences can be measured by comparing two texts. While young poets learn most of their craft by studying the writing of their elders, some of their most important relationships remain beneath the surface of the printed page. Some writers affect one deeply not because of their style or subjects but because of their character. Young writers not only need to learn their craft well. They must also shape their values and aspirations to resist the manifold temptations to write cheaply or dishonestly in the fashionable ways. They need to develop a character strong enough to withstand both failure and success.

For some of us coming to maturity in the late sixties and early seventies, Bishop's personal example deeply influenced our sense of what it meant to be a serious poet. This assertion may seem odd to those who remember how little was known about her life at that point, but her determined privacy was an essential part of her attraction. One tends to

consider a writer's character mostly in cases where the life has become famous enough to color one's vision of the work. Knowing about Osip
Mandelstam's courageous independence under Stalin and T. S. Eliot's
acceptance of Anglo-Catholicism affects one's reading of their poetry.
Sometimes a single fact like Hart Crane's suicide at sea sets off a chain reaction of associations that changes one's notion of a particular writer's
development. However much literary theory from New Criticism to de-
constructionism insists that one separate the life from the work, there remains a human impulse to judge the two together and apply the lessons
to one's own situation. An established writer's life provides a standard by
which a younger writer assesses his or her own.

But a writer can also choose to remain invisible. Bishop was a poet
who existed publicly only in her work. Yet how clearly one saw her values
in the poetry. It reflected a modest woman who prized honesty, clarity,
and exactitude. The voice was personal, even intimate, but never forward
or indecorous. While speaking openly, it also asserted that some things
needed to remain private. This reticence made one appreciate her confi-
dences all the more. Avoiding all sweeping theories, her poems insisted
on the specificity of truth and the complexity of experience. Her character
also came across in her standards. She published very little, but everything was both carefully crafted and meticulously observed.

One also sensed the integrity of her character in what she declined
to do. She eschewed the publicity other writers so assiduously courted.
She never vied for literary power. She seemed unconcerned with trends
and reputations. Like her own early model, Wallace Stevens, she remained by choice outside the public sphere of literary life. She did not directly criticize the trivialities of the intellectual establishment, but as with
Stevens her refusal to leave her desk and join her contemporaries in profitable self-promotion made the unmistakable statement that a poet's true
task was to write.

To appreciate the importance of Bishop's example one needs only to
reflect on the carnival atmosphere of American poetry over the past three
decades. My generation was the first in centuries to meet contemporary
poets not on the page but at the podium. Encountering a writer for the
first time at a public reading can often create difficulties in separating the
substance from the show—not only for the audience but for the author.
Nowhere was poetry more a performing art than in the San Francisco
Bay area, where I attended college. When Charles Bukowski stumbled on

stage carrying a six-pack of beer, the crowd would squeal with delight. They hardly cared what was said as long as he kept in character. When Robert Bly donned a pig mask and spoke in funny voices or Allen Ginsberg jingled his finger-cymbals like a Hollywood gypsy, the resulting art form often had less to do with poetry than with TV wrestling.

Twenty years ago Bishop was not a famous poet like Ginsberg or Lowell. Nor was she yet as fashionable among the literary intelligentsia as Berryman or Sexton. Although most large anthologies contained a little of her work, it was rarely assigned in classes. Plath already occupied the token slot most surveys gave to a contemporary female poet. Bishop belonged to no movement, she illustrated no trends. Her verse moved independently from the generalizations that ruled the professional overviews of recent American poetry—neither Beat nor Confessional, Modernist nor feminist, Black Mountain nor New York School. She was, of course, already a poet's poet, celebrated by a small knowledgeable circle of writers. But for those of us beginners who knew no poets—knowledgeable or otherwise—she seemed like an anomalous figure. One usually came across her work by accident while reading an anthology for pleasure or by seeing her name mentioned in print by an admirer like Lowell or Jarrell. Her work did not make a dramatic first impression, but it stuck with one in the odd way true poetry does—not in the themes or archetypes but in specific images or situations memorably expressed. A line or two would become fixed in one's ear for good:

> More delicate than the historians' are the map-makers' colors.

or:

> Should we have stayed at home and thought of here?

My own discovery of Bishop occurred not only outside the classroom or lecture hall but also off the printed page. I first encountered her poetry as the lyrics of a song—Ned Rorem's powerful setting of "Visits to St. Elizabeths" (which, to Rorem's credit, was composed not only before Bishop became well known but also before the poem even appeared between hard covers in *Questions of Travel*). This song made such a deep impression on me that I tracked down more of her work by locating poems in various anthologies, since the local public library had none of her books. I was then a high-school student spending much of my free time listening to, studying, and trying, without notable success, to compose music. Except for the work of W. H. Auden, which I had loved at first sight, I hadn't cared for the contemporary poetry I had been assigned in school. But listening to the vocal music of contemporary composers, especially Rorem and his colleague, William Flanagan, I became interested in three poets my English teachers had never mentioned— Theodore Roethke, Howard Moss, and Elizabeth Bishop. I loved them all the more because they were private discoveries.

A few years later I was an undergraduate at Stanford. Having abandoned music for literature, I found myself in English classes where I was taught to admire poetry such as:

> Holy! Holy! Holy! Holy! Holy! Holy! Holy! Holy! Holy! Holy!
>   Holy! Holy! Holy! Holy! Holy!
> The world is holy! The soul is holy! The skin is holy! The nose is holy!
>   The tongue and cock and hand and asshole holy!
> Everything is holy! everybody's holy! everywhere is holy! everyday is
>   in eternity! Everyman's an angel!

Even in my unsubtle teens, I knew language was capable of more than slogan shouting. Truth seemed more complex and elusive than easy formulas, and literary power did not depend exclusively on volume. If poetry hoped to get at the heart of things, it needed more subtlety and precision, more openness to experience and less reliance on gross generalities. The sort of contemporary poetry I admired achieved clarity and immediacy without sinking into simplification and clichés. It used contemporary language musically without becoming metronomic. It sounded like this:

> There are too many waterfalls here; the crowded streams
> hurry too rapidly down to the sea,
> and the pressure of so many clouds on the mountaintops
> makes them spill over the sides in soft slow-motion,
> turning to waterfalls under our very eyes.
> —For if those streaks, those mile-long, shiny, tearstains,
> aren't waterfalls yet,
> in a quick age or so, as ages go here,
> they probably will be.

I noticed that most of my teachers—professors and graduate students alike—talked most comfortably about contemporary poetry when they could reduce it to ideology. The Beats espoused political, moral, and social revolution; hence they deserved attention. The feminists demanded a fundamental revision of traditional sexual identities; therefore their poetry became important. This utilitarian aesthetic transformed poetry into a secular version of devotional verse. The reading lists covering contemporary poetry rarely seemed to originate from genuine love or excitement about the work itself but rather from some dutiful sense of its value in illustrating some theoretically important trend. This dreary moral and aesthetic didacticism had little to do with the "lonely impulse of delight" that had brought me to poetry.

Likewise I found it hard to consider Ginsberg or Ferlinghetti revolutionary when I first encountered them as classroom texts in an elite private university. To me they represented the conventional values—most of which, incidentally, I accepted—of the establishment I had just entered. Moreover, its novel trappings aside, their work often appeared predictable, prolix, and sentimental. By contrast, Bishop seemed original without being ostentatious, conversational without becoming verbose, and emotional without seeming maudlin. Her childhood reminiscence "First Death in Nova Scotia" worked all the more powerfully by being restrained. Her short narrative poem "House Guest" explored the subtle psychology of class relations more convincingly by being so insistently personal. She explored moral dilemmas without having a predetermined destination. Despite its familiar feel, her poetry almost always surprised one.

In this atmosphere, reading Bishop—without ever having her assigned—became a refreshingly revolutionary act. If indeed all literary texts make political statements, what could be more subversive to established authority than her quiet insistence on the individual's right to her own sensibility and values? She never argued overtly for this position. She simply assumed it as a natural human inheritance. She rejected all general theories by ignoring them and built her own beliefs from the ground up with empirical precision. Her "ideology" was therefore irrefutable because she spoke only of specifics. Admittedly her truths remained personal, the observations of one woman living in a particular time and place. Yet even when she wrote about private events in her most reticent manner, one immediately felt the emotional impulse of the poem. Her imagination worked with the prosy stuff of everyday affairs, and though she heightened it into poetry, she never distorted its reality.

Her poems still offered a common world that the reader and author could share. But both Brooklyn and Brazil became universal without losing their quirky specificity. She made the ordinary seem exotic and the foreign turn familiar.

Ultimately Bishop reminded one of the poet's duty to be true to his or her own sensibility and experience, no matter how deeply at odds they might be with prevailing fashions. She demonstrated that originality depended on more than novelty. She implied that while style might not in itself be character, it was certainly the product of character, and that excellence came from imaginative integrity rather than any method. In a confusing time she affirmed poetry's freedom to move in delight and discovery. Her presence was gentle and reassuring, but her lessons were difficult. If today one finds it hard to identify her students by any obvious family resemblance, then she proved a most successful teacher.

The Poet
in an Age of Prose

IF POETRY REPRESENTS, as Ezra Pound maintained, "the most concentrated form of verbal expression," it achieves its characteristic concision and intensity by acknowledging how words have been used before. Poems do not exist in isolation but share and exploit the history and literature of the language in which they are written. Although each new poem seeks to create a kind of temporary perfection in and of itself, it accomplishes this goal by recognizing the reader's lifelong experience with words, images, symbols, stories, sounds, and ideas outside of its own text. By successfully employing the word or image that triggers a particular set of associations, a poem can condense immense amounts of intellectual, sensual, and emotional meaning into a single line or phrase.

When R. P. Blackmur noted that "when a word is used in a poem it should be the sum of all its appropriate history made concrete and particular in the individual context," he may have sounded abstract and coldly analytical. But Blackmur was a poet as well as a critic, and his observation reflects the practical problems of writing genuine poetry. A poet knows that a reader will bring the sum of his experience in both life and literature to a poem, and the text must bear the weight of that attention. Good poetry never underestimates its readers. It actively seeks their imaginative and intellectual collaboration by assuming and exploiting a common frame of reference.

Judging exactly what constitutes that common framework at any given moment is part of the poet's task, since any living literary tradition constantly changes. Defining the tradition becomes—implicitly or explicitly—part of the creative act. Composed from that portion of the reader's cultural experience that a poet can use assumptively as a foundation for new work, this framework constitutes an era's available tradition.

One always risks being misunderstood when using the word *tradition*.

Even in 1917 T. S. Eliot observed that the term was seldom employed "except in a phrase of censure." To speak of tradition summons images of old books in musty libraries or rows of marble busts gathering dust along a wall. But in speaking of "available tradition" I intend something less grand and more practical—namely that small portion of the past a poet finds usable at a particular moment in history. The available tradition is not a fixed entity but a dynamic concept. It changes—and indeed must change—not only from generation to generation but also from audience to audience.

The composition of a poem requires—either consciously or intuitively—the notion of an audience. To create language of requisite precision and intensity, the writer must assume a reader's specific response to every word, idea, or image. Some authors, like Shakespeare, knew their audience directly. Others, like Wallace Stevens, simply supposed an invisible reader of deeply sympathetic intelligence. Still others, like Pound in his *Cantos,* sought to invent, through the poem itself, an ideal reader who did not yet exist. Whatever the case, the author's idea of his audience helps shape the poems he creates. In the past the relationship between the poet and the public did not seem especially problematic. Societies were more compact and homogeneous. Cultural traditions changed very slowly, and readers shared a common fund of knowledge and concerns. Writers—even innovative ones like William Blake or Walt Whitman—were usually able to choose an audience whose sensibilities they understood (if not entirely endorsed) and whose general cultural assumptions they shared.

Today a poet faces a practical problem in trying to define a common cultural tradition available to both him and his readers. The difficulty originates in contemporary society, where the continuous proliferation of information has increasingly fragmented audiences into specialized subcultures that share no common frame of reference. The situation is further aggravated by the culture's shift away from the printed word as its primary source of information and entertainment. Although this problem is not specifically literary, it does affect the poet more severely than other artists because it destroys the referential framework that gives poetry its particular concentration and intensity. How does an intertextual art like poetry sustain its force in a culture that no longer studies and esteems the written text? And how, if the poet limits his audience to people for whom the written word maintains its importance, does he write for readers who have lost touch with verse as a serious artistic medium?

Merely to mention the atomization of American cultural life is guaranteed to set off alarms in every ideological camp. But—for the space of this essay—I ask the reader to put aside not only all theories of why this fragmentation has occurred but also whether the change was a positive or negative event. The relevant factor here is only that the notion of tradition a serious poet entertained in 1940 no longer exists. We live in a country where the average college freshman doesn't know in what century the Civil War was fought, cannot identify the language spoken in ancient Rome, and cannot name a single Romantic poet. Not only has this student probably never read a single page of Milton, he probably could not understand it if he did. The epigraph to a recent Edgar Bowers poem aptly summarizes the situation. Quoting a student, it reads, "Who's Apollo?" Students, of course, do not fully represent the American reader, but they do serve, to borrow a phrase from economists, as a reliable leading indicator of general cultural trends.

Since the poet can no longer write assumptively to a diverse audience using a common framework of history, literature, science, myth, and religion, he faces a series of distressing compromises. He can strip his language free of most references and create a kind of minimalist verse that achieves clarity at the expense of comprehensiveness and intensity. Or the poet can substitute a private frame of reference (which in our narcissistic society is almost inevitably autobiographical) for the lost public tradition. This confessional method gains immediacy at the price of breadth and relevance. Or the poet can adopt a public ideology (usually a particular political or religious creed) to provide a predetermined framework. This method gains accessibility and depth but usually at the cost of immediacy and independence. Or, finally, the poet can limit his audience to an educated coterie that still understands the traditional literary codes—a decision that maintains the art's intensity but risks its vitality and general relevance.

One might easily view the history of recent American poetry as a series of rebellions against and reconciliations to the writer's cultural predicament. Most major innovations have originated in the frustration generated by poetry's sequestration in the academy. Each significant new movement has attempted to form some meaningful coalition outside the university—both to link its poetry to a living cultural tradition and to revitalize it with genuine social purpose. The Beats, for example, linked their literary vision to the nonconformist attitudes of the countercultural Left. Black poets sought to become the voice of their own disenfranchised race. Protest poets in the late sixties mythologized the political framework of the Vietnam era into a publicly accessible literary tradition. Women writers adopted the ideological structure of feminism to give their poetry great social relevance. Whatever one thinks of the artistic success of these movements, one must recognize the initial jolt of energy each delivered by reestablishing poetry's link with the broader culture. (But, ironically, each rebellion from the academy was almost immediately calmed by assimilating its ringleaders into the university, and the impact on the general culture ultimately proved limited.)

NEW FORMALISM represents the latest in this series of rebellions against poetry's cultural marginality. The generational change in literary sensibility, which would eventually be called New Formalism, began twenty years ago when a group of young writers created—admittedly, only in their own minds—a new audience for poetry. Alienated from the kind of verse being praised and promulgated in the university, these young poets—like every new generation of writers—sought to define their own emerging art in relation to an imaginary audience. For obvious reasons, their ideal readers were not the poetry professionals of the Creative Writing department who had quite explicitly rejected formal metrics and narrative verse. Nor were they the contemporary literature experts of the English department who often prized difficulty for its own sake.

At odds with the small but established institutional audience for new poetry, these young writers imagined instead readers who loved literature and the arts but had either rejected or never studied contemporary poetry. This was not the mass audience of television or radio, for whom the written word was not a primary means of information. It was an audience of prose readers—intelligent, educated, and sophisticated individuals who, while no longer reading poetry, enjoyed serious novels, film, drama, jazz, dance, classical music, painting, and the other modern arts. While these prose readers had limited experience with contemporary poetry, they also displayed few preconceptions about what it should or should not be. For them, formal and narrative verse did not violate any preordained theoretical taboos, since they unself-consciously enjoyed rhyme, meter, and storytelling as natural elements of the popular arts like rock, musical theater, and motion pictures. In writing for a general audience that poetry had long ago lost, the New Formalists chose to embrace rather than repudiate the broader cultural trends of their era. Rather than be bards for the poetry subculture, they aspired to become the poets for an age of prose.

Whether or not the New Formalists have actually ever reached this large audience is immaterial here. The crucial consideration is that—like the Beats or the black power poets before them—they tried to break the cultural deadlock strangling their art. In the New Formalists' case, the attempt involved the creation of an idealized common reader to define the cultural traditions available to them as poets. They took the risk of courting a prose audience generally indifferent to serious verse rather than addressing the existing academic coterie. In doing so, they openly broke ranks with the prevailing models of contemporary poetry, rejecting the hypersophisticated or highly intellectualized aesthetics of academically fashionable writers like Ashbery, Olson, Creeley, or Merwin whose work seemed targeted primarily at an elite readership of critics and fellow artists.

Less obvious, at least initially, was the fact that the young poets also departed from the example of the most influential formalists of the older generation (such as Merrill, Hecht, or Hollander), who saw themselves as guardians of the imperiled traditions of European high culture. The first break was announced with fierce rhetoric by the poets of the new movement, since most of them felt little sympathy with the academic mainstream. The second break, however, was not so clearly articulated, since the young writers generally admired the older formal poets and looked on them as literary allies. The subsequent direction of New Formalist poetry, however, indicates that the aesthetics of the older and younger schools are in many respects irreconcilable.

Since there was no open conflict between the older and younger generations, some critics have conflated the two schools. There has been a common criticism by detractors that the New Formalists are doing nothing new. These young poets, the complaint goes, are epigones not innovators, since they represent merely a continuation of the American formalist tradition of the 1940s and 1950s. This line of reasoning has the virtue of simplicity, but, unfortunately, it betrays little familiarity with what the young poets have actually written. One need only compare a poem by Merrill or Hollander with one by Tom Disch or Molly Peacock to see how radically they differ in terms of audience, genre, tone, cultural heritage, and even prosody. The confusion between these two related but divergent generations originates, one suspects, in the term *New Formalism* itself, which is misleadingly reductive. One need not subscribe to the philosophical tradition of nominalism to appreciate that anyone hoping to understand an artistic movement—be it New Formalism, Modernism, or Romanticism—must make a distinction between the name itself and the phenomena it tries to describe. Responsible investigation begins with the actual works of art the movement produces, not uninformed generalizations about the name literary journalists first applied dismissively to its earliest manifestations.

By focusing attention solely on the revival of formal metrics, the term *New Formalism* has obscured the broader change in sensibility that these young poets represent. The use of rhyme and meter is only one aspect of a deeper aesthetic shift away from the coterie culture of the universities. The new sensibility also has led to the return of verse narrative, the exploration of popular culture for both forms and subjects, the rejection of avant-garde posturing, the distrust of narrowly autobiographical thematics, the unembarrassed employment of heightened popular speech, and the restoration of direct, unironic emotion. Seen from this perspective, the movement might be more accurately described by the alternate term *Expansive* poetry. This expression captures the eclectic interests and broad cultural ambitions of the movement. While it is possible to focus profitably on the revival of formal metrics, such a narrow perspective risks missing the broader cultural issues at stake. It also distorts the relationship between the young formal and narrative poets and their predecessors.

There are some continuities between the New Formalist and New Critical poets. Both groups endorse rhyme and meter as legitimate and "organic" modes of literary composition. They also consider the finished poem a consciously crafted artifact rather than a spontaneous or aleatory creation. And both schools believe that poetry is an essentially intertextual art. They maintain, in other words, that poetry refers to life only through the intricately self-referential prism of language and that the individual poem discloses its full meaning only in relation to its broader literary context.

In other respects, however, the aesthetics of the New Formalist and New Critical poets stand in radical disagreement. If they share a belief in the necessity of placing new poems in relation to a tradition, they differ irreconcilably in terms of defining what traditions are available to them as contemporary artists. If both recognize the importance of the idea of an audience in shaping a poem, each group has chosen different audiences. That choice, in turn, has indeed taken the tone, style, and subject of their work in fundamentally different directions despite the occasional similarity of their prosody. And, finally, their divergent sense of available tradition and intended audience has led them to pursue different modes and genres of literary expression. That these two literary schools differ so substantially is not surprising, however, since each emerged in a different historical moment.

The older generation of formalists came to maturity during World War II, and their emergence as writers coincided with the postwar period of American cultural ascendance. The intellectual assumptions behind their work reflect the ebullient confidence of America's new international dominance. Touring Europe as soldiers or Fulbright scholars (or both), they were determined to meet the Old World on equal terms by demonstrating their mastery of its traditional modes of discourse. Likewise, these older writers were the first generation of poets in the history of American literature to move *en masse* into the university—an environment they found intellectually and artistically congenial. Here, too, they resolved to address their scholarly colleagues on equal footing. They wrote poems that displayed their full command of the traditions of English literature, informed and energized by international Modernism. Having, in many cases, risked their lives to defend (and later staked their careers to teach) Western Culture, they assumed—as a central ideological foundation—the reader's deep familiarity with traditional literature. Their work was designed to bear the full weight of tradition and withstand the scrutiny of critical examination. Their work was intellectually demanding, aesthetically self-conscious, emotionally detached, and intricately constructed. Their audience was, by definition, limited to fellow members of the academy's intellectual and artistic elite.

The New Formalists emerged in less optimistic and assumptive times. They came to maturity in the cultural disintegration of the Vietnam era, when a series of ideological revolutions challenged the conventional notions of literary value and intellectual objectivity that had shaped the older generation's aesthetic. The idea of tradition—even including its corollary principles of genre, diction, prosody, and form—was rejected. The notion of a common canon of universally acknowledged master-pieces was exploded into splinters of competing traditions, each grounded in its own exclusionary aesthetic. Art was divorced from pleasure and bound to ideology—especially to the reductive notion of the perpetual avant-garde, which proclaimed that literary styles, like the blueprints for microchip hardware, constantly evolved only to become immediately outmoded by the next innovation.

Having found high culture in shambles, the New Formalists looked to popular culture for perspective. In film, rock music, science fiction, and other popular arts, they found the traditional forms and genres, which the academy had discredited for ideological reasons in high art, still being actively used. Innocent of theory, the general public had somehow failed to appreciate that rhyme and meter, genre and narrative were elitist modes of discourse designed to subjugate their individuality. The poor fools actually found such outmoded artistic technology interesting and enjoyable. The gap between what the academy declared represented democratic art and what the *demos* itself actually preferred was imagina-tively provocative. The young writers realized that, while after the revolu-tion the public might clamor for projectivist verse and neodadaist mime shows, in the corrupt present a more accessible kind of art was called for.

What the New Formalists—and their counterparts in music, art, sculp-ture, and theater—imagined was a new imaginative mode that took the materials of popular art—the accessible genres, the genuinely emotional subject matter, the irreverent humor, the narrative vitality, and the linguis-tic authenticity—and combined it with the precision, compression, and ambition of high art. They remained committed to the standards of excel-lence embodied in high culture but recognized that the serious arts had grown remote and inbred. Just as the English and German Romantic poets had sought to reform eighteenth-century Neoclassicism by the adaptation of idealized folk song, legend, and colloquial language, the New Formalists undertook the reclamation of contemporary poetry by mixing democratic and elitist models into a new synthesis.

The imaginative enterprise of combining high and popular culture has resulted in the confusion of most academic critics who have tried to ex-amine New Formalism according to the orthodox conventions of their discipline. Since the movement makes no sense in the progressive Mod-ernist framework commonly used in the university to discuss contemporary poetry, it can be viewed only as some recidivist manifestation, a throwback to the generation of Wilbur and Nemerov. Likewise, since the forms and subject matter drawn from popular culture lie outside the university's canonic modes of contemporary literature, those clarifying precedents remain either invisible or puzzling to most critics. While many influential literary theorists passionately discuss popular culture in general terms, they rarely show much enthusiasm about its gaudy particulars. Since their interest is primarily ideological, politics not pleasure becomes their governing principle. Unlike the actual audiences for popular art, they view it generically in abstract terms—often with an unconscious element of professorial condescension. Although they aspire to a classless political consciousness, they cannot escape the social conditioning of their elitist university caste. When discussing popular art, they instinctively feel obliged to signal their Brahmin taste by demonstrating a sophisticated detachment from and intellectual superiority to the lowbrow material under review. Consequently, the notion that serious artists would employ popular forms in an unironic, undetached, and apolitical manner leaves these *au courant* theorists not merely dumbfounded but embarrassed.

Few early critics, for instance, understood the centrality of narrative poetry to the New Formalist enterprise. Although superficially unrelated to the use of rhyme and meter, the revival of narrative verse allowed the young writers to address several of the same broad cultural problems that had initially led them back to formal poetry. First, it gave them an inclusive literary mode that, however out of favor with academic theorists, nonetheless had immediate appeal to the nonspecialist reader of novels and short stories. Second, narrative provided young poets with a genre that avoided the excessive narcissism of the confessional style (which had often vitiated the work of the older generation) and yet allowed them to write directly about highly emotional situations. Third, it gave them the opportunity for innovation because narrative poetry had not been actively explored by American writers since the days of Frost and Jeffers. Finally—and most subtly—narrative poetry helped fill the void left by the diminishment of the common cultural context. A story, by definition, creates its own context as it progresses. The self-contained psychological, social, and cultural contexts that fiction constructs in the reader's mind allow the narrative to tighten at certain moments and achieve powerfully lyric moments—"epiphanies," as a Joycean might call them—that represent the quintessential poetic effect. The impoverishment of public culture made it difficult to achieve these allusive connections in lyric poetry without limiting one's audience to the elite. But by creating their own *ad hoc* context within a narrative poem, the New Formalists pursued such imaginative epiphanies in a broadly accessible mode.

The new mode, however, did not prove especially accessible to the academy, which had set notions of what contemporary poems should or should not be. Frederick Turner's epic science-fiction poem, *The New World,* for instance, was met with bewilderment or abuse by academic commentators, even while it earned high praise in nonacademic journals. Likewise, Vikram Seth's novel in verse (patterned in some ways after a soap opera), *The Golden Gate,* was dismissed by a neo-avant-garde apologist like Marjorie Perloff but was greeted enthusiastically by thousands of sophisticated fiction readers. Many critics have not understood the obvious point that writers in the movement—like Timothy Steele or R. S. Gwynn—have revitalized love poetry, satire, and verse narratives, not out of literary antiquarianism but because both the authors and their non-academic readers actually enjoy these genres. It is not coincidental, I think, that the critics most committed to the "new" are often the ones who miss what is most original in New Formalism. Nor is it an accident that so many of the leading New Formalist writers either work outside the university or, if they are teachers, often did graduate work in literature rather than creative writing. As Perloff and other critics have noted, the movement is both a generational and contrarian response to the torpor of mainstream American academic poetry.

The generational and contrarian nature of New Formalism is ultimately the source of both its strengths and weaknesses. If the new movement has the vitality and confidence of youth, it often also displays the naïveté and recklessness of inexperience. It also has the toughness of a group that defined itself in opposition to mainstream practice. But if that genesis endowed the poets with a feisty independence and healthy disregard for the critical fashions and professional protocol that enervated much current poetry, it also encouraged a certain narrow self-righteousness. One sees this parochialism most clearly among a hard-core faction of young formalists who are essentially anti-Modernists. As critics, they are more apt to fight than explore new ideas, and, as poets, they are more likely to imitate than innovate. The ardent traditionalists, however, represent only a small part of a large, heterogeneous movement.

New Formalism remains a young movement still in the process of development and self-definition. Despite the active opposition of the middle-aged generation that dominates the poetry establishment, the new movement has not only gained notoriety but has changed the agenda of contemporary American poetry in several important ways. First, it has shifted the concerns of contemporary poetics by bringing serious attention to considerations of form, meter, mode, and genre after decades of neglect. Second, New Formalist poetry and criticism have democratized literary discourse. The poetry is accessible to nonspecialist readers. Likewise, whatever their limitations as critics, the New Formalists have written about poetry in a public idiom and thereby both enlivened and demystified critical discourse. Finally, the return to form, narrative, and traditional genres has changed the notion of the usable past by reviving dormant possibilities in twentieth-century American poetry. Previously peripheral narrative masters like Frost, Jeffers, and Robinson now seem central to contemporary poetic practice. At the moment the changes wrought by New Formalism are still coming too rapidly, and the amount of new poetry appearing is too overwhelming, to make any cogent judgments about its long-term place, but there is no question that the movement has both transformed and expanded the possibilities of American poetry.

DANA GIOIA was born in Los Angeles in 1950. He received his B.A. and M.B.A. degrees from Stanford University. He also has an M.A. in Comparative Literature from Harvard University. For fifteen years, he worked as a business executive in New York before quitting in 1992 to write full-time. He has published three collections of poetry—*Daily Horoscope* (1986), *The Gods of Winter* (1991), and *Interrogations at Noon* (2001), which won the American Book Award. He has also written an opera libretto, *Nosferatu* (2001). The first edition of *Can Poetry Matter?* (1992) was a finalist for the National Book Critics Circle Award. A prolific essayist, reviewer, and translator, Gioia has also published nine anthologies of poetry and fiction. He lives in Sonoma County, California, with his wife and two sons.

This book was designed by Ann Sudmeier.
It is set in Galliard type by Stanton Publication Services, Inc.,
and manufactured by Bang Printing on acid-free paper.

Graywolf Press is a not-for-profit, independent press. The books we publish include poetry, literary fiction, essays, and cultural criticism. We are less interested in best-sellers than in talented writers who display a freshness of voice coupled with a distinct vision. We believe these are the very qualities essential to shape a vital and diverse culture.

Thankfully, many of our readers feel the same way. They have shown this through their desire to buy books by Graywolf writers; they have told us this themselves through their e-mail notes and at author events; and they have reinforced their commitment by contributing financial support, in small amounts and in large amounts, and joining the "Friends of Graywolf."

If you enjoyed this book and wish to learn more about Graywolf Press, we invite you to ask your bookseller or librarian about further Graywolf titles; or to contact us for a free catalog; or to visit our award-winning web site that features information about our forthcoming books.

We would also like to invite you to consider joining the hundreds of individuals who are already "Friends of Graywolf" by contributing to our membership program. Individual donations of any size are significant to us: they tell us that you believe that the kind of publishing we do *matters*. Our web site gives you many more details about the benefits you will enjoy as a "Friend of Graywolf"; but if you do not have online access, we urge you to contact us for a copy of our membership brochure. www.graywolfpress.org

Graywolf Press
2402 University Avenue, Suite 203
Saint Paul, MN 55114
Phone: (651) 641-0077
Fax: (651) 641-0036
E-mail: wolves@graywolfpress.org

Other Graywolf titles you might enjoy:

Feeling as a Foreign Language:
The Good Strangeness of Poetry
by Alice Fulton

By Herself: Women Reclaim Poetry,
edited by Molly McQuade

After Confession: Poetry as Autobiography,
edited by Kate Sontag and David Graham

Readings
by Sven Birkerts

Burning Down the House: Essays on Fiction
by Charles Baxter

If You Want to Write:
A Book about Art, Independence and Spirit
by Brenda Ueland

A Hundred White Daffodils
by Jane Kenyon